KAIJUMAX
SEASON THREE
KING OF THE MONSTAS

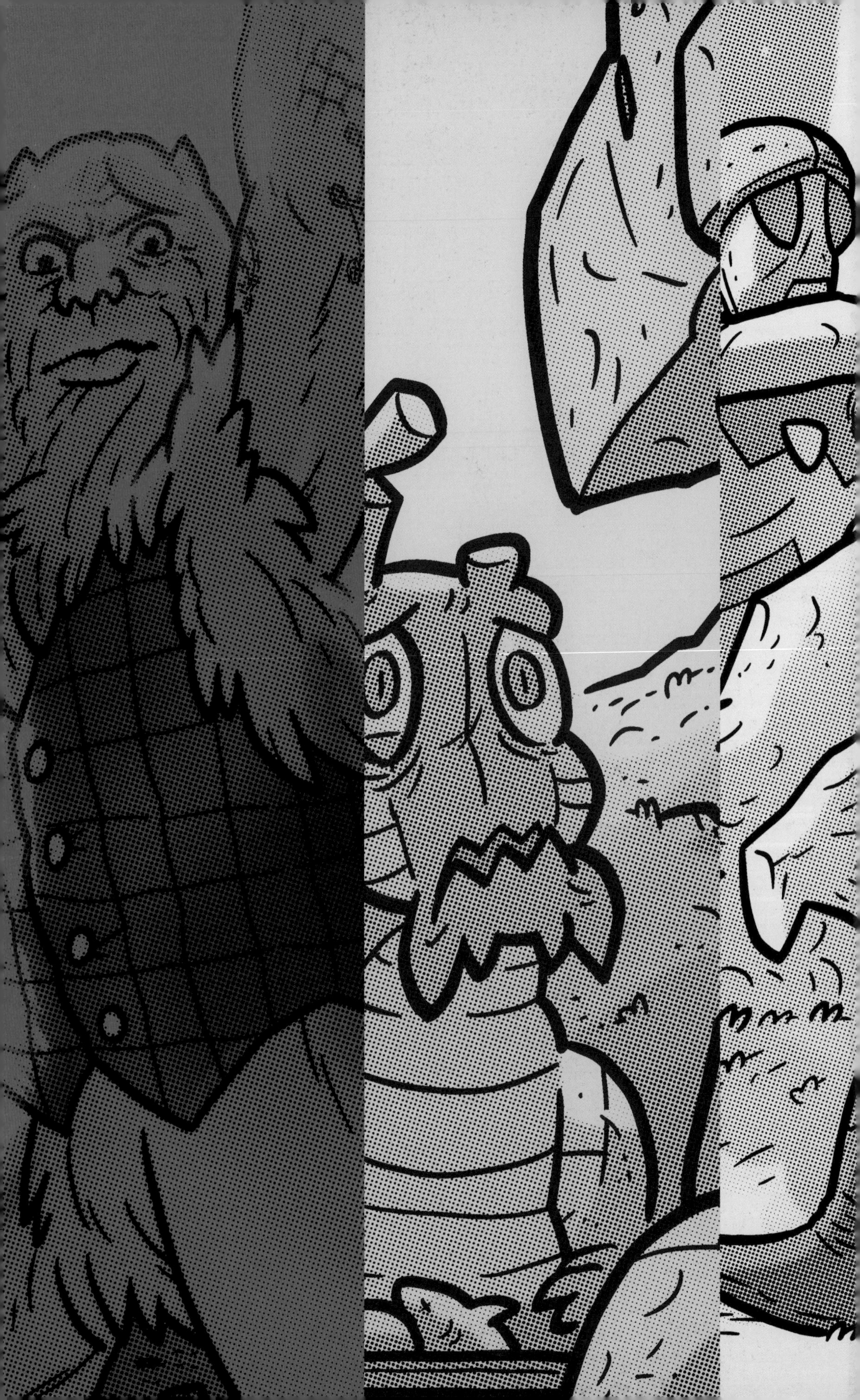

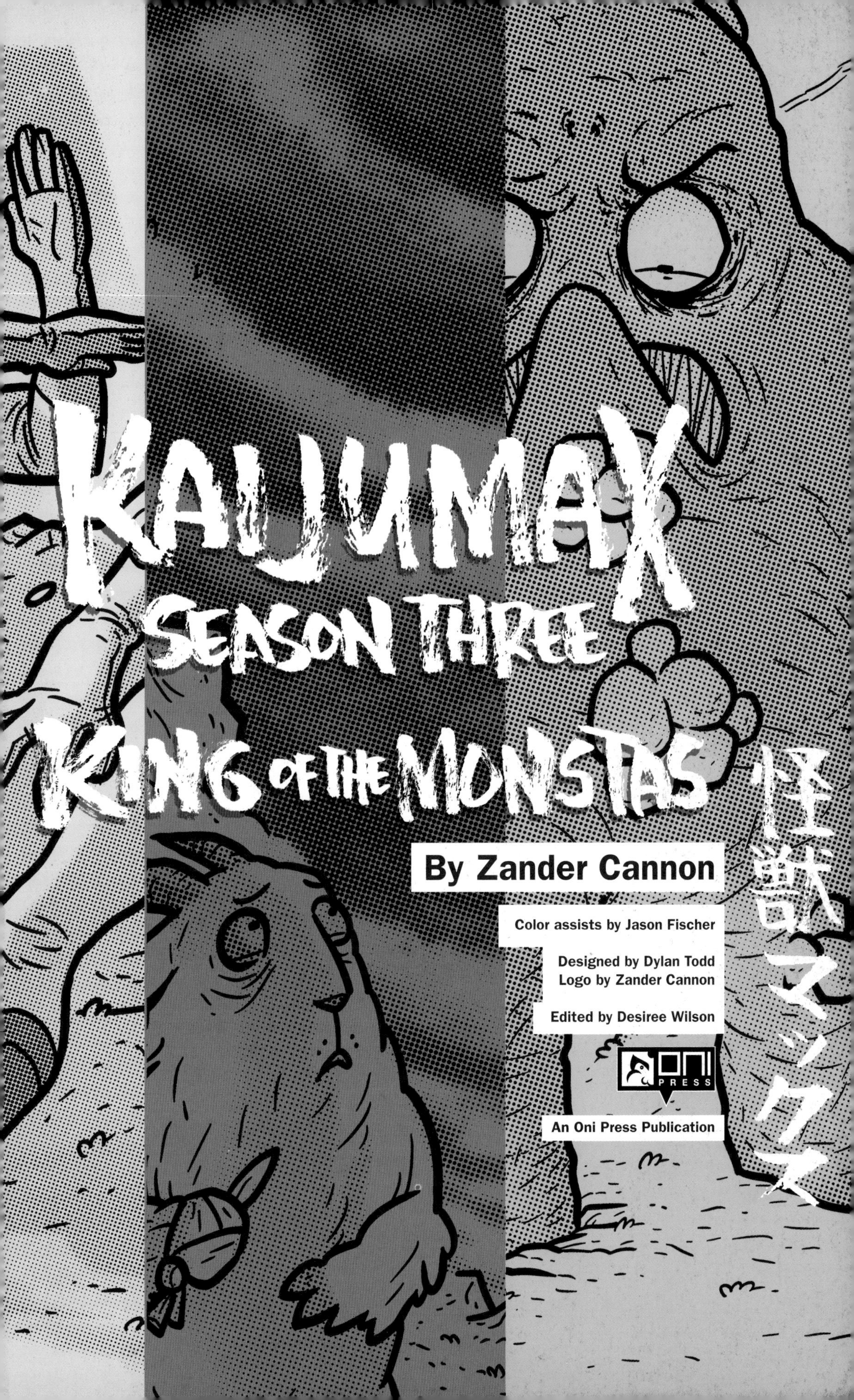

KAIJUMAX SEASON THREE
KING OF THE MONSTAS

怪獣マックス

By Zander Cannon

Color assists by Jason Fischer

Designed by Dylan Todd
Logo by Zander Cannon

Edited by Desiree Wilson

An Oni Press Publication

ON A REMOTE ISLAND IN THE SOUTH PACIFIC LIES KAIJUMAX,

the infamous prison for the world's most terrible monsters. Fiercely divided into gangs, the inmates do their time in a world of shifting alliances, dark moral compromise, and flame breath.

The Creature from Devil's Creek has found himself in the unenviable position of being low mon in the Cryptid Brotherhood hierarchy, and he has begun looking desperately for anything to change his fortune.

As the prison emerges from a month-long lockdown after Electrogor and The Green Humongo's well-publicized escape, the J-Pop gang of Japanese kaiju adjusts to a new leader, Whoofy, the woefully unprepared son of legendary monster Ape-Whale.

Whoofy's sinister consiglieri, the mysterious Li'l Boy, has been whispering advice in his ear all along, but to what end?

EPISODE 1

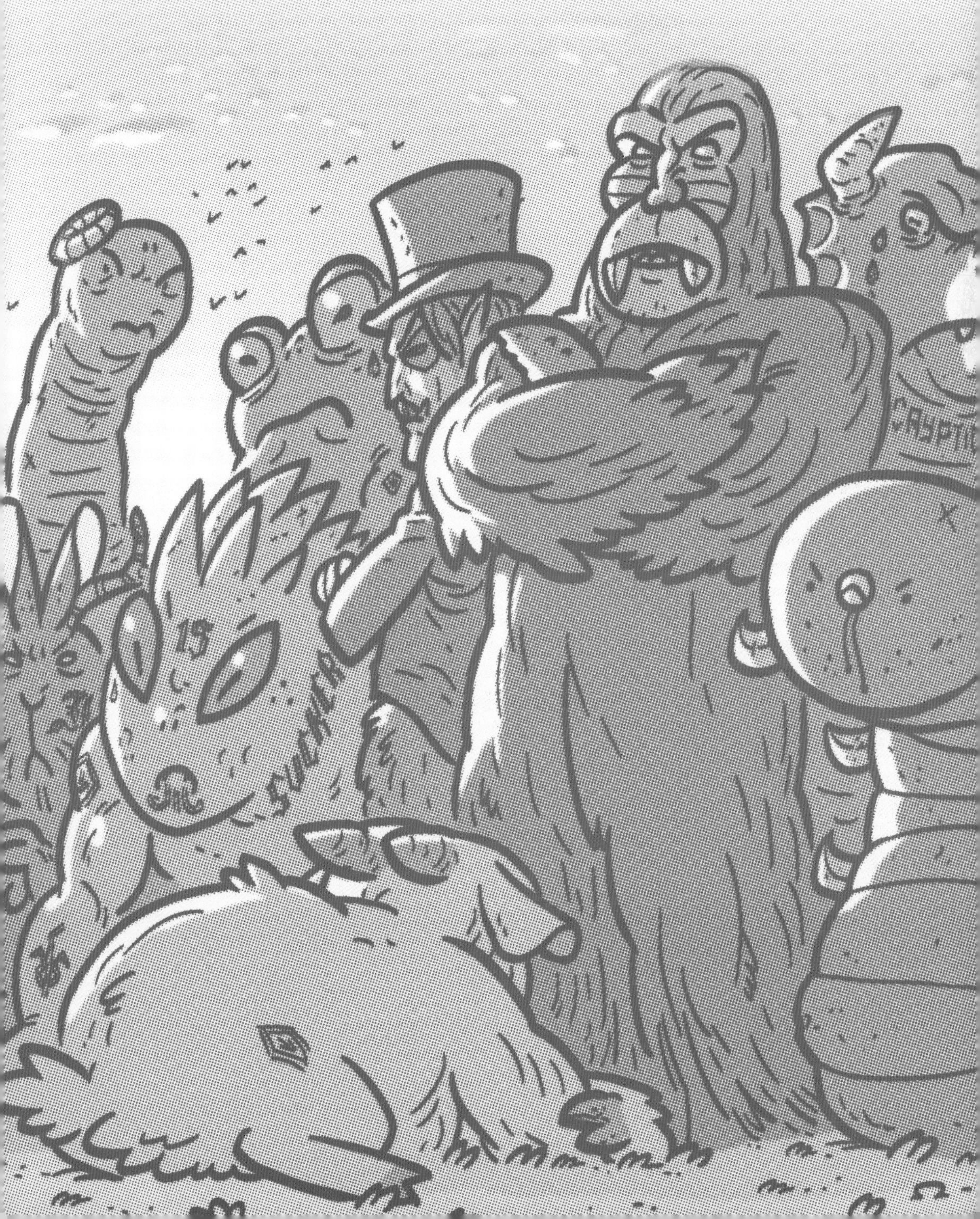

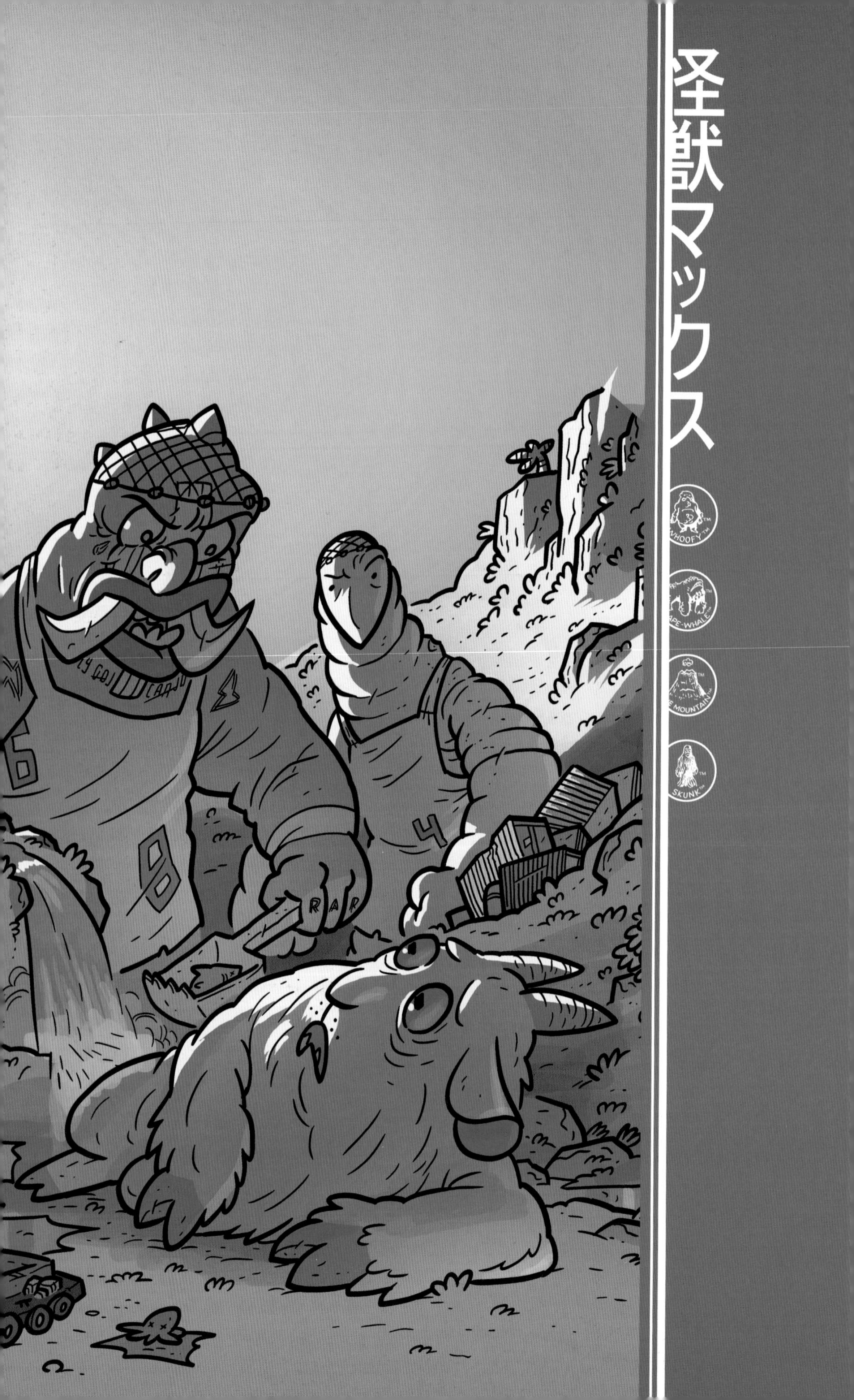
怪獣マックス
WHOOFY
SKUNK

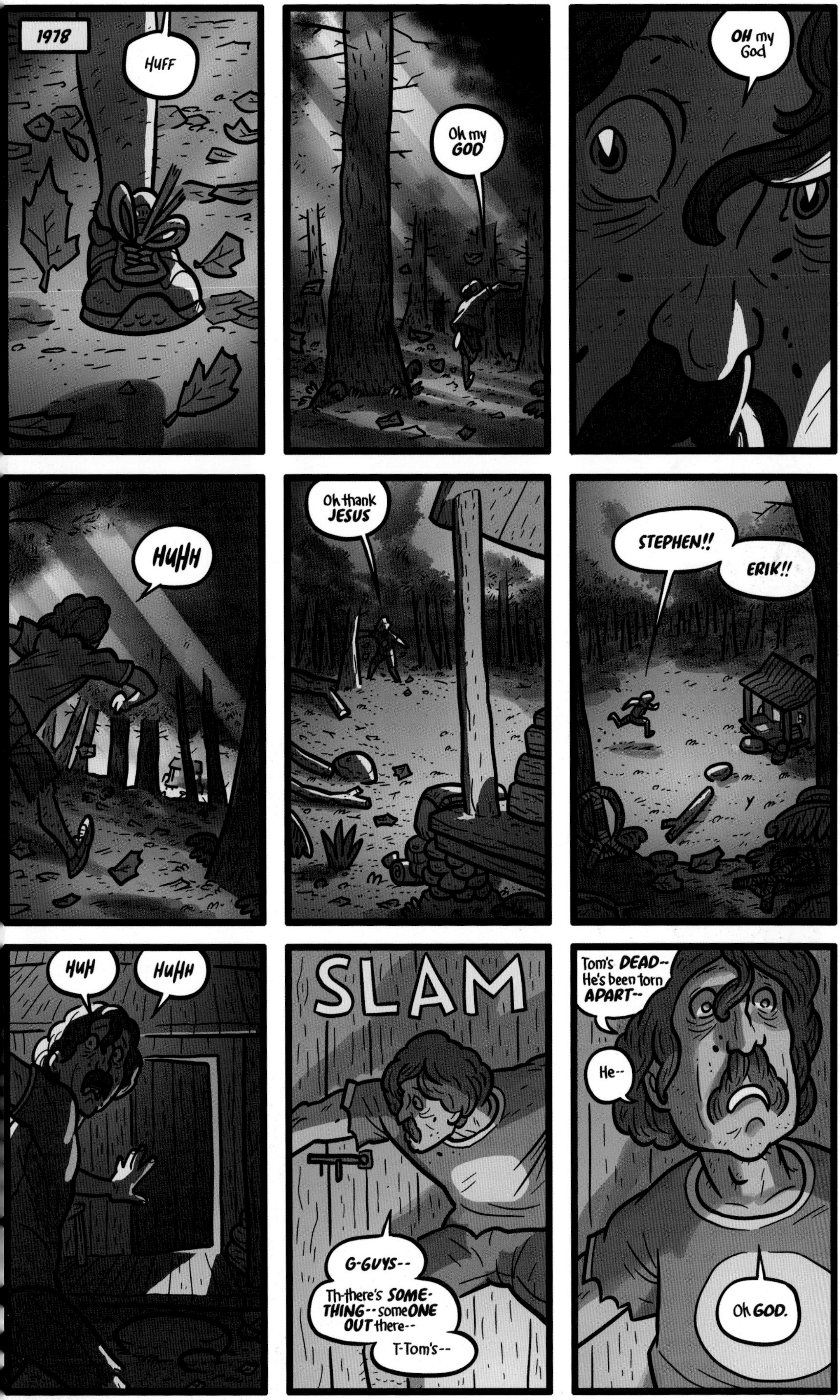
1978
HUFF
Oh my GOD
OH my God
HUHH
Oh thank JESUS
STEPHEN!!
ERIK!!
HUH
HUHH
SLAM
G-GUYS--
Th-there's SOME-THING--someONE OUT there--
T-Tom's--
Tom's DEAD--
He's been torn APART--
He--
Oh GOD.

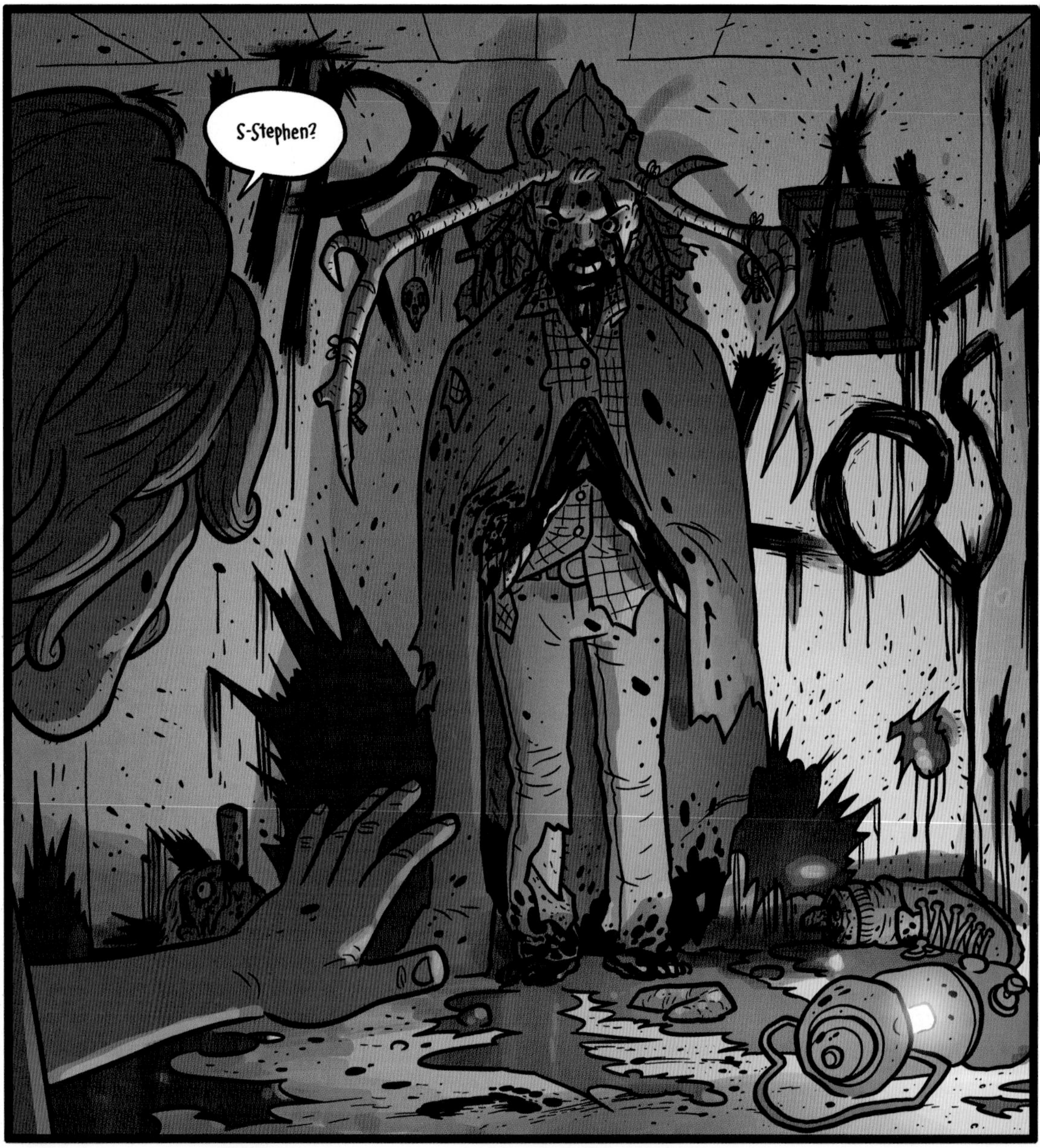
S-Stephen?

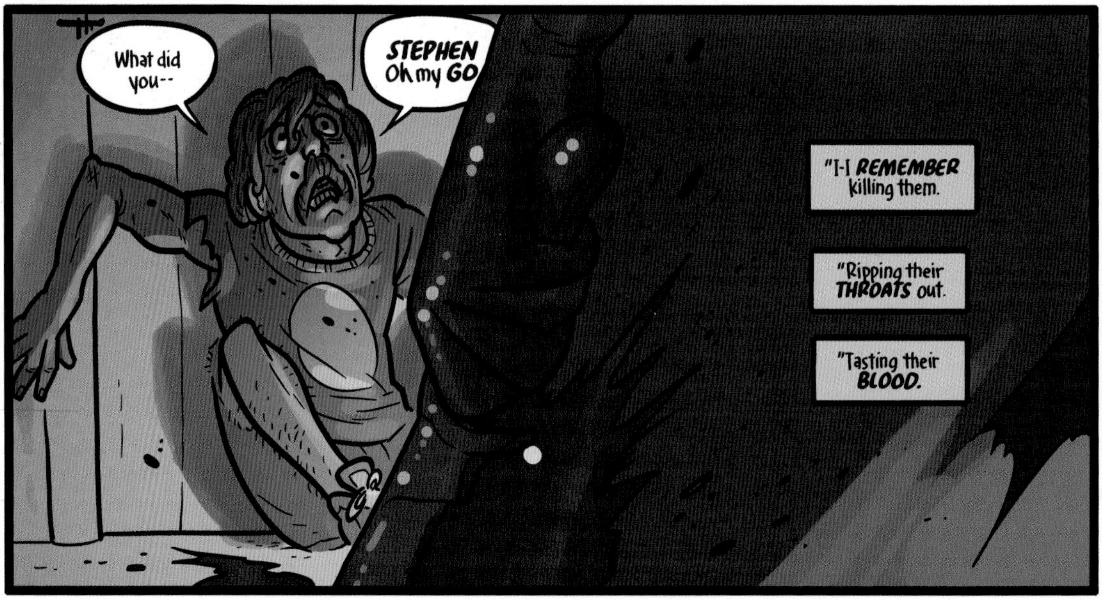
What did you--
STEPHEN Oh my GO
"I-I REMEMBER killing them.
"Ripping their THROATS out.
"Tasting their BLOOD.

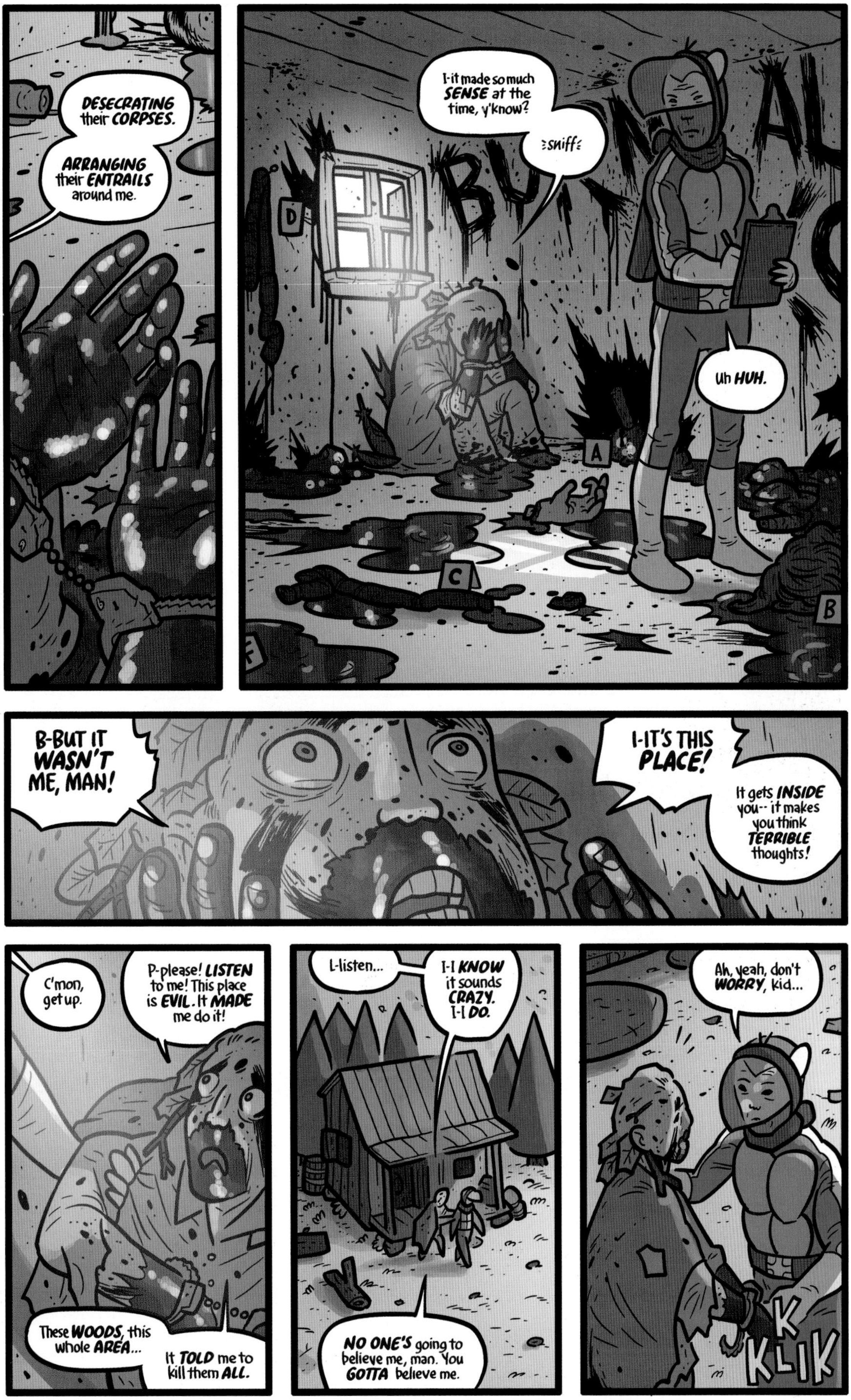
DESECRATING their CORPSES.
ARRANGING their ENTRAILS around me.
BU
D
I-it made so much SENSE at the time, y'know?
sniff
Uh HUH.
A
C
B
B-BUT IT WASN'T ME, MAN!
I-IT'S THIS PLACE!
It gets INSIDE you-- it makes you think TERRIBLE thoughts!
C'mon, get up.
P-please! LISTEN to me! This place is EVIL. It MADE me do it!
These WOODS, this whole AREA...
It TOLD me to kill them ALL.
L-listen...
I-I KNOW it sounds CRAZY. I-I DO.
NO ONE'S going to believe me, man. You GOTTA believe me.
Ah, yeah, don't WORRY, kid...
KLIK

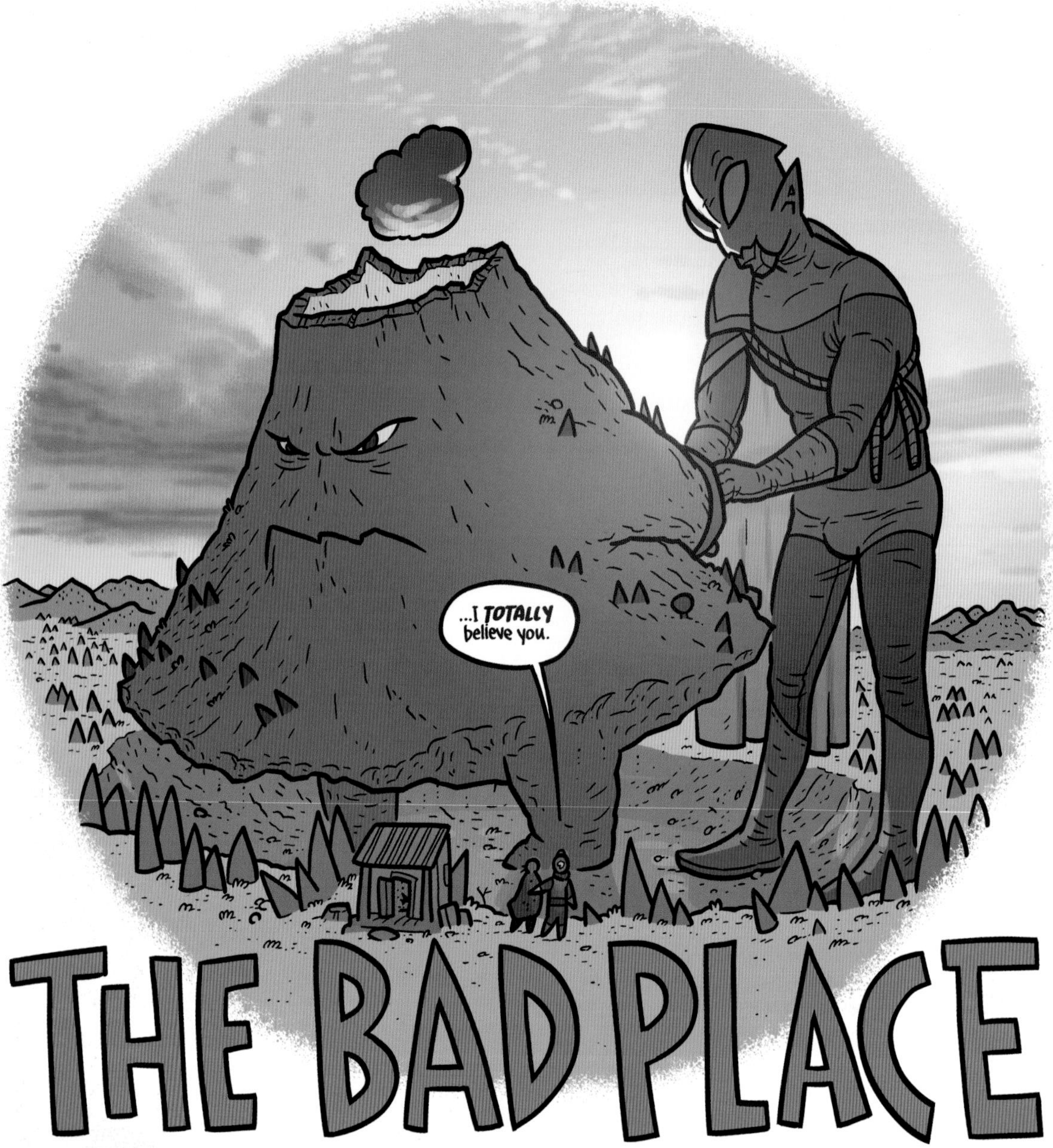
...I TOTALLY believe you.

THE BAD PLACE

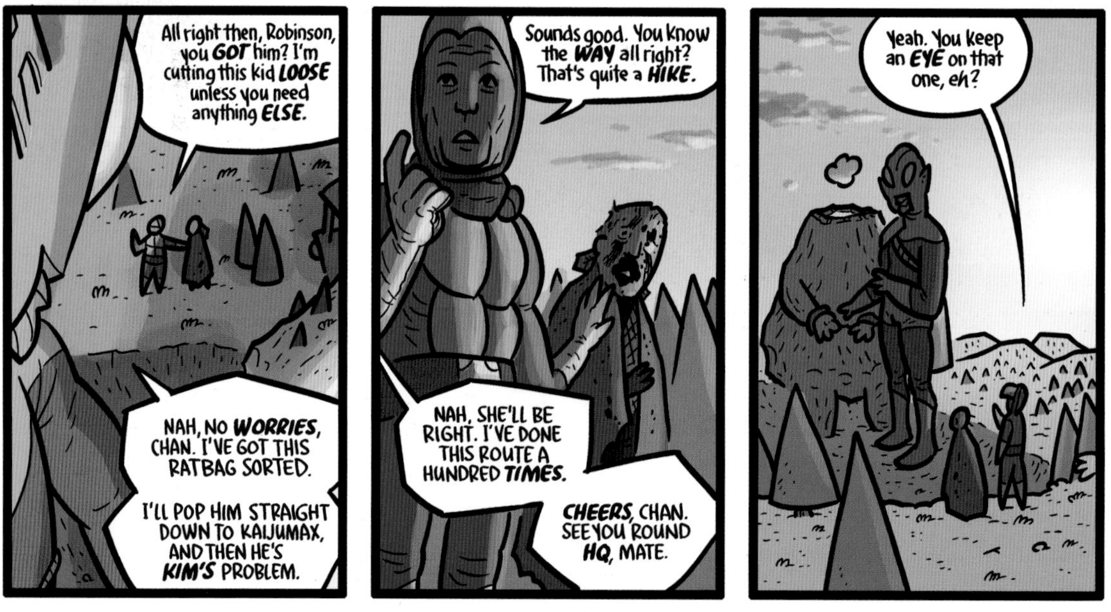
All right then, Robinson, you GOT him? I'm cutting this kid LOOSE unless you need anything ELSE.
NAH, NO WORRIES, CHAN. I'VE GOT THIS RATBAG SORTED.
I'LL POP HIM STRAIGHT DOWN TO KAIJUMAX, AND THEN HE'S KIM'S PROBLEM.
Sounds good. You know the WAY all right? That's quite a HIKE.
NAH, SHE'LL BE RIGHT. I'VE DONE THIS ROUTE A HUNDRED TIMES.
CHEERS, CHAN. SEE YOU ROUND HQ, MATE.
Yeah. You keep an EYE on that one, eh?

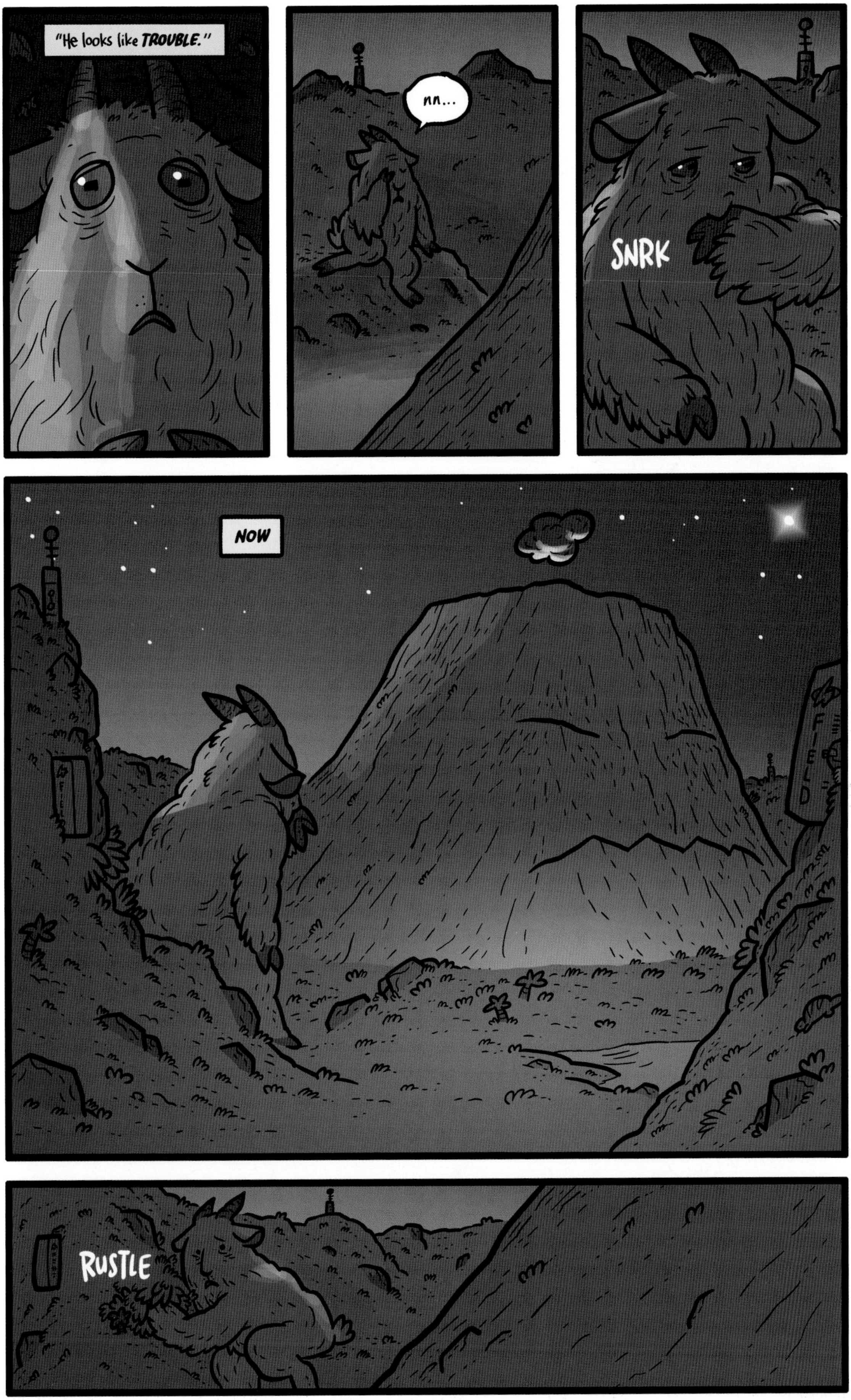
"He looks like TROUBLE."
nn...
SNRK
NOW
FIELD
RUSTLE

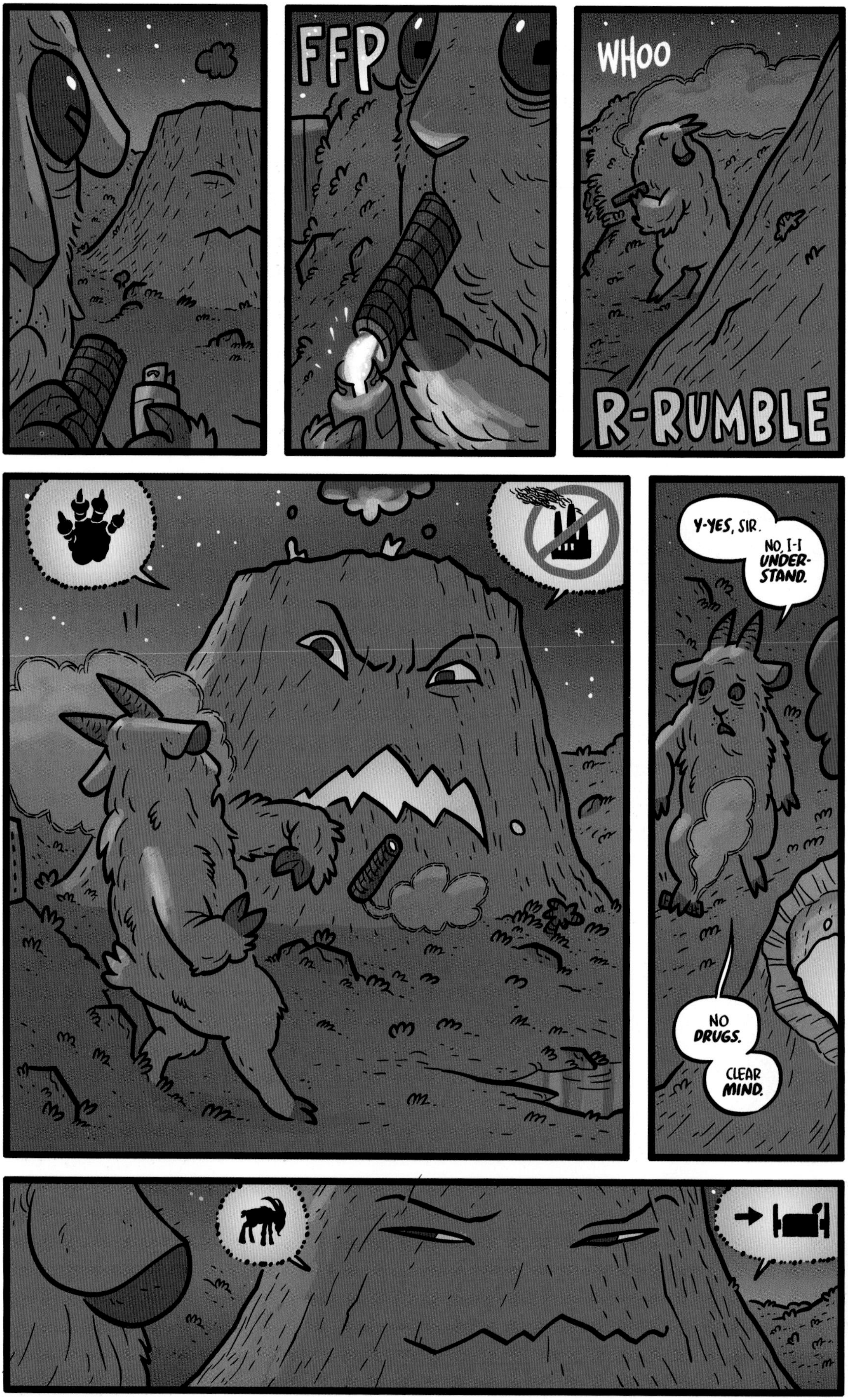

FFP
WHOO
R-RUMBLE
Y-YES, SIR.
NO, I-I UNDERSTAND.
NO DRUGS.
CLEAR MIND.

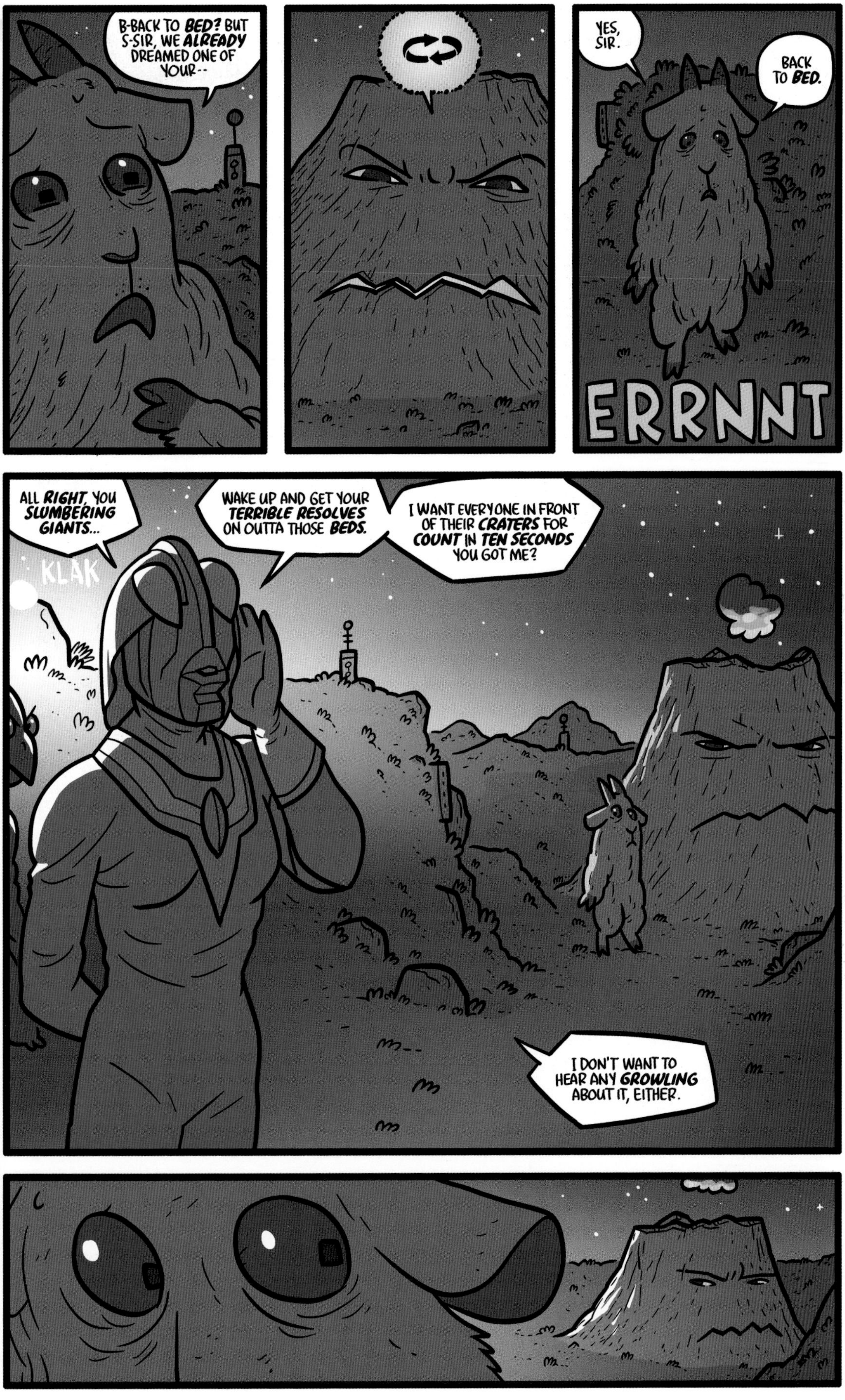
B-BACK TO BED? BUT S-SIR, WE ALREADY DREAMED ONE OF YOUR--
YES, SIR.
BACK TO BED.
ERRNNT
ALL RIGHT, YOU SLUMBERING GIANTS...
KLAK
WAKE UP AND GET YOUR TERRIBLE RESOLVES ON OUTTA THOSE BEDS.
I WANT EVERYONE IN FRONT OF THEIR CRATERS FOR COUNT IN TEN SECONDS YOU GOT ME?
I DON'T WANT TO HEAR ANY GROWLING ABOUT IT, EITHER.

SPLAP

YO, **WHAT?** THAT'S **IT?**

MY LIZZA, WHAT KIND OF LUNCH IS **THIS** FOR YOUR **HOMEBOY,** HUH?

C'MON, YO, WE BOTH FROM THE **BIG J.** WHY DON'T YOU HOOK A LIZZA **UP?**

PFF. YOU AIN'T NO HOMEBOY OF **MINE.**

WE AIN'T EVEN PART OF THE SAME **ZEITGEIST,** KNOW WHAT I'M SAYIN'?

WHY DON'T YOU TAKE YOUR **MEAL 'N' GO** ON AND **BE THE BEST THERE EVER WAS** WITH Y'**OWN** CREW.

NAH, NAH, C'MON, I'M **DOWN** WITH IT, LIZZA.

YOU **J-POPS** KNOW WHERE IT'S AT. SPECTER OF **WAR?** ECOLOGICAL **COLLAPSE?** I'M ALL **ABOUT** THAT, YOU HEARD?

YOU GOT MORE IN COMMON WITH THE **MAKETO GANG** THAN YOU **THINK,** KNOW WHAT I'M **SAYIN'?**

YOU GOT A NEW **LEADER,** RIGHT? **APE-WHALE'S** KID? WORD **IS,** THE DON'S TALKIN' ABOUT REACHIN' OUT, MAKIN' AN **ALLIANCE.**

huh.

SO WHY DO **WE** CARE WHAT THE DON HAS TO SAY?

I HEARD THAT **MEGAFAUNA** WAS IN **HIDING** AFTER HE KILLED A **COP.**

NAH, YO, IT WASN'T A **COP,** IT WAS JUST **SECURITY** OR SOMETHING AT THE **GYM.** SAID YOU GOT TO **BATTLE** HIM TO GET IN, WELL, THE DON **GAVE** HIM A BATTLE.

YOU CAN'T BE STEPPIN' TO THE **BIG MON** WITHOUT EXPECTIN' TO GET **FRIED.**

I FEEL YOU, BUT LIKE, THAT **DON** A' YOURS AIN'T COMIN' TO **GEN-POP** IF THEY FIND HIM.

STOMPIN' ON A CITY'S **ONE** THING, MY LIZZA, BUT YOU KILL ONE OF THEIR **OWN,** YOU'RE GOIN' TO THE **CHAIR.**

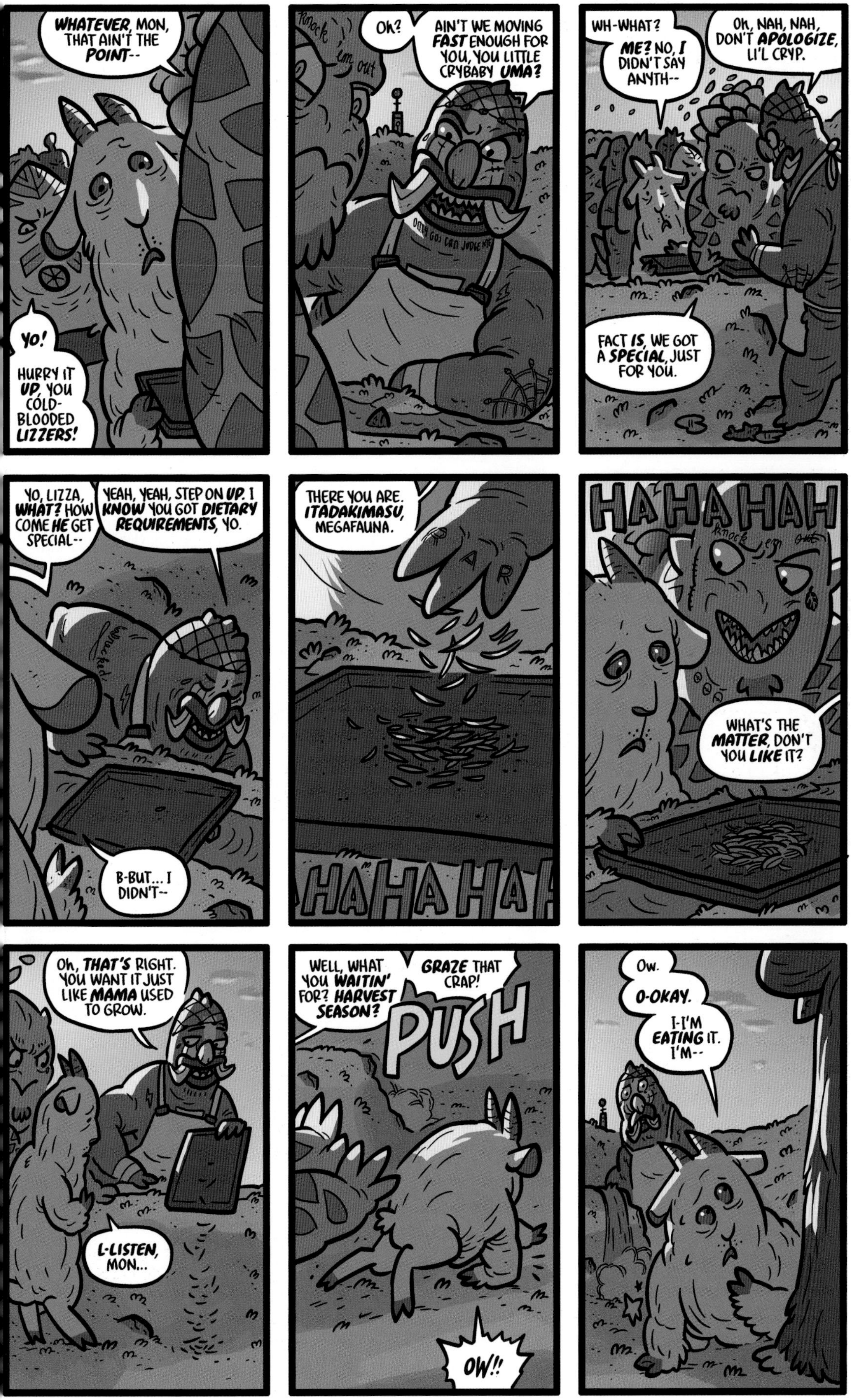
WHATEVER, MON, THAT AIN'T THE POINT--
YO!
HURRY IT UP, YOU COLD-BLOODED LIZZERS!
OH?
AIN'T WE MOVING FAST ENOUGH FOR YOU, YOU LITTLE CRYBABY UMA?
WH-WHAT?
ME? NO, I DIDN'T SAY ANYTH--
OH, NAH, NAH, DON'T APOLOGIZE, LI'L CRYP.
FACT IS, WE GOT A SPECIAL, JUST FOR YOU.
YO, LIZZA, WHAT? HOW COME HE GET SPECIAL--
YEAH, YEAH, STEP ON UP. I KNOW YOU GOT DIETARY REQUIREMENTS, YO.
B-BUT... I DIDN'T--
THERE YOU ARE. ITADAKIMASU, MEGAFAUNA.
HAHAHAHA
HAHAHAH
WHAT'S THE MATTER, DON'T YOU LIKE IT?
OH, THAT'S RIGHT. YOU WANT IT JUST LIKE MAMA USED TO GROW.
L-LISTEN, MON...
WELL, WHAT YOU WAITIN' FOR? HARVEST SEASON?
GRAZE THAT CRAP!
PUSH
OW!!
OW.
O-OKAY.
I-I'M EATING IT. I'M--

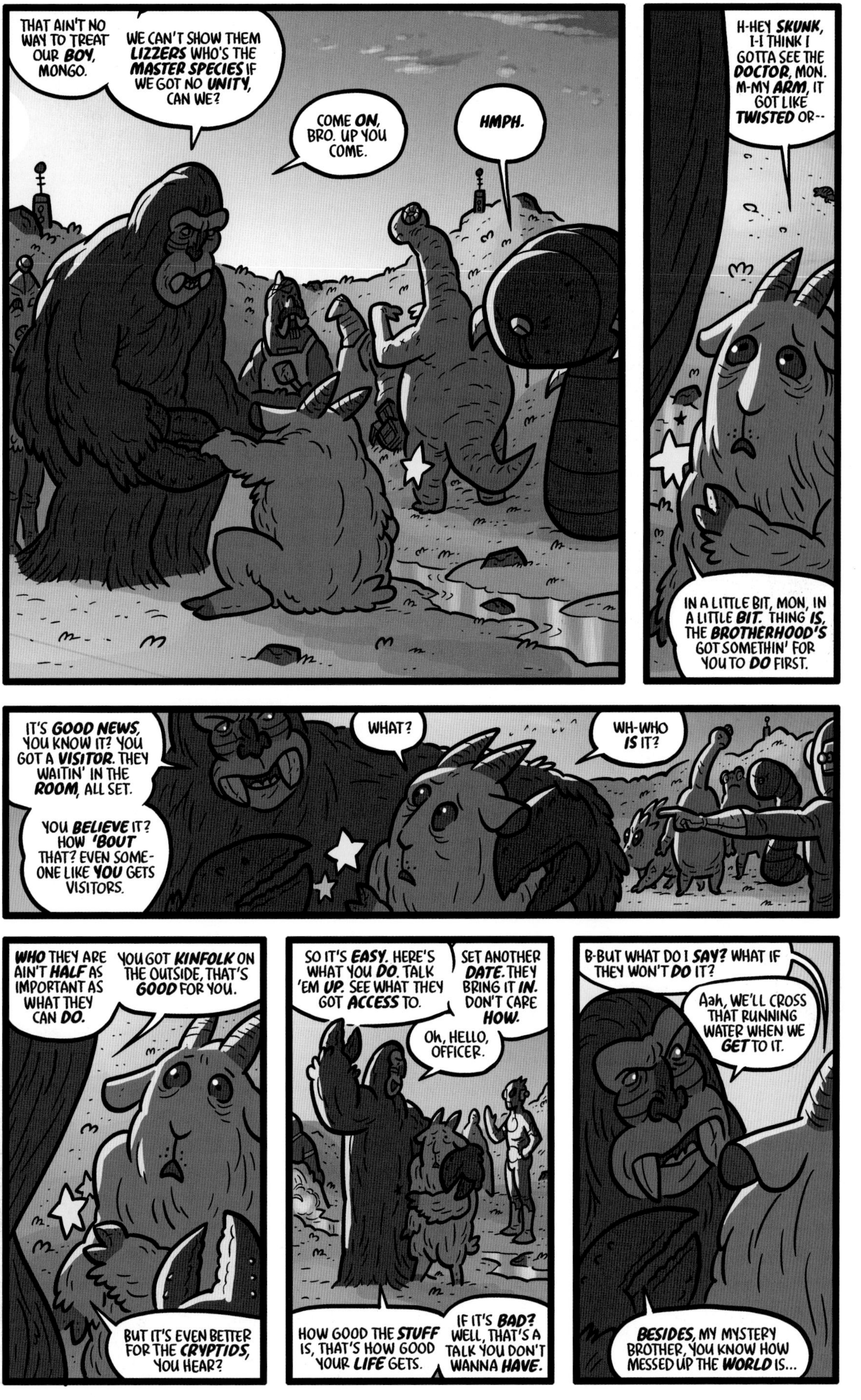
THAT AIN'T NO WAY TO TREAT OUR **BOY**, MONGO.
WE CAN'T SHOW THEM **LIZZERS** WHO'S THE **MASTER SPECIES** IF WE GOT NO **UNITY**, CAN WE?
COME **ON**, BRO. UP YOU COME.
HMPH.
H-HEY **SKUNK**, I-I THINK I GOTTA SEE THE **DOCTOR**, MON. M-MY **ARM**, IT GOT LIKE **TWISTED** OR--
IN A LITTLE BIT, MON, IN A LITTLE **BIT.** THING' **IS**, THE **BROTHERHOOD'S** GOT SOMETHIN' FOR YOU TO **DO** FIRST.
IT'S **GOOD NEWS**, YOU KNOW IT? YOU GOT A **VISITOR**. THEY WAITIN' IN THE **ROOM**, ALL SET.
YOU **BELIEVE** IT? HOW **'BOUT** THAT? EVEN SOME-ONE LIKE **YOU** GETS VISITORS.
WHAT?
WH-WHO **IS** IT?
WHO THEY ARE AIN'T **HALF** AS IMPORTANT AS WHAT THEY CAN **DO**.
YOU GOT **KINFOLK** ON THE OUTSIDE, THAT'S **GOOD** FOR YOU.
BUT IT'S EVEN BETTER FOR THE **CRYPTIDS**, YOU HEAR?
SO IT'S **EASY**. HERE'S WHAT YOU **DO**. TALK 'EM **UP**. SEE WHAT THEY GOT **ACCESS** TO.
SET ANOTHER **DATE**. THEY BRING IT **IN**. DON'T CARE **HOW**.
Oh, HELLO, OFFICER.
HOW GOOD THE **STUFF** IS, THAT'S HOW GOOD YOUR **LIFE** GETS.
IF IT'S **BAD**? WELL, THAT'S A TALK YOU DON'T WANNA **HAVE**.
B-BUT WHAT DO I **SAY**? WHAT IF THEY WON'T **DO** IT?
Aah, WE'LL CROSS THAT RUNNING WATER WHEN WE **GET** TO IT.
BESIDES, MY MYSTERY BROTHER, YOU KNOW HOW MESSED UP THE **WORLD** IS...

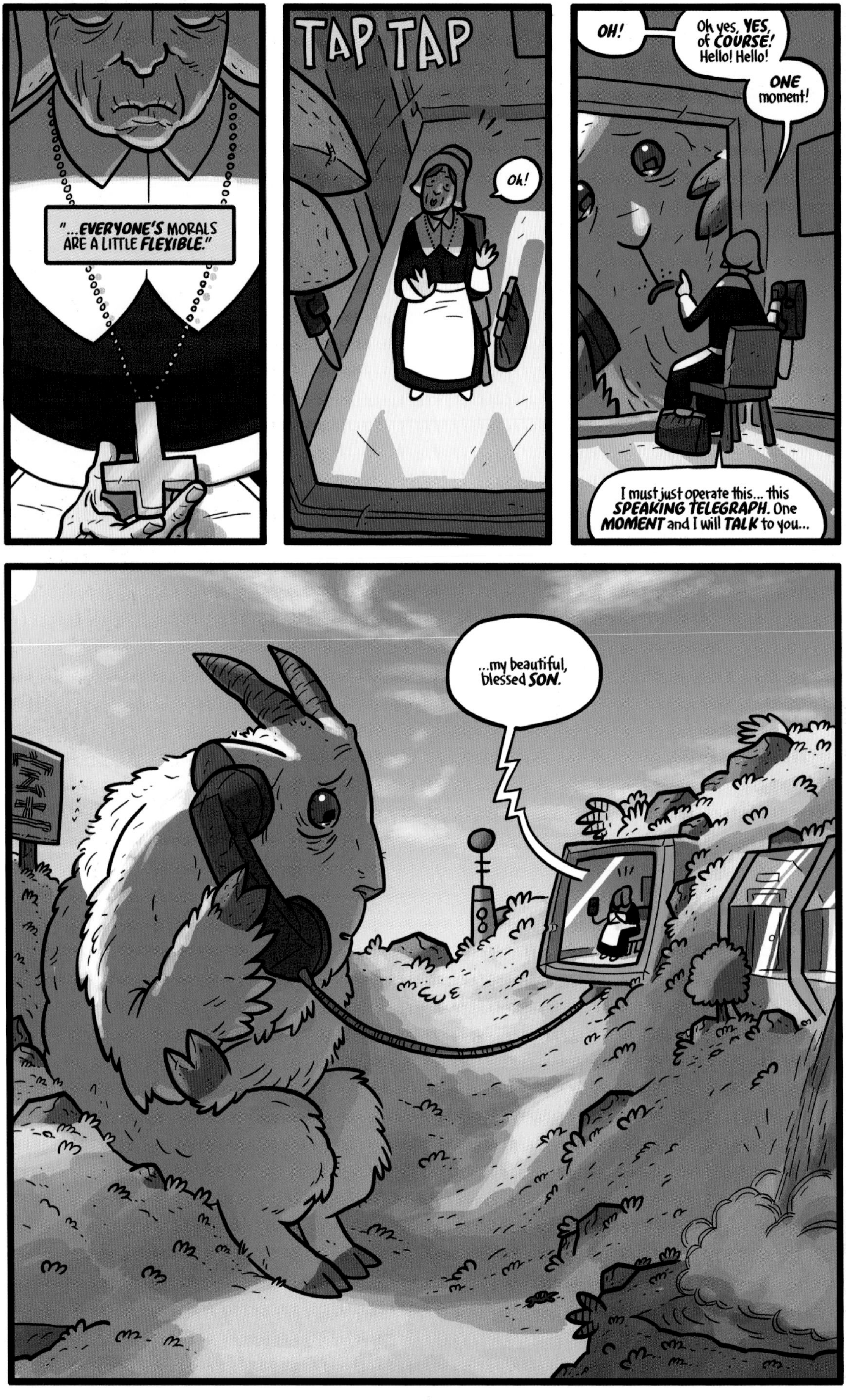
"...EVERYONE'S MORALS ARE A LITTLE FLEXIBLE."
TAP TAP
Oh!
OH!
Oh yes, YES, of COURSE! Hello! Hello!
ONE moment!
I must just operate this... this SPEAKING TELEGRAPH. One MOMENT and I will TALK to you...
...my beautiful, blessed SON.

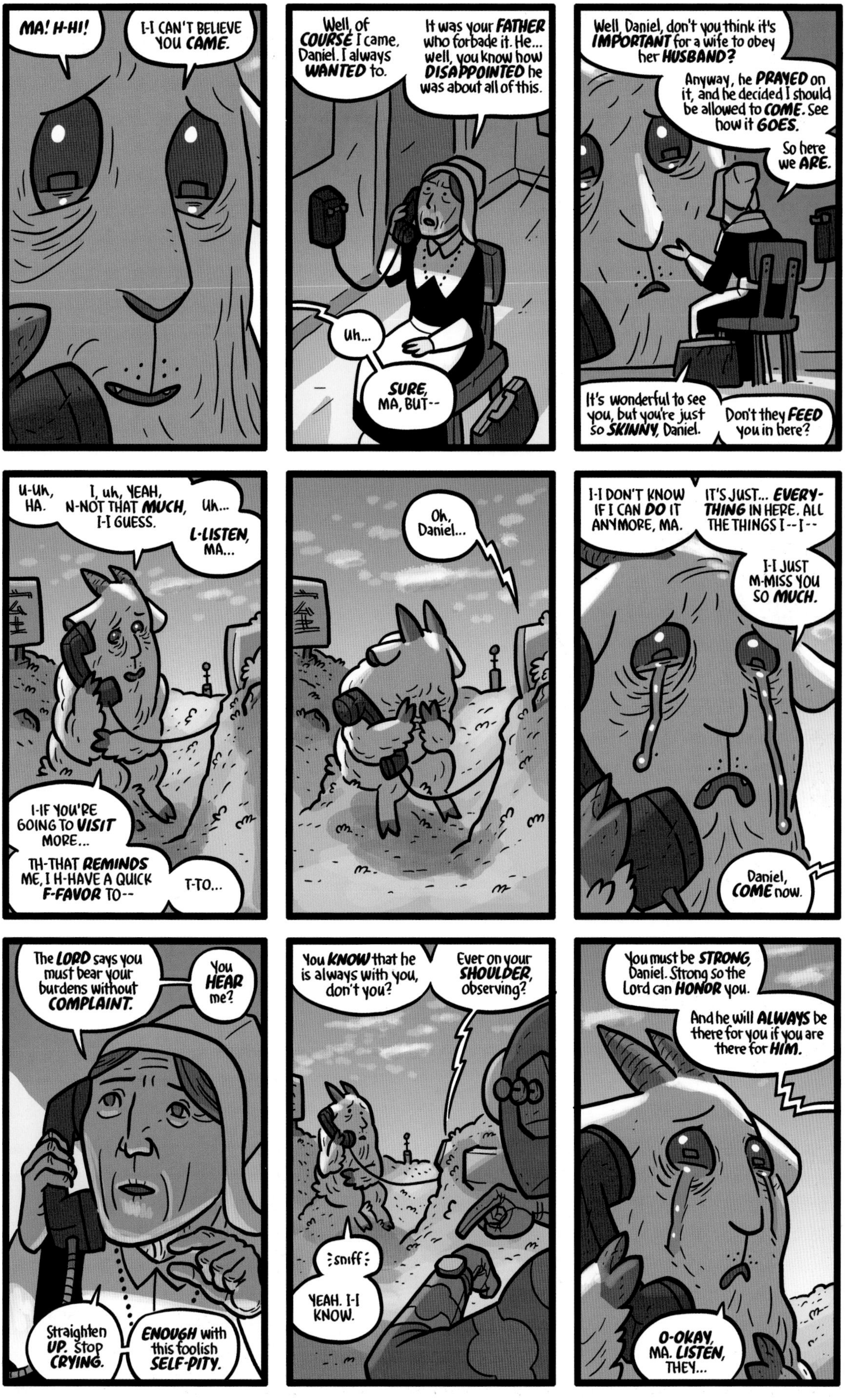
MA! H-HI!
I-I CAN'T BELIEVE YOU CAME.
Well, of COURSE I came, Daniel. I always WANTED to.
It was your FATHER who forbade it. He... well, you know how DISAPPOINTED he was about all of this.
Uh...
SURE, MA, BUT--
Well, Daniel, don't you think it's IMPORTANT for a wife to obey her HUSBAND?
Anyway, he PRAYED on it, and he decided I should be allowed to COME. See how it GOES.
So here we ARE.
It's wonderful to see you, but you're just so SKINNY, Daniel.
Don't they FEED you in here?
U-Uh, HA.
I, uh, YEAH, N-NOT THAT MUCH, I-I GUESS.
Uh...
L-LISTEN, MA...
I-IF YOU'RE GOING TO VISIT MORE...
TH-THAT REMINDS ME, I H-HAVE A QUICK F-FAVOR TO--
T-TO...
Oh, Daniel...
I-I DON'T KNOW IF I CAN DO IT ANYMORE, MA.
IT'S JUST... EVERYTHING IN HERE. ALL THE THINGS I--I--
I-I JUST M-MISS YOU SO MUCH.
Daniel, COME now.
The LORD says you must bear your burdens without COMPLAINT.
You HEAR me?
Straighten UP. Stop CRYING.
ENOUGH with this foolish SELF-PITY.
You KNOW that he is always with you, don't you?
Ever on your SHOULDER, observing?
sniff
YEAH. I-I KNOW.
You must be STRONG, Daniel. Strong so the Lord can HONOR you.
And he will ALWAYS be there for you if you are there for HIM.
O-OKAY, MA. LISTEN, THEY...

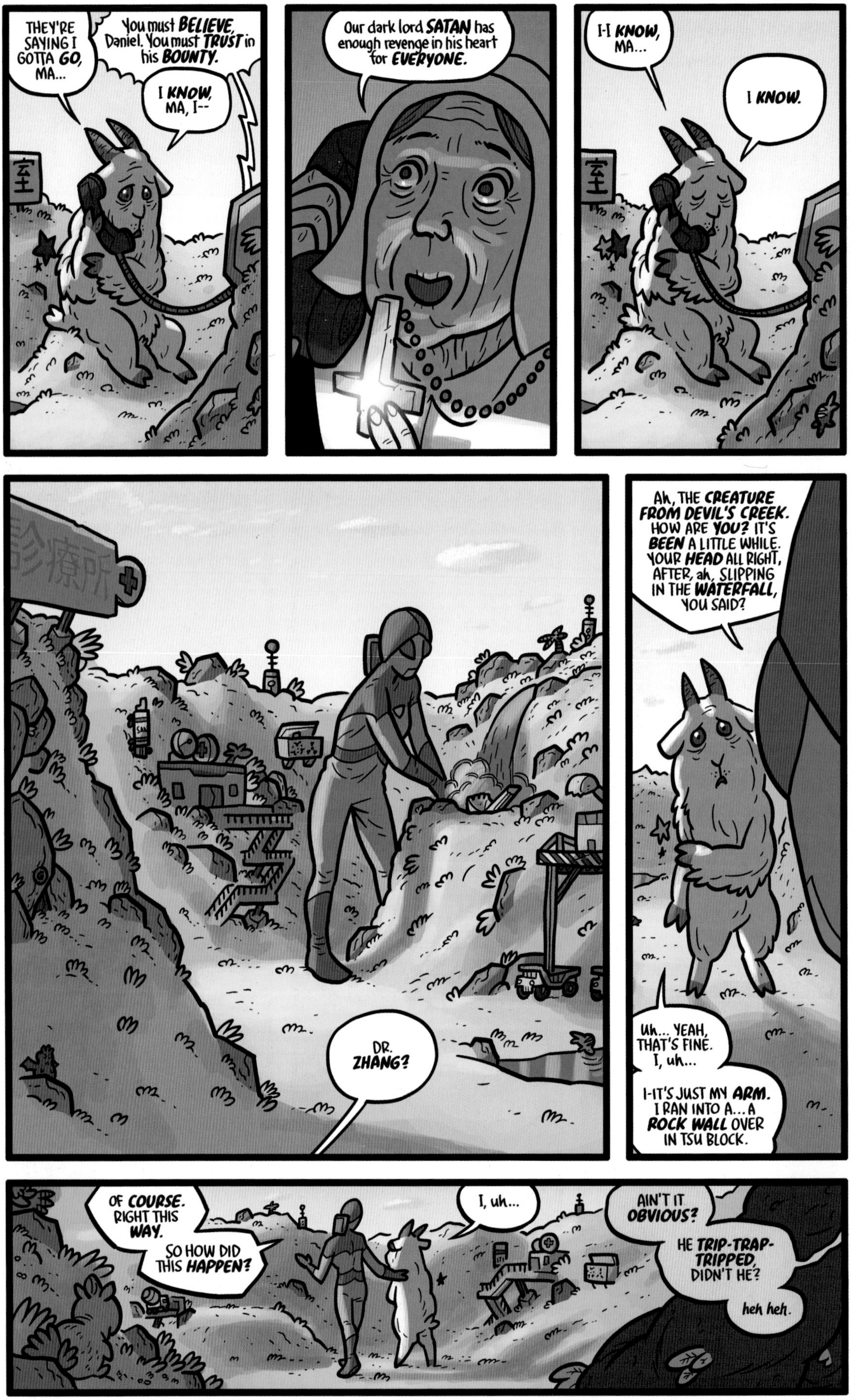

THEY'RE SAYING I GOTTA GO, MA...
You must BELIEVE, Daniel. You must TRUST in his BOUNTY.
I KNOW, MA, I--
Our dark lord SATAN has enough revenge in his heart for EVERYONE.
I-I KNOW, MA...
I KNOW.
DR. ZHANG?
Ah, THE CREATURE FROM DEVIL'S CREEK. HOW ARE YOU? IT'S BEEN A LITTLE WHILE. YOUR HEAD ALL RIGHT, AFTER, ah, SLIPPING IN THE WATERFALL, YOU SAID?
Uh... YEAH, THAT'S FINE. I, uh...
I-IT'S JUST MY ARM. I RAN INTO A... A ROCK WALL OVER IN TSU BLOCK.
OF COURSE. RIGHT THIS WAY.
SO HOW DID THIS HAPPEN?
I, uh...
AIN'T IT OBVIOUS?
HE TRIP-TRAP-TRIPPED, DIDN'T HE?
heh heh.

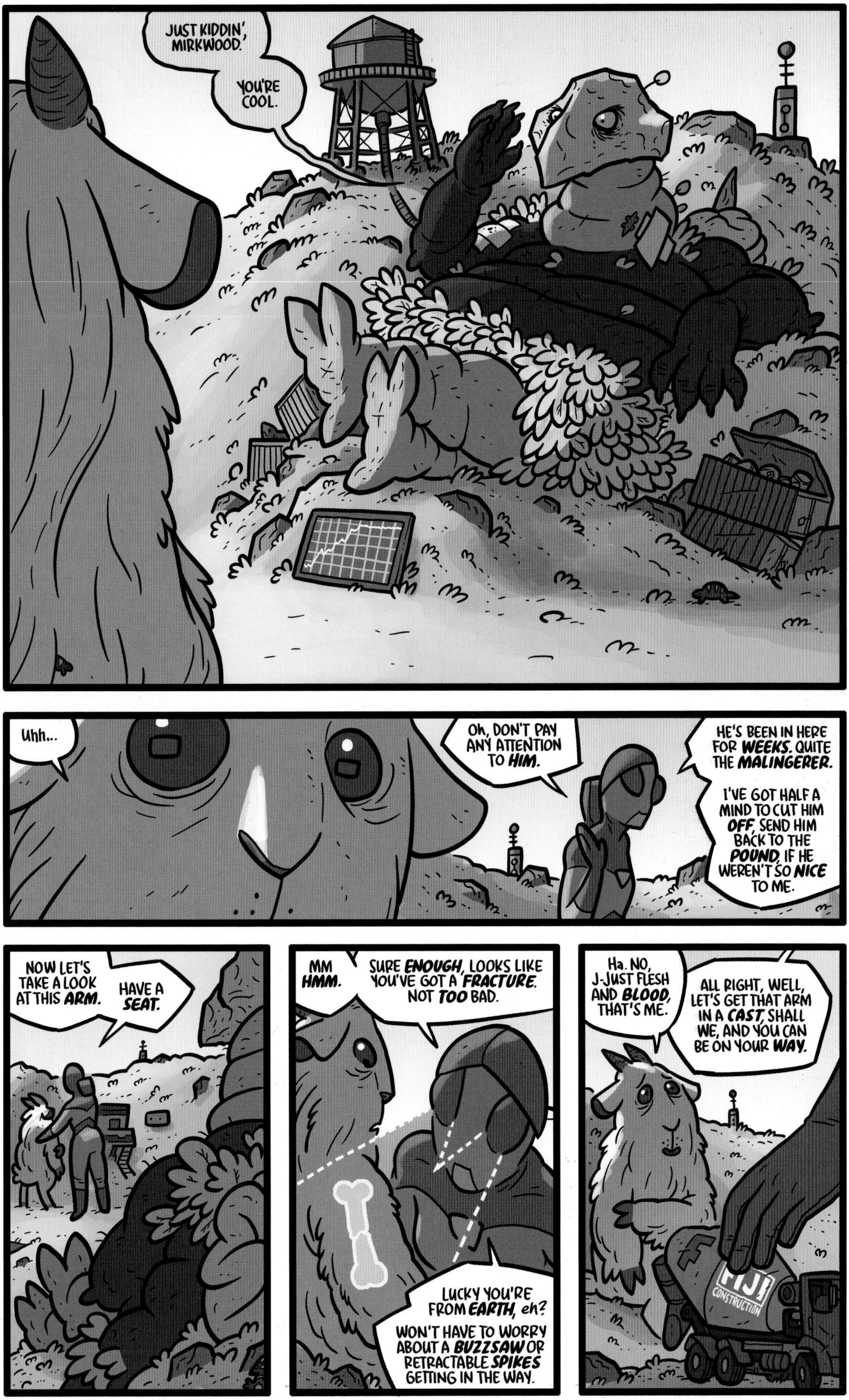
JUST KIDDIN', MIRKWOOD.
YOU'RE COOL.
Uhh...
Oh, DON'T PAY ANY ATTENTION TO HIM.
HE'S BEEN IN HERE FOR WEEKS. QUITE THE MALINGERER.
I'VE GOT HALF A MIND TO CUT HIM OFF, SEND HIM BACK TO THE POUND, IF HE WEREN'T SO NICE TO ME.
NOW LET'S TAKE A LOOK AT THIS ARM.
HAVE A SEAT.
MM HMM.
SURE ENOUGH, LOOKS LIKE YOU'VE GOT A FRACTURE. NOT TOO BAD.
LUCKY YOU'RE FROM EARTH, eh?
WON'T HAVE TO WORRY ABOUT A BUZZSAW OR RETRACTABLE SPIKES GETTING IN THE WAY.
Ha. NO, J-JUST FLESH AND BLOOD, THAT'S ME.
ALL RIGHT, WELL, LET'S GET THAT ARM IN A CAST, SHALL WE, AND YOU CAN BE ON YOUR WAY.
FIJI
CONSTRUCTION

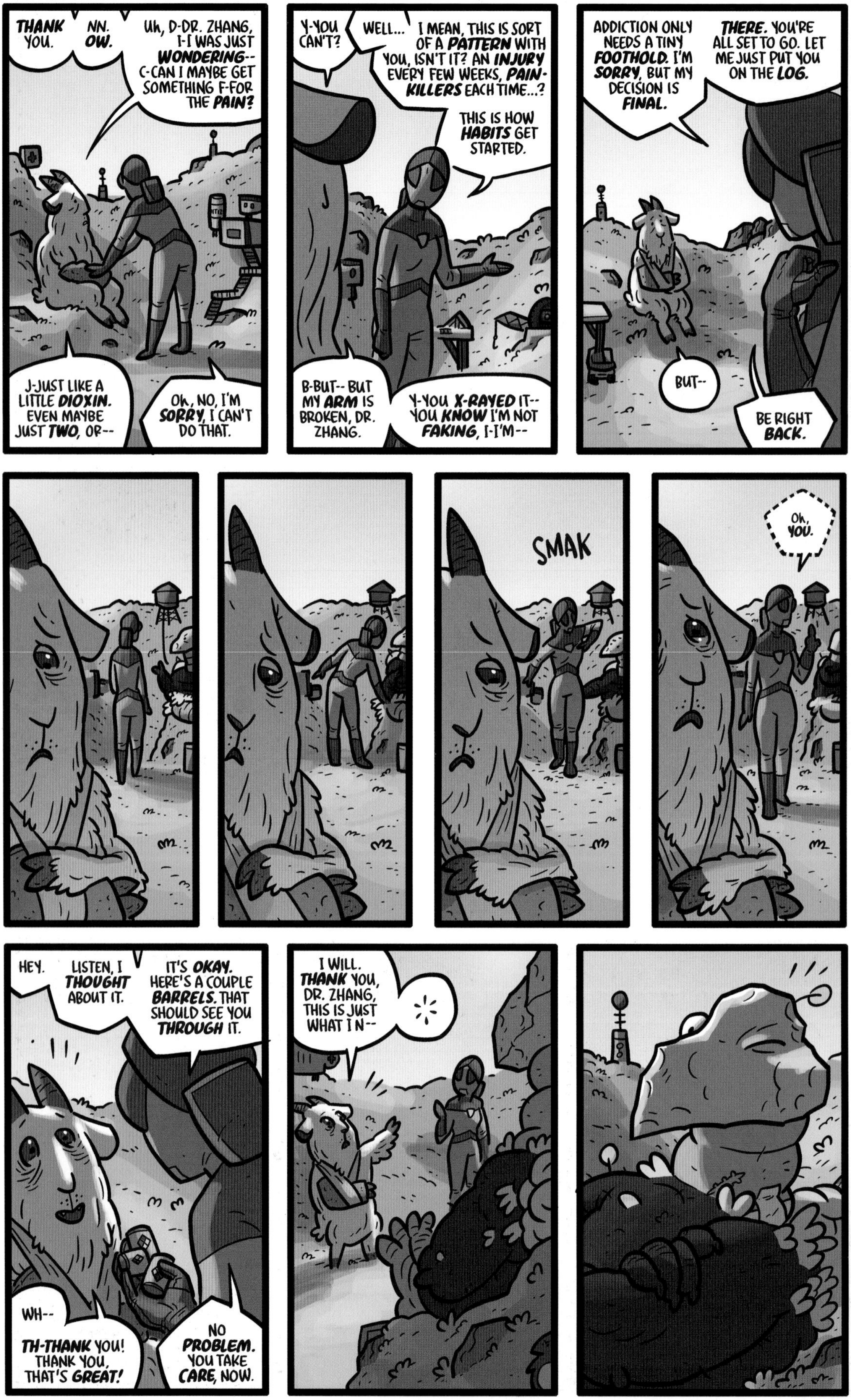
THANK YOU.
NN. OW.
Uh, D-DR. ZHANG, I-I WAS JUST WONDERING-- C-CAN I MAYBE GET SOMETHING F-FOR THE PAIN?
J-JUST LIKE A LITTLE DIOXIN. EVEN MAYBE JUST TWO, OR--
Oh, NO, I'M SORRY, I CAN'T DO THAT.
Y-YOU CAN'T?
WELL...
I MEAN, THIS IS SORT OF A PATTERN WITH YOU, ISN'T IT? AN INJURY EVERY FEW WEEKS, PAIN-KILLERS EACH TIME...?
THIS IS HOW HABITS GET STARTED.
B-BUT-- BUT MY ARM IS BROKEN, DR. ZHANG.
Y-YOU X-RAYED IT-- YOU KNOW I'M NOT FAKING, I-I'M--
ADDICTION ONLY NEEDS A TINY FOOTHOLD. I'M SORRY, BUT MY DECISION IS FINAL.
THERE. YOU'RE ALL SET TO GO. LET ME JUST PUT YOU ON THE LOG.
BUT--
BE RIGHT BACK.
SMAK
Oh, YOU.
HEY.
LISTEN, I THOUGHT ABOUT IT.
IT'S OKAY. HERE'S A COUPLE BARRELS. THAT SHOULD SEE YOU THROUGH IT.
WH--
TH-THANK YOU! THANK YOU, THAT'S GREAT!
NO PROBLEM. YOU TAKE CARE, NOW.
I WILL. THANK YOU, DR. ZHANG, THIS IS JUST WHAT I N--

Oh no.

YO, LOOK WHO'S *BACK!*

MR. *POPULAR!*

ALL RIGHT, THEN, BALLER, WHAT'D YOU *GET?*

YEAH, YOUR GIRL-FRIEND BRING SOME *URANIUM* STUFFED UP IN HER GILLS?

HA!

NAH, YO, YOU THINK *HE'S* GOT A *GIRLFRIEND?*

MEGAFAUNA'S GOTTA SHARE THAT LONELY *FARMER* JUST LIKE THE WHOLE *REST* OF HIS FLOCK, KNOW WHAT I'M SAYIN'?

HA HA HA HA HA HA HA

OKAY, FOR *REAL,* THEN, WOOD, WHAT YOU *GOT?*

L-LOOK, SKUNK, I-I MEAN...

C-CAN WE KEEP THIS ON THE *DEEP,* A LITTLE? M-MY VISITOR, I MEAN...

I-IT'S MY *MA-SH*-SHE CAN'T SMUGGLE *NOTHING* IN HERE.

I MEAN, SHE'S *TINY.*

HEY, HEY, CHINNY-CHIN UP, LITTLE BILLY GOAT.

DON'T YOU WORRY ABOUT *THAT* NONE.

YOU *KNOW* WE TAKE CARE OF OUR OWN.

W-WELL, uh...

OKAY THEN, MONGO, YOU *GOT* HIM?

WHAT?

23

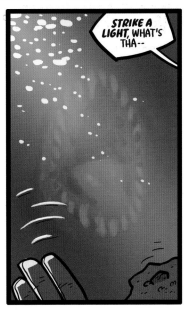

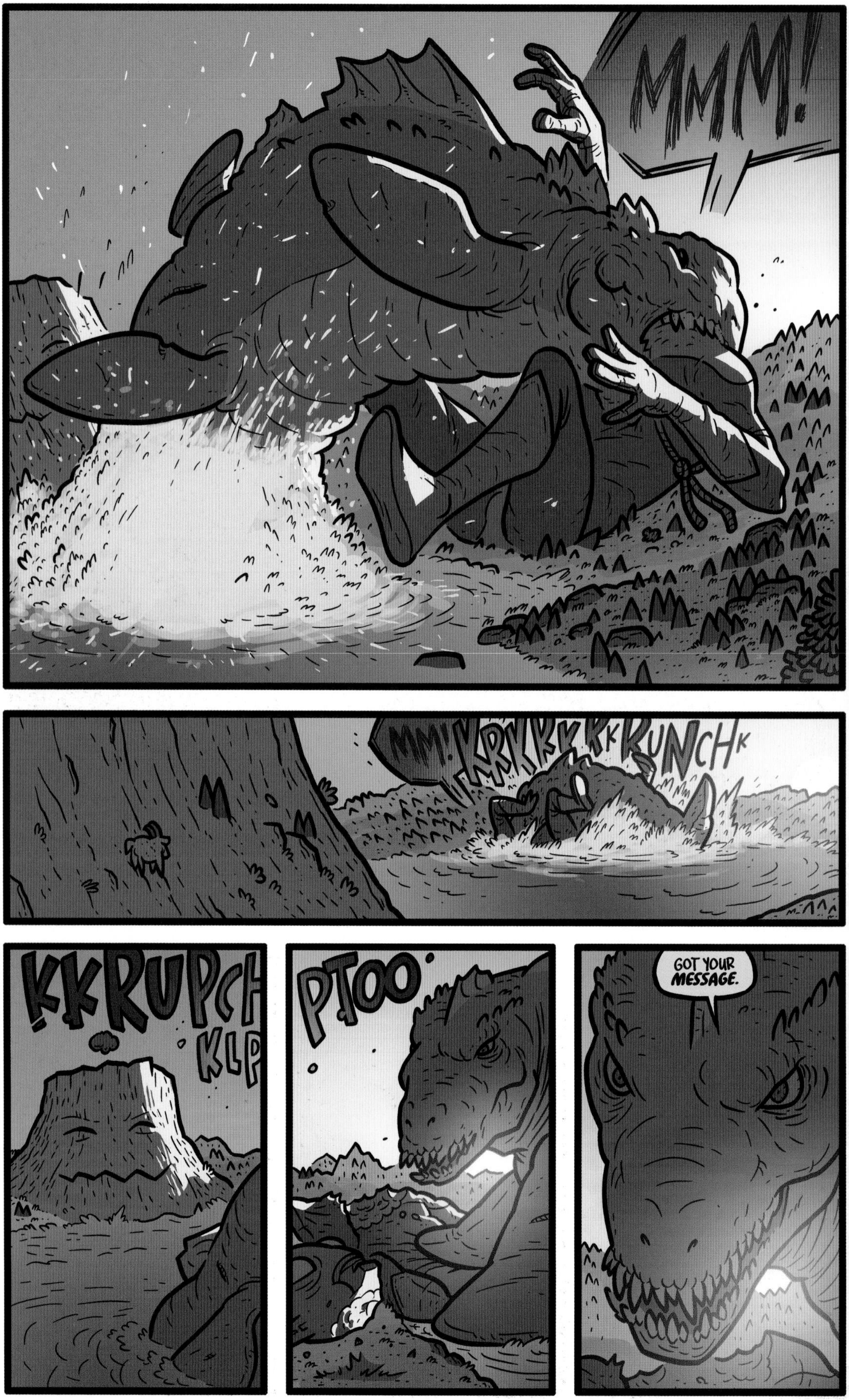

MMM!
MM!
KRKKKKKRUNCHK
KKRUPCH
KLP
PTOO
GOT YOUR MESSAGE.

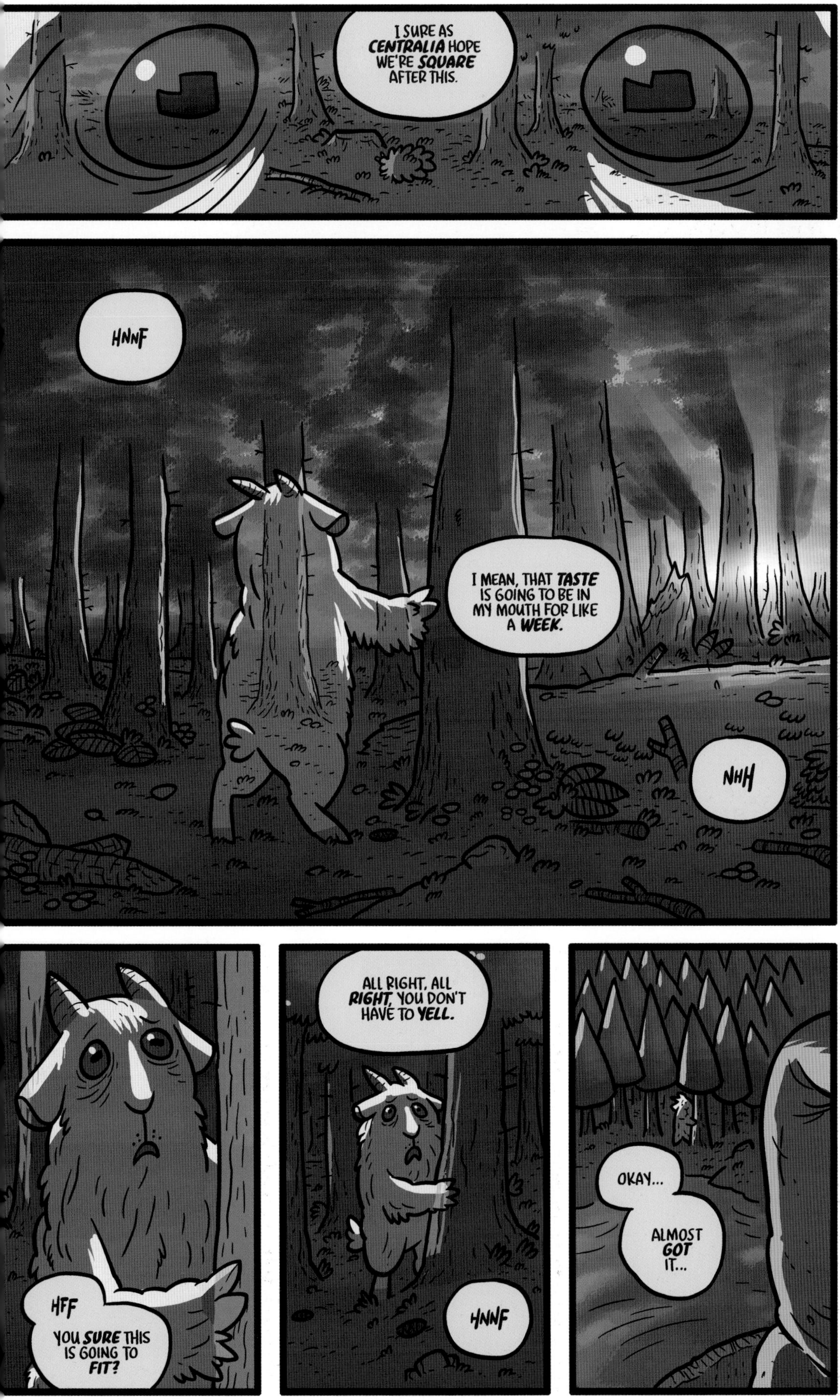
I SURE AS CENTRALIA HOPE WE'RE SQUARE AFTER THIS.
HNNF
I MEAN, THAT TASTE IS GOING TO BE IN MY MOUTH FOR LIKE A WEEK.
NHH
HFF
YOU SURE THIS IS GOING TO FIT?
ALL RIGHT, ALL RIGHT, YOU DON'T HAVE TO YELL.
HNNF
OKAY...
ALMOST GOT IT...

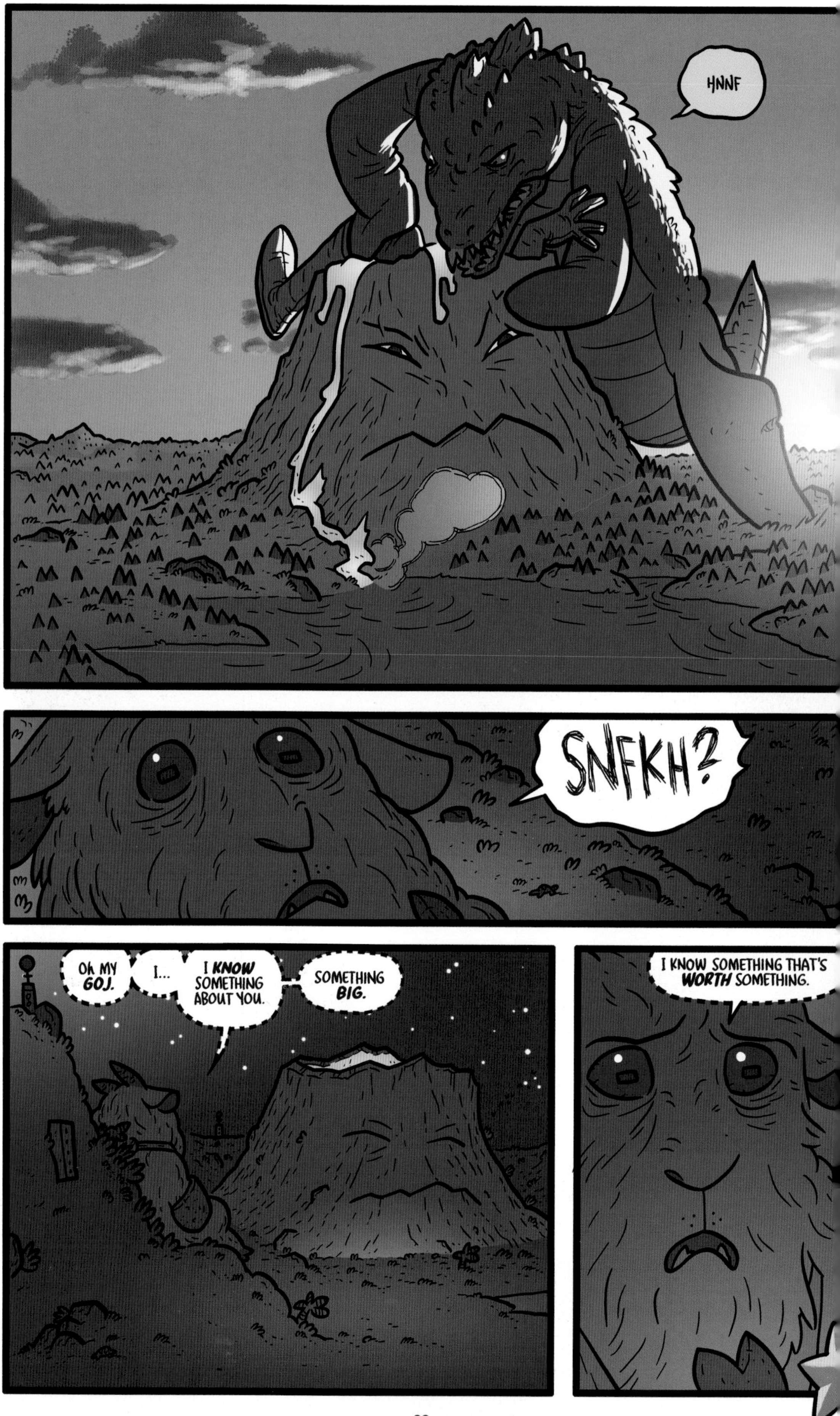
HNNF
SNFKH?
Oh MY GOJ.
I...
I KNOW SOMETHING ABOUT YOU.
SOMETHING BIG.
I KNOW SOMETHING THAT'S WORTH SOMETHING.

EPISODE 2

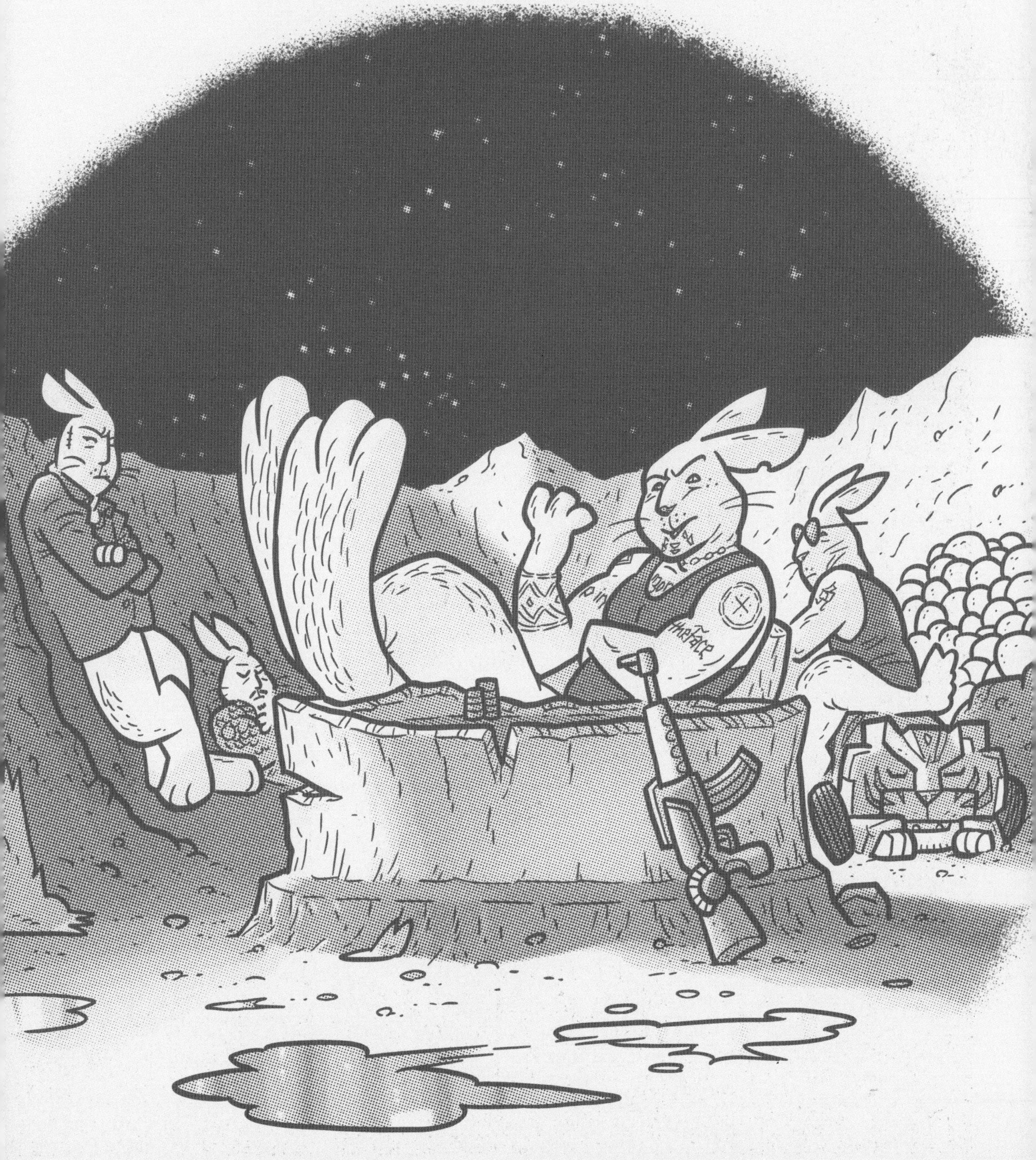

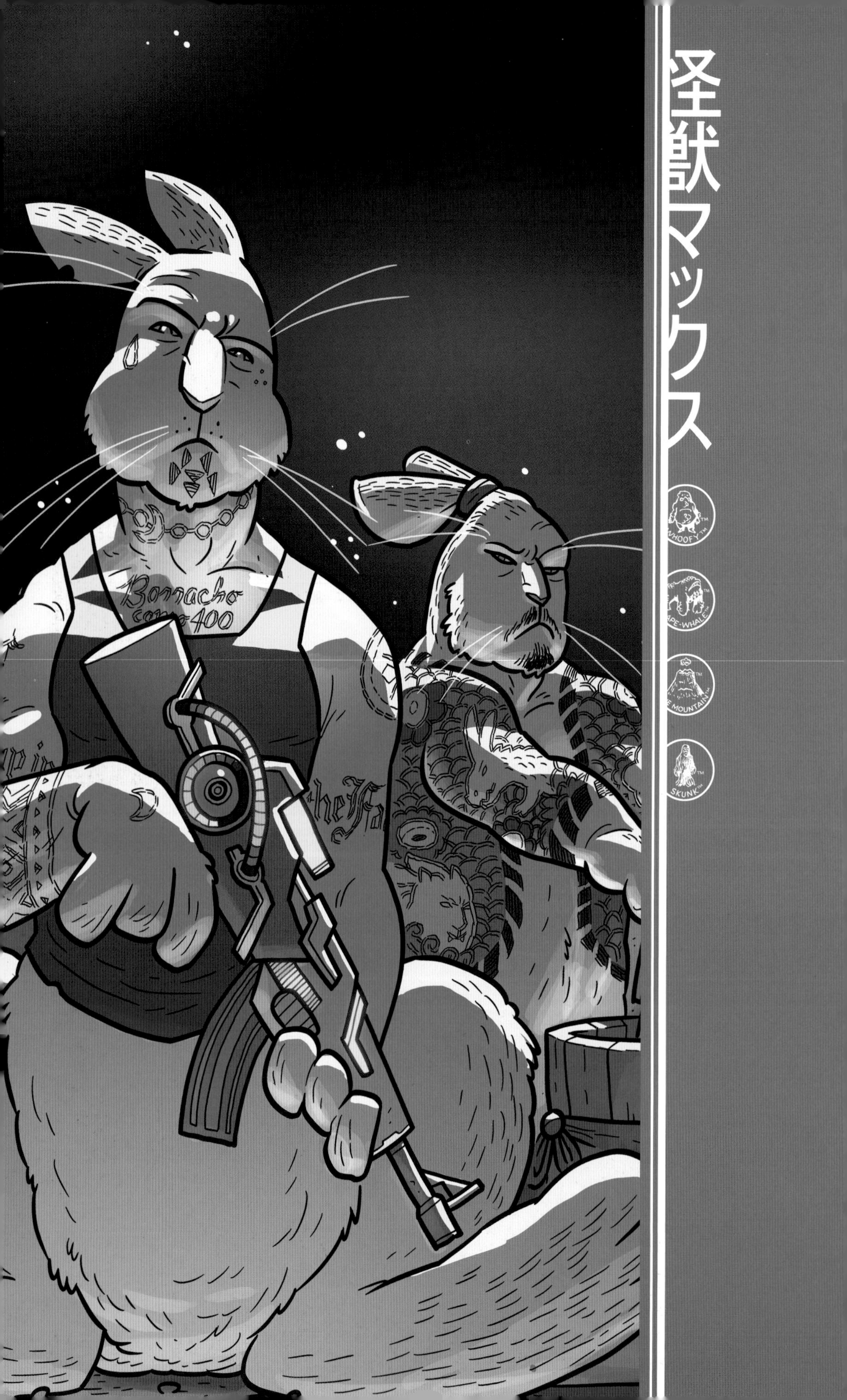
怪獣マックス
Borracho
APE-WHALE
SKUNK

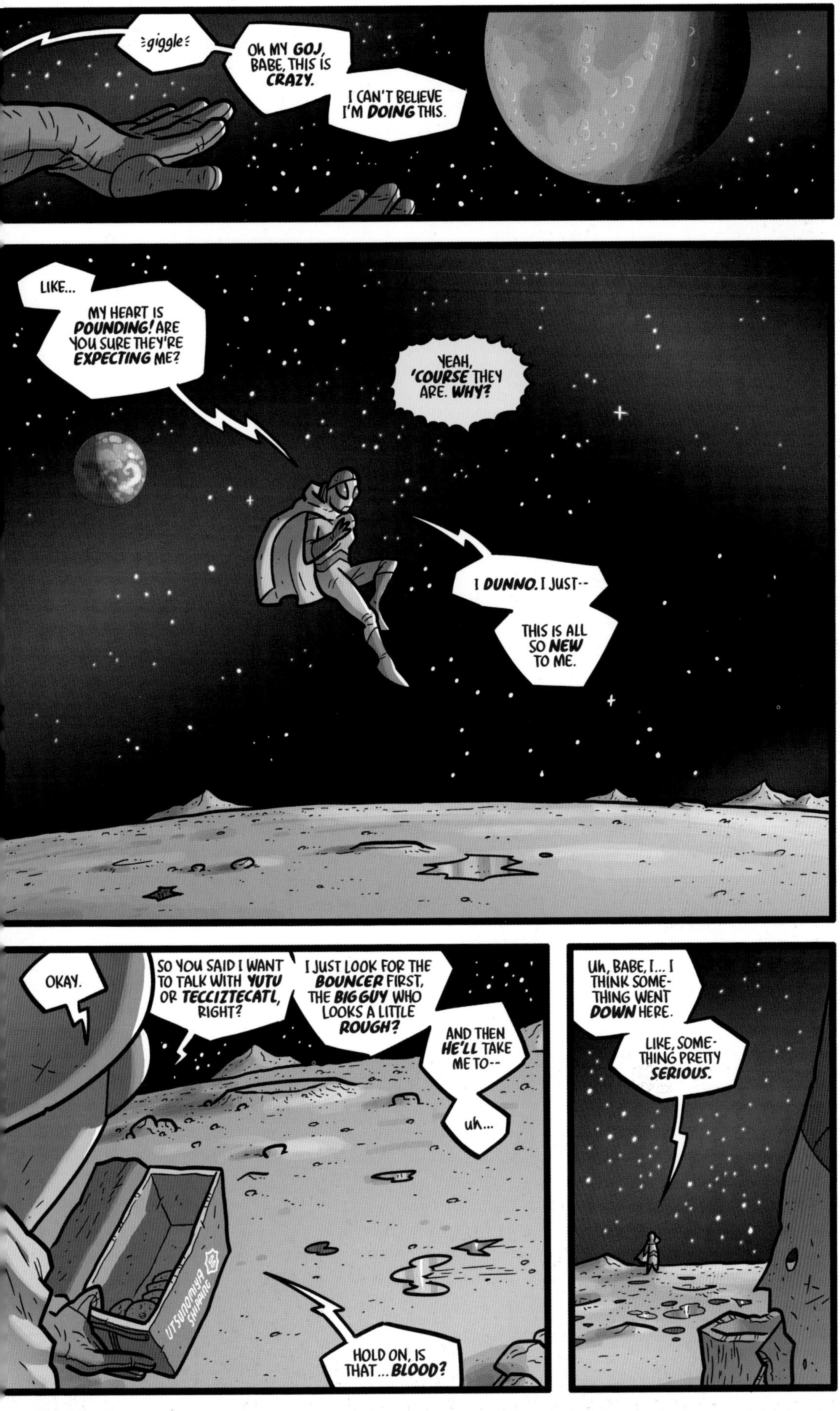

giggle
Oh MY GOJ, BABE, THIS IS CRAZY.
I CAN'T BELIEVE I'M DOING THIS.
LIKE...
MY HEART IS POUNDING! ARE YOU SURE THEY'RE EXPECTING ME?
YEAH, 'COURSE THEY ARE. WHY?
I DUNNO. I JUST--
THIS IS ALL SO NEW TO ME.
OKAY.
SO YOU SAID I WANT TO TALK WITH YUTU OR TECCIZTECATL, RIGHT?
I JUST LOOK FOR THE BOUNCER FIRST, THE BIG GUY WHO LOOKS A LITTLE ROUGH?
AND THEN HE'LL TAKE ME TO--
uh...
HOLD ON, IS THAT... BLOOD?
UTSUNOMIYA SHIPPING
Uh, BABE, I... I THINK SOME-THING WENT DOWN HERE.
LIKE, SOME-THING PRETTY SERIOUS.

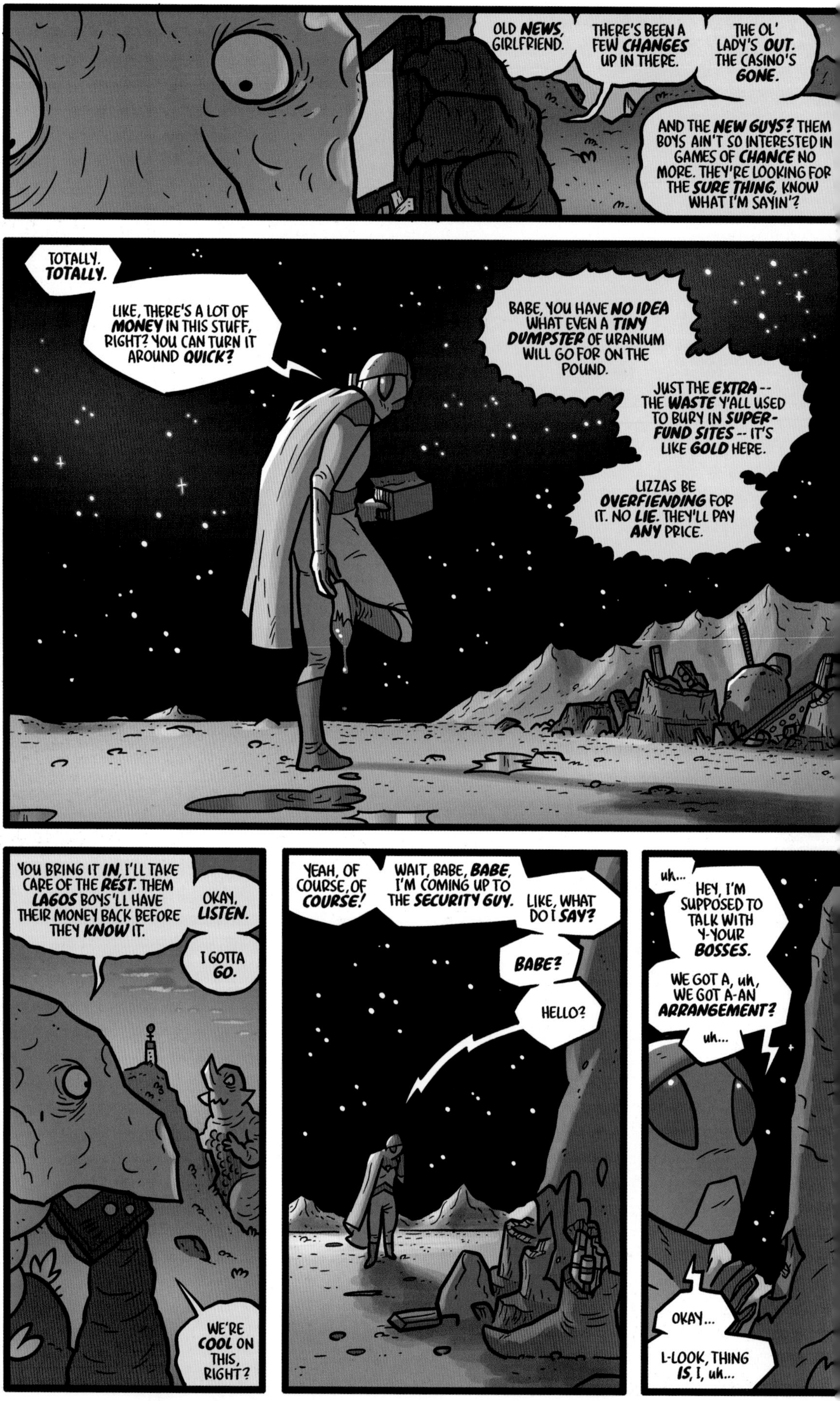

OLD NEWS, GIRLFRIEND.
THERE'S BEEN A FEW CHANGES UP IN THERE.
THE OL' LADY'S OUT. THE CASINO'S GONE.
AND THE NEW GUYS? THEM BOYS AIN'T SO INTERESTED IN GAMES OF CHANCE NO MORE. THEY'RE LOOKING FOR THE SURE THING, KNOW WHAT I'M SAYIN'?
TOTALLY. TOTALLY.
LIKE, THERE'S A LOT OF MONEY IN THIS STUFF, RIGHT? YOU CAN TURN IT AROUND QUICK?
BABE, YOU HAVE NO IDEA WHAT EVEN A TINY DUMPSTER OF URANIUM WILL GO FOR ON THE POUND.
JUST THE EXTRA -- THE WASTE Y'ALL USED TO BURY IN SUPER-FUND SITES -- IT'S LIKE GOLD HERE.
LIZZAS BE OVERFIENDING FOR IT. NO LIE. THEY'LL PAY ANY PRICE.
YOU BRING IT IN, I'LL TAKE CARE OF THE REST. THEM LAGOS BOYS'LL HAVE THEIR MONEY BACK BEFORE THEY KNOW IT.
OKAY, LISTEN.
I GOTTA GO.
WE'RE COOL ON THIS, RIGHT?
YEAH, OF COURSE, OF COURSE!
WAIT, BABE, BABE, I'M COMING UP TO THE SECURITY GUY.
LIKE, WHAT DO I SAY?
BABE?
HELLO?
uh...
HEY, I'M SUPPOSED TO TALK WITH Y-YOUR BOSSES.
WE GOT A, uh, WE GOT A-AN ARRANGEMENT?
uh...
OKAY...
L-LOOK, THING IS, I, uh...

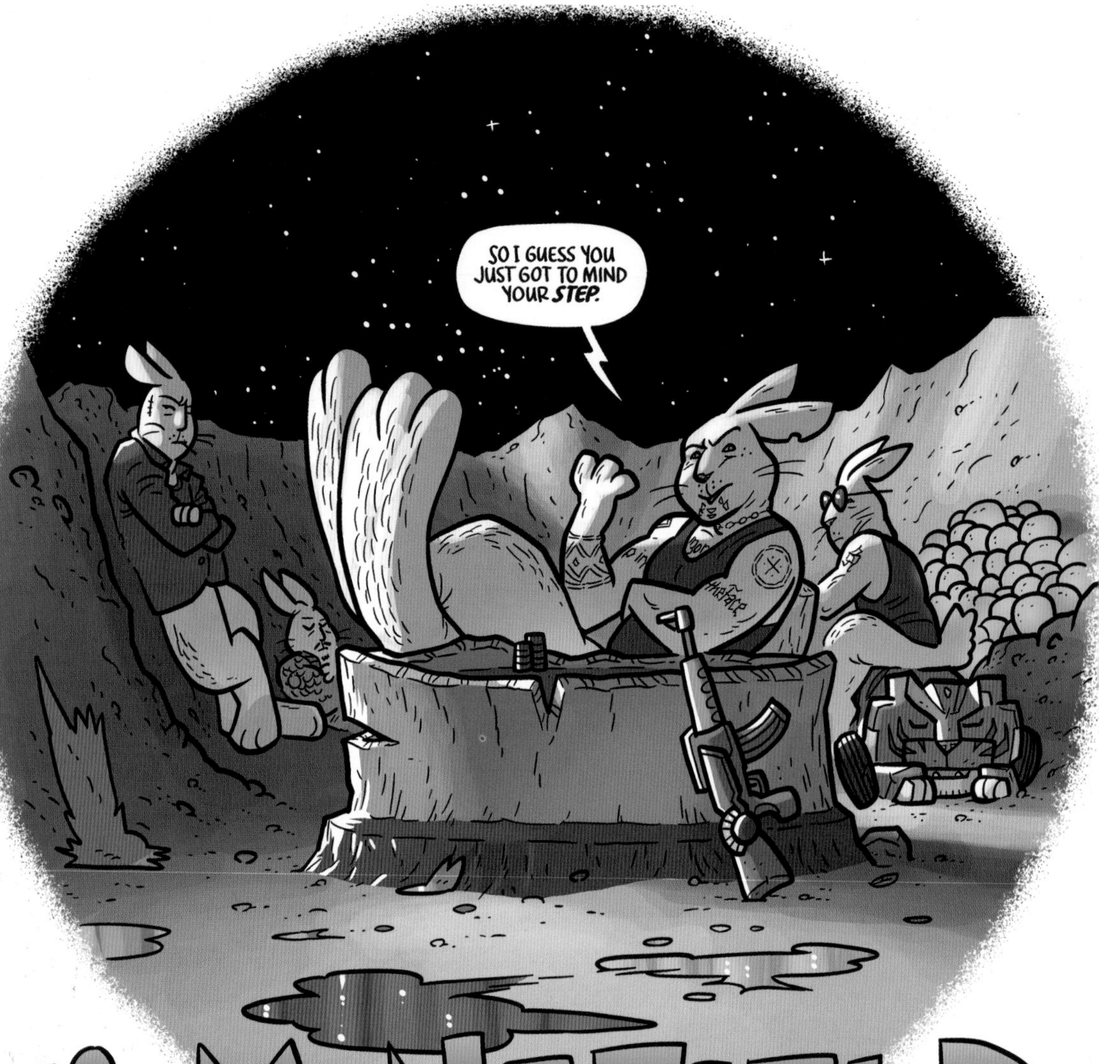
SO I GUESS YOU JUST GOT TO MIND YOUR STEP.

the MINEFIELD

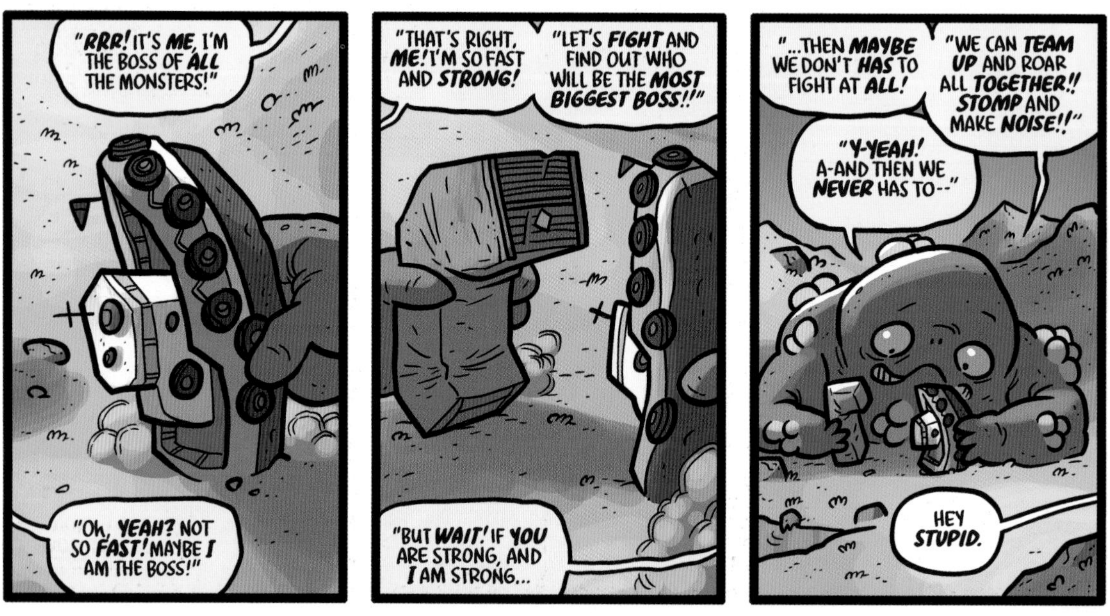
"RRR! IT'S ME, I'M THE BOSS OF ALL THE MONSTERS!"
"Oh, YEAH? NOT SO FAST! MAYBE I AM THE BOSS!"
"THAT'S RIGHT, ME! I'M SO FAST AND STRONG!
"LET'S FIGHT AND FIND OUT WHO WILL BE THE MOST BIGGEST BOSS!!"
"BUT WAIT! IF YOU ARE STRONG, AND I AM STRONG...
"...THEN MAYBE WE DON'T HAS TO FIGHT AT ALL!
"WE CAN TEAM UP AND ROAR ALL TOGETHER!! STOMP AND MAKE NOISE!!"
"Y-YEAH! A-AND THEN WE NEVER HAS TO--"
HEY STUPID.

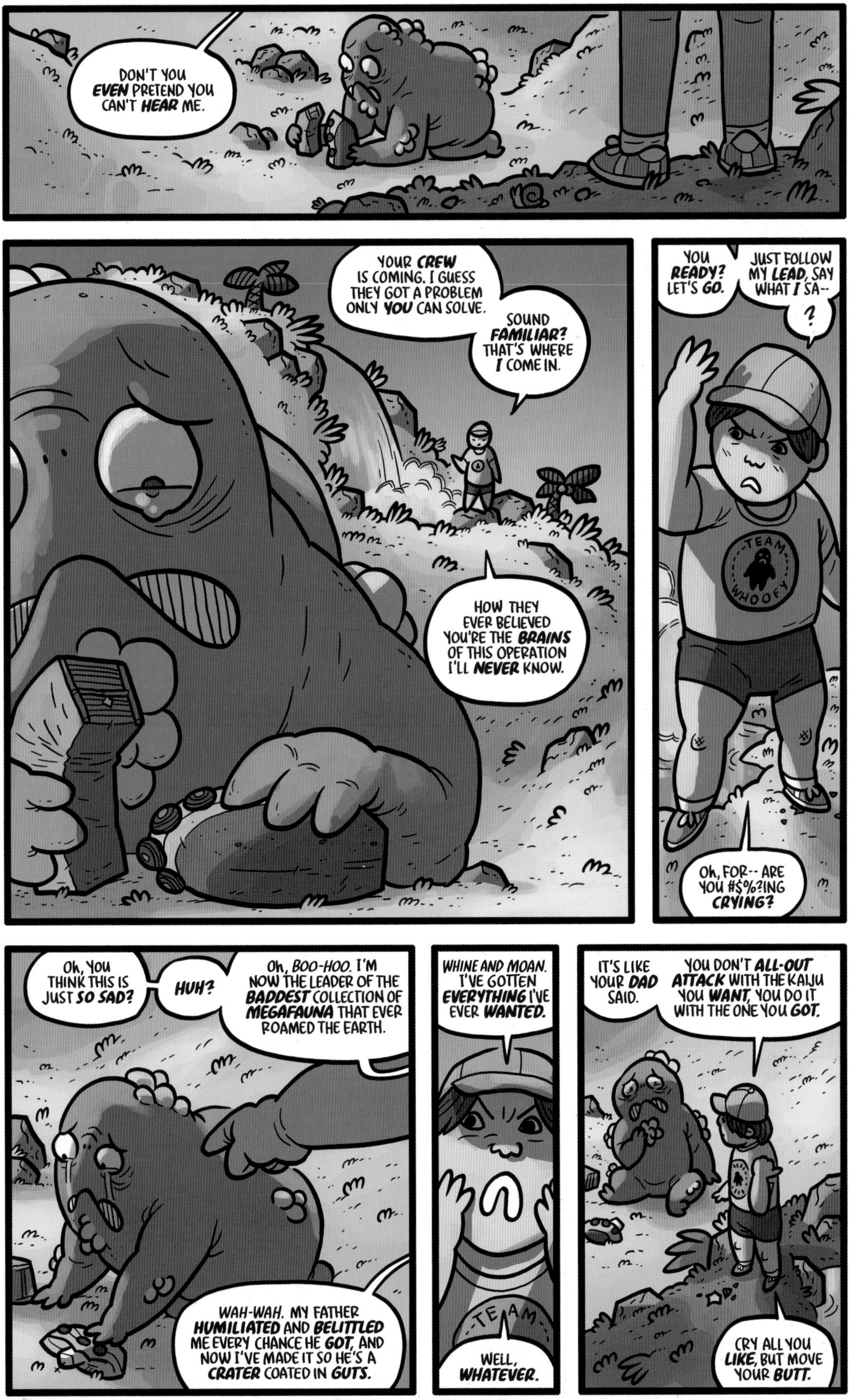
DON'T YOU EVEN PRETEND YOU CAN'T HEAR ME.
YOUR CREW IS COMING. I GUESS THEY GOT A PROBLEM ONLY YOU CAN SOLVE.
SOUND FAMILIAR? THAT'S WHERE I COME IN.
HOW THEY EVER BELIEVED YOU'RE THE BRAINS OF THIS OPERATION I'LL NEVER KNOW.
YOU READY? LET'S GO.
JUST FOLLOW MY LEAD, SAY WHAT I SA--
?
TEAM WHOOFY
Oh, FOR-- ARE YOU #$%?ING CRYING?
Oh, YOU THINK THIS IS JUST SO SAD?
HUH?
Oh, BOO-HOO. I'M NOW THE LEADER OF THE BADDEST COLLECTION OF MEGAFAUNA THAT EVER ROAMED THE EARTH.
WAH-WAH. MY FATHER HUMILIATED AND BELITTLED ME EVERY CHANCE HE GOT, AND NOW I'VE MADE IT SO HE'S A CRATER COATED IN GUTS.
WHINE AND MOAN. I'VE GOTTEN EVERYTHING I'VE EVER WANTED.
TEAM
WELL, WHATEVER.
IT'S LIKE YOUR DAD SAID.
YOU DON'T ALL-OUT ATTACK WITH THE KAIJU YOU WANT, YOU DO IT WITH THE ONE YOU GOT.
CRY ALL YOU LIKE, BUT MOVE YOUR BUTT.

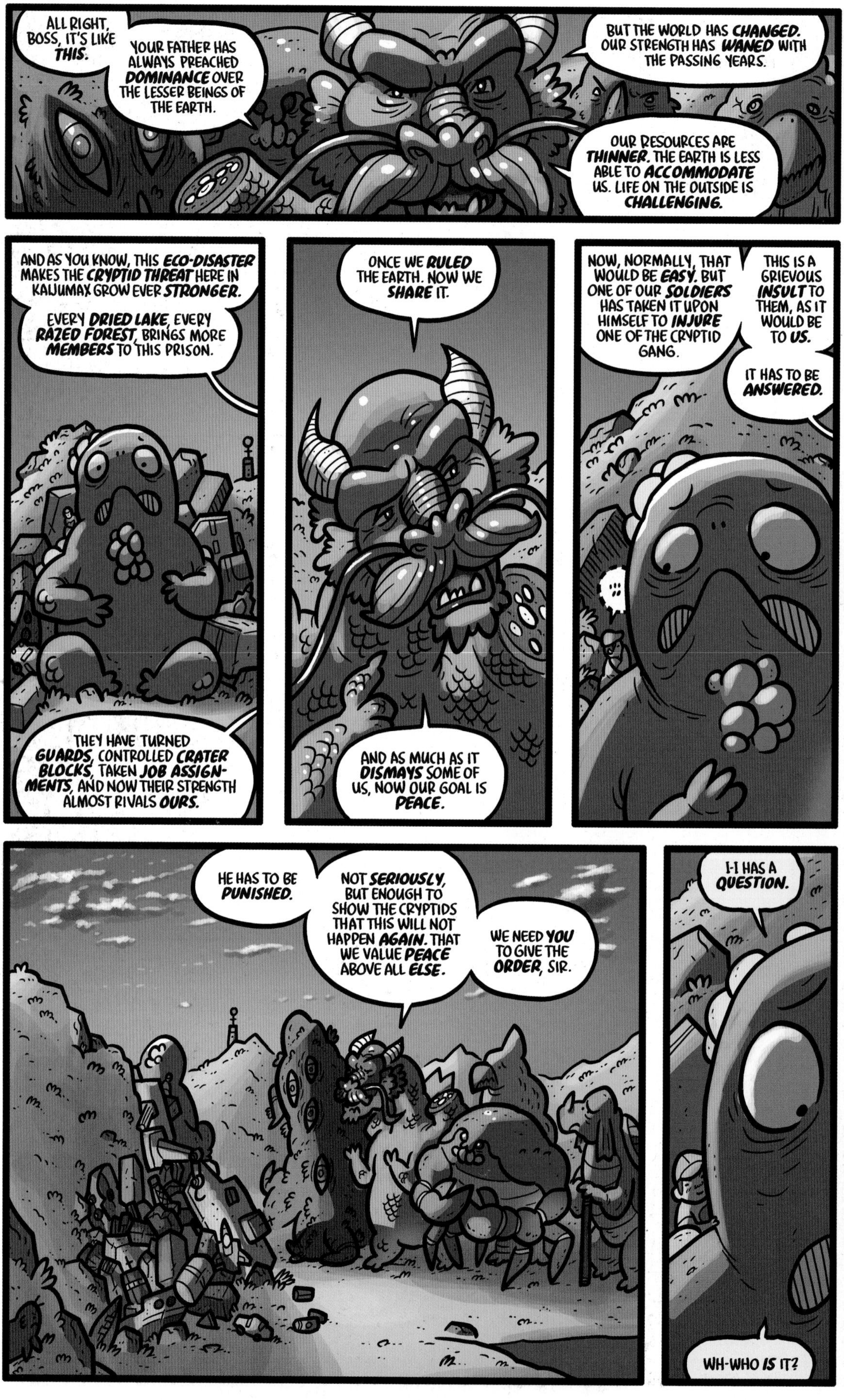
ALL RIGHT, BOSS, IT'S LIKE THIS.
YOUR FATHER HAS ALWAYS PREACHED DOMINANCE OVER THE LESSER BEINGS OF THE EARTH.
BUT THE WORLD HAS CHANGED. OUR STRENGTH HAS WANED WITH THE PASSING YEARS.
OUR RESOURCES ARE THINNER. THE EARTH IS LESS ABLE TO ACCOMMODATE US. LIFE ON THE OUTSIDE IS CHALLENGING.
AND AS YOU KNOW, THIS ECO-DISASTER MAKES THE CRYPTID THREAT HERE IN KAIJUMAX GROW EVER STRONGER.
EVERY DRIED LAKE, EVERY RAZED FOREST, BRINGS MORE MEMBERS TO THIS PRISON.
THEY HAVE TURNED GUARDS, CONTROLLED CRATER BLOCKS, TAKEN JOB ASSIGN-MENTS, AND NOW THEIR STRENGTH ALMOST RIVALS OURS.
ONCE WE RULED THE EARTH. NOW WE SHARE IT.
AND AS MUCH AS IT DISMAYS SOME OF US, NOW OUR GOAL IS PEACE.
NOW, NORMALLY, THAT WOULD BE EASY. BUT ONE OF OUR SOLDIERS HAS TAKEN IT UPON HIMSELF TO INJURE ONE OF THE CRYPTID GANG.
THIS IS A GRIEVOUS INSULT TO THEM, AS IT WOULD BE TO US.
IT HAS TO BE ANSWERED.
HE HAS TO BE PUNISHED.
NOT SERIOUSLY, BUT ENOUGH TO SHOW THE CRYPTIDS THAT THIS WILL NOT HAPPEN AGAIN. THAT WE VALUE PEACE ABOVE ALL ELSE.
WE NEED YOU TO GIVE THE ORDER, SIR.
I-I HAS A QUESTION.
WH-WHO IS IT?

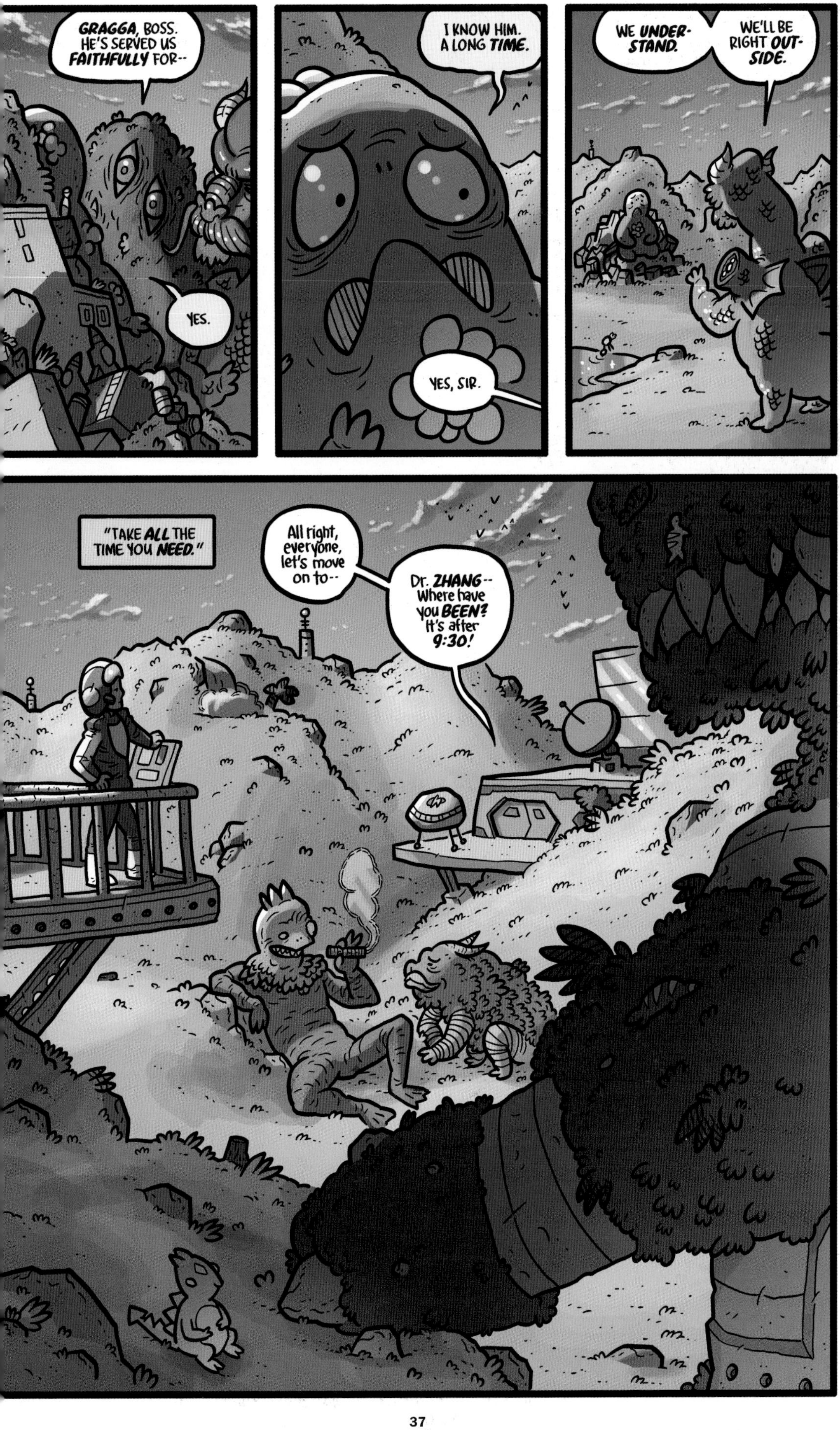
GRAGGA, BOSS. HE'S SERVED US FAITHFULLY FOR--
YES.
I KNOW HIM. A LONG TIME.
YES, SIR.
WE UNDER-STAND.
WE'LL BE RIGHT OUT-SIDE.
"TAKE ALL THE TIME YOU NEED."
All right, everyone, let's move on to--
Dr. ZHANG-- Where have you BEEN? It's after 9:30!

LISTEN, man, if **Z-43** taught us **ANYTHING** in the last week, it's that these lizzers have been getting away with **WAY** too much for **WAY** too long--

AHEM. Okay, now we don't--

Oh, yeah, '*SCUSE* **ME**, we can't **CALL** 'em that anymore.

I'm sayin' this: I got this **CRYSTAL BADGE** from the far side of the **NEBULA OF THE ETERNAL SUNRISE**, and if any of those cloakers want to step to that...

HA HA HA HA HA

...they're gonna get a beam of **DARK ENERGY** right up where the **SUN** don't shine.

Okay, okay. I **GET** it. But **LISTEN**.

Some of these kaiju are sentenced to a full **LIFE-CYCLE**.

They have **NOTHING** better to do than to **MESS** with you, you can't go all **REDMAN** on 'em every single **TIME**.

So choose your **MEGA-BATTLES**.

When it comes down **TO** it, there's a lot more of **THEM** than there are of **US**. If they **WANT** to take this prison, they **CAN**.

Sure, they all hate each other **NOW**...

...but if they agree that **HUMANS** are the enemy, they'll team up and take us **DOWN**...

"...no matter **HOW** strange their bedfellows are."

NNF

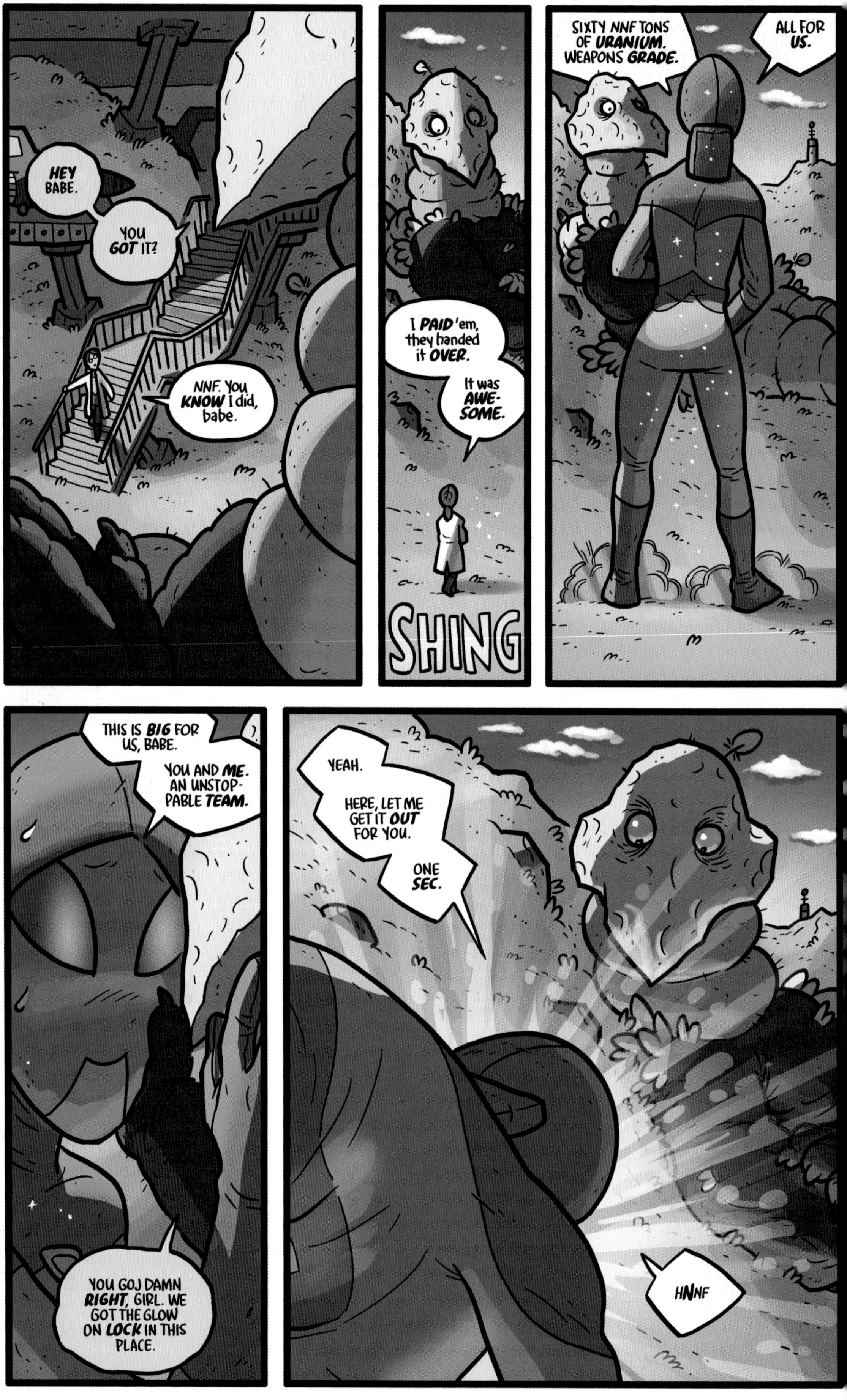
HEY BABE.
YOU GOT IT?
NNF. YOU KNOW I did, babe.
I PAID 'em, they handed it OVER.
It was AWE-SOME.
SHING
SIXTY NNF TONS OF URANIUM. WEAPONS GRADE.
ALL FOR US.
THIS IS BIG FOR US, BABE.
YOU AND ME. AN UNSTOP-PABLE TEAM.
YOU GOJ DAMN RIGHT, GIRL. WE GOT THE GLOW ON LOCK IN THIS PLACE.
YEAH.
HERE, LET ME GET IT OUT FOR YOU.
ONE SEC.
HNNF

41

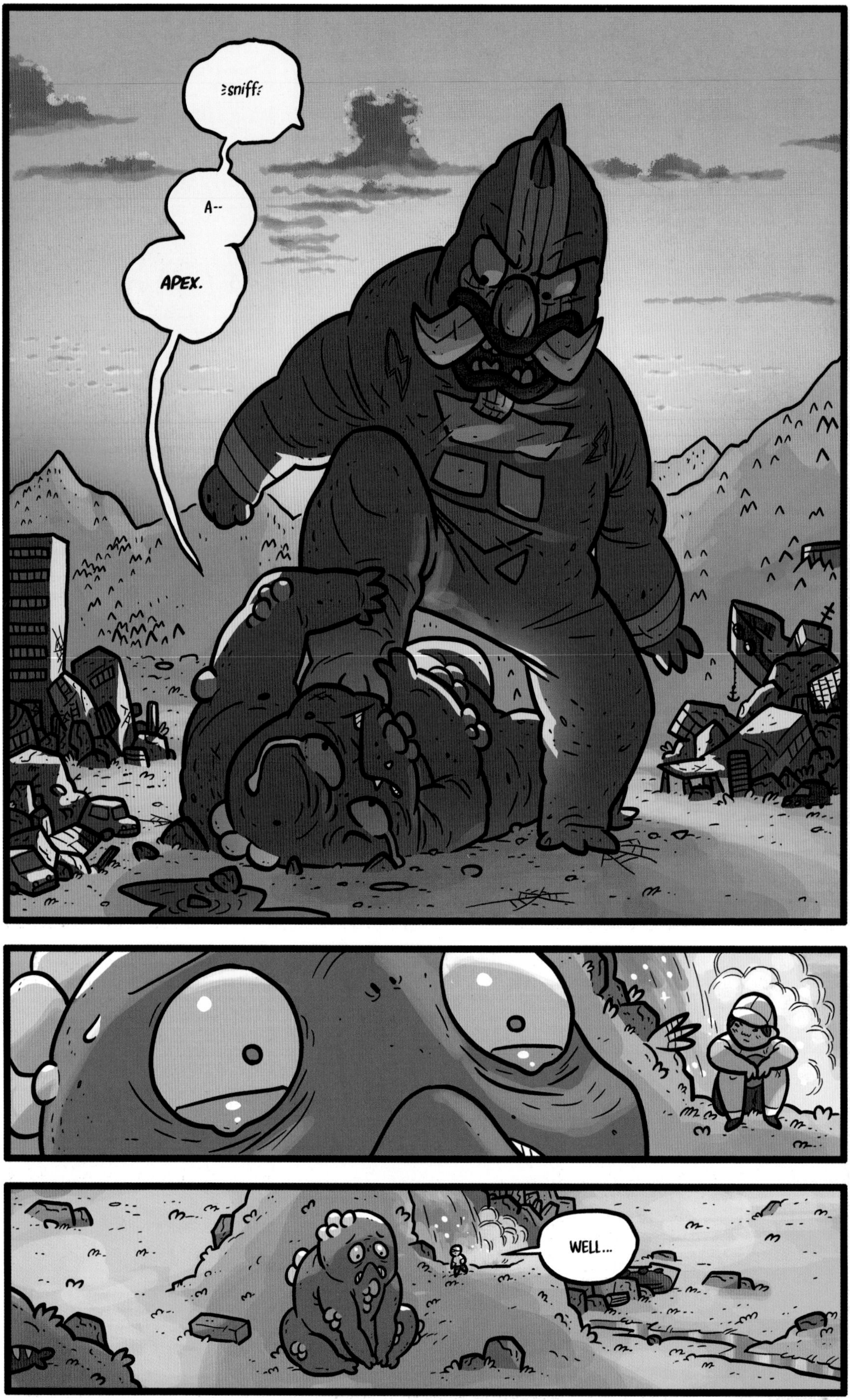

:sniff:
A--
APEX.
WELL...

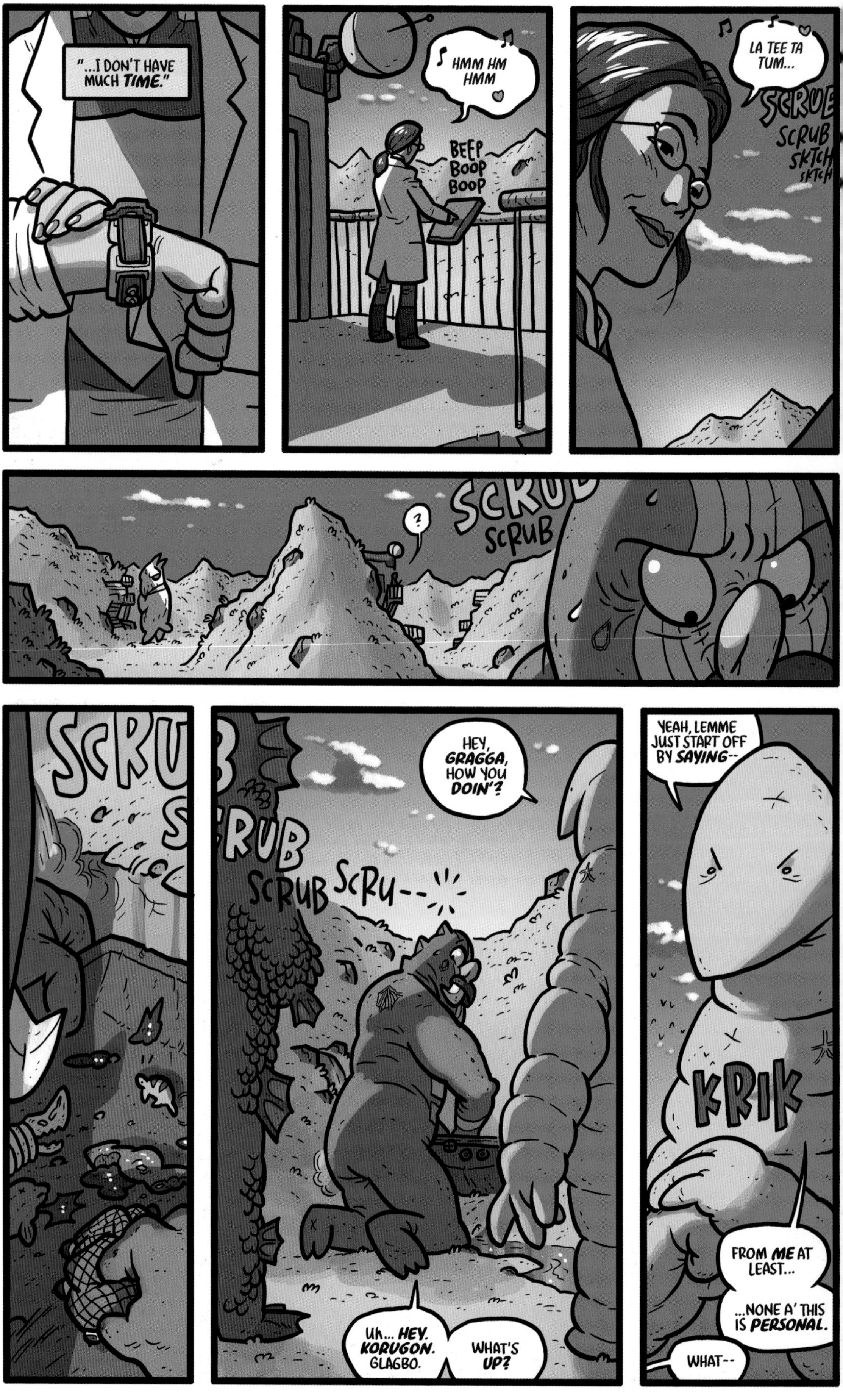
"...I DON'T HAVE MUCH TIME."
HMM HM HMM
BEEP BOOP BOOP
LA TEE TA TUM...
SCRUB SCRUB SKTCH SKTCH
?
SCRUB SCRUB
SCRUB
SCRUB SCRUB SCRU--
HEY, GRAGGA, HOW YOU DOIN'?
Uh... HEY. KORUGON. GLAGBO.
WHAT'S UP?
YEAH, LEMME JUST START OFF BY SAYING--
KRIK
FROM ME AT LEAST...
...NONE A' THIS IS PERSONAL.
WHAT--

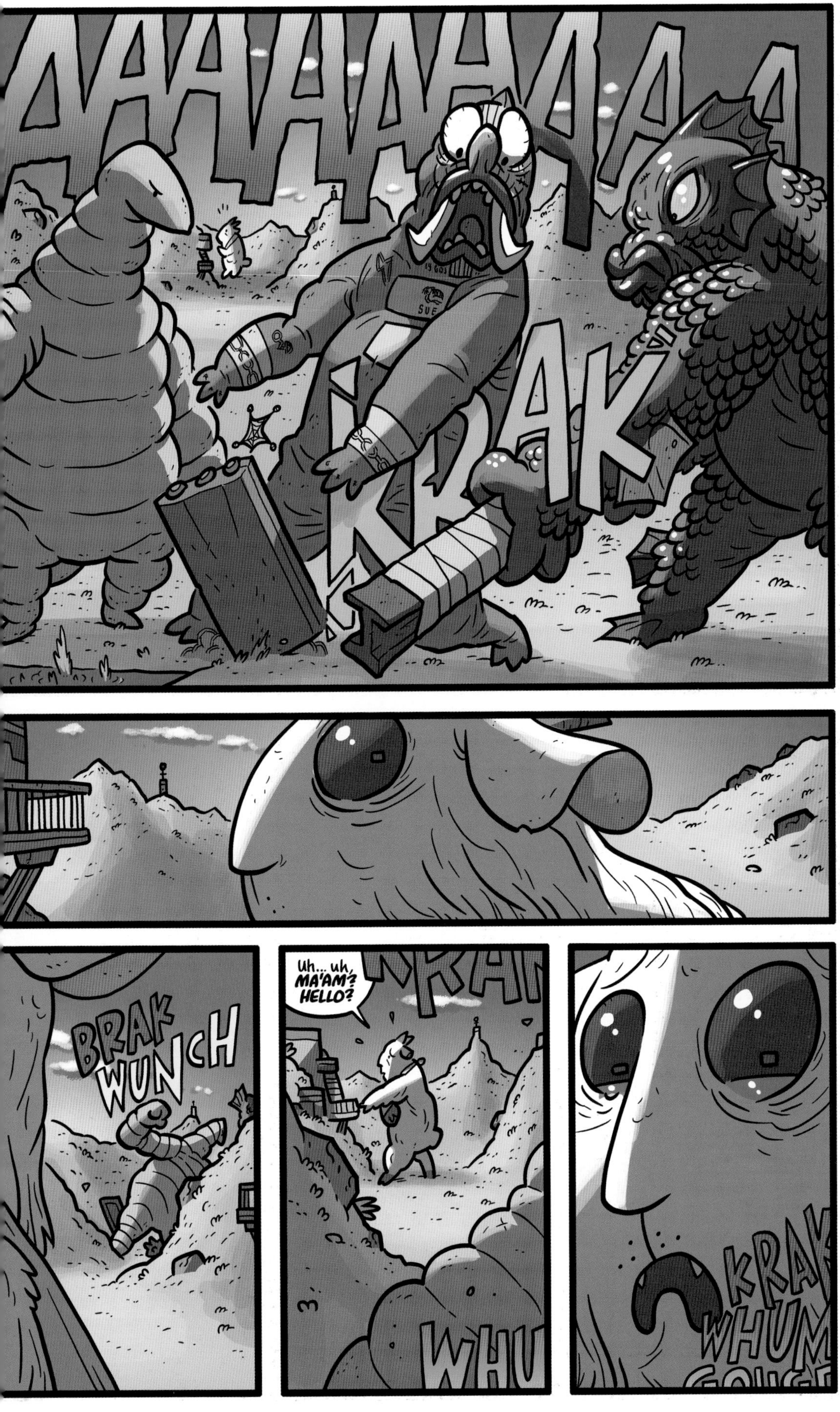
AAAAAAAAA
KRAK
BRAK
WUNCH
Uh... uh, MA'AM? HELLO?
KRAK
WHU
KRAK
WHUM

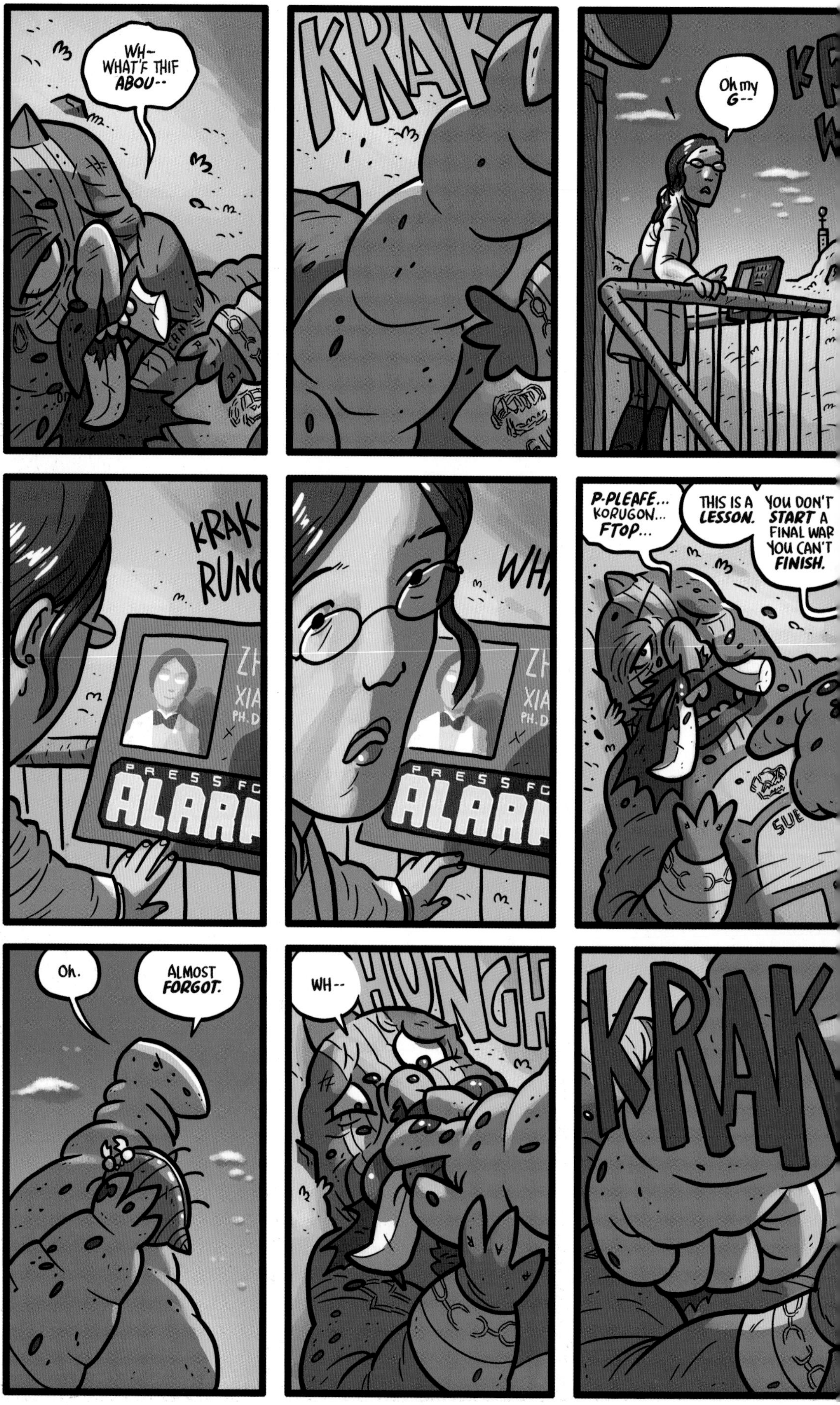
WH- WHAT'F THIF ABOU--
KRAK
Oh my G--
KRAK
PRESS FO
ALAR
P-PLEAFE... KORUGON... FTOP...
THIS IS A LESSON.
YOU DON'T START A FINAL WAR YOU CAN'T FINISH.
SUE
Oh.
ALMOST FORGOT.
WH--
HUNGH
KRAK

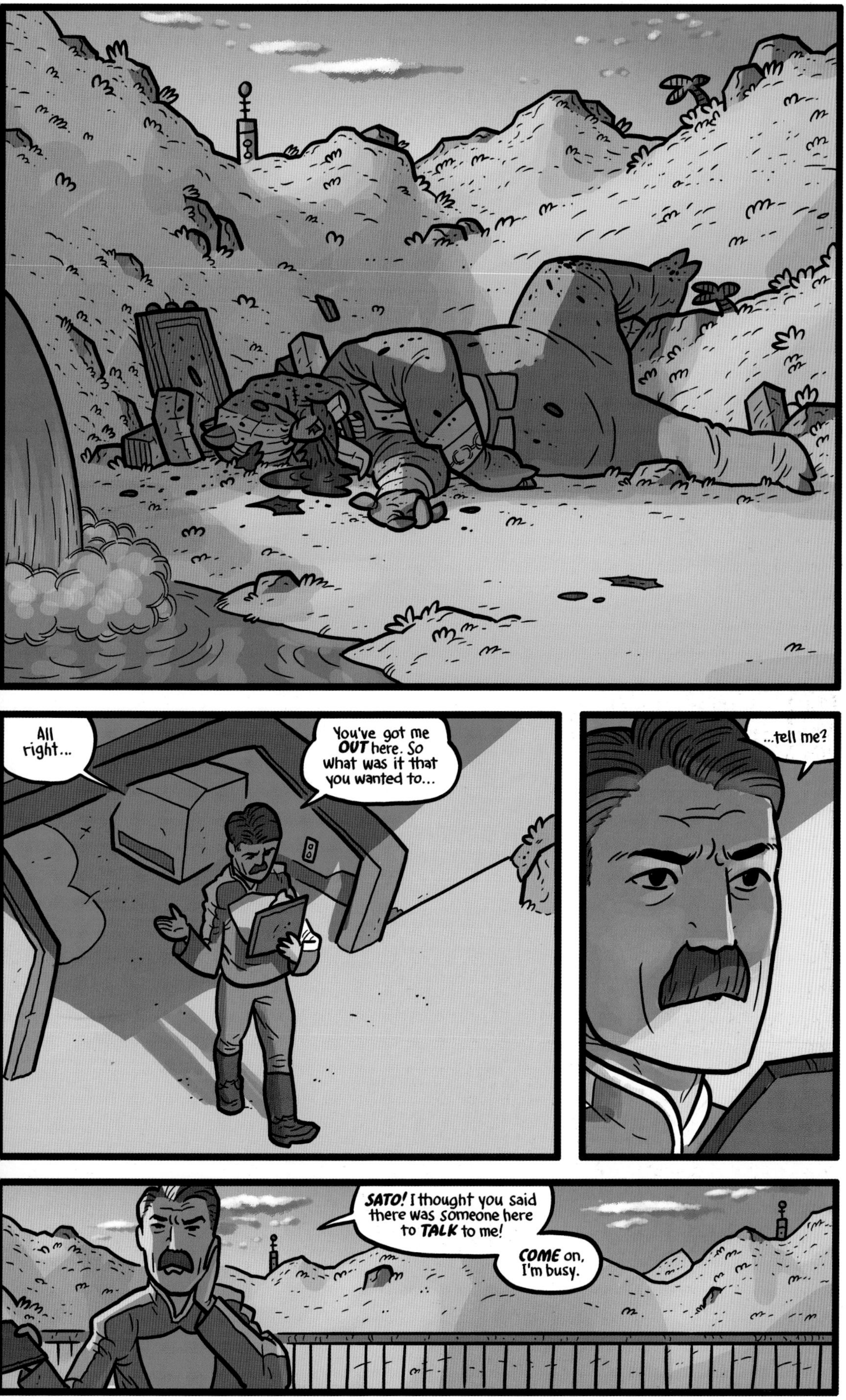
All right...
You've got me OUT here. So what was it that you wanted to...
...tell me?
SATO! I thought you said there was someone here to TALK to me!
COME on, I'm busy.

"I've got *NO* time for *FOOLISHNESS.*"

ZONN!

LISTEN, WE NEED TO GET THAT *MONEY,* AND WE NEED TO GET IT *NOW.*

HMH?

EVEN JUST A *BIT,* Y-YOU KNOW, TO SHOW SOME *GOOD FAITH* BEFORE YOU GET THE *REST.*

PFF!

C'MON, BABE.

WHAT'S A BIG *DEAL* ALL A SUDDEN?

NOTHING'S THE BIG DEAL, IT'S JUST...

...I-IT'S JUST WE JUST NEED TO STAY ON *TOP* OF THIS STUFF IF--

WAIT A SEC-- HAVE YOU EVEN *MOVED?*

MOVED? WHY?

THERE'S NO *NEED,* BABE. *YELLOWHORNS* SENT SOME-ONE BY TO *COLLECT.*

THE MONEY I BORROWED FOR *THIS,* PLUS WHAT I OWED THEM FROM *BEFORE.*

IS *COOL.* THEY JUST TOOK SOME OF THE *URANIUM* AS PAYMENT AND WE'RE *SQUARE.*

WHAT?!

SQUARE WITH *THEM,* BUT WHAT ABOUT THE FRIGGIN' *BUNNIES* ON THE *MOON?*

HUH?

THEY'RE GONNA NEED THEIR *MONEY* BACK IN LESS THAN--

??!

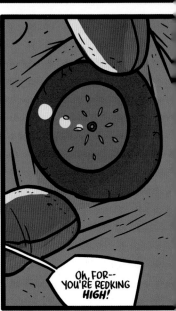

OH, FOR-- YOU'RE REDKING *HIGH!*

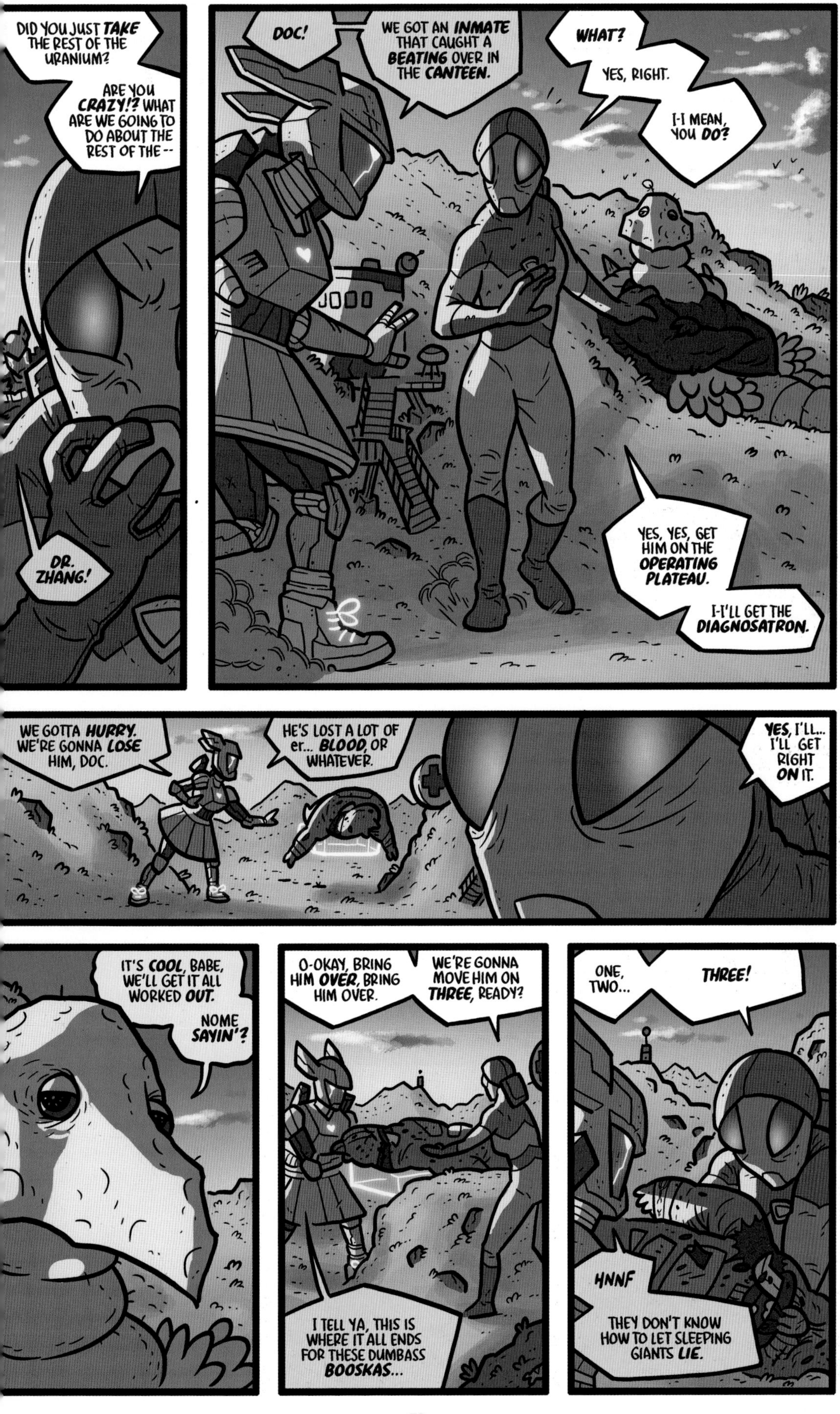
DID YOU JUST TAKE THE REST OF THE URANIUM?
ARE YOU CRAZY!? WHAT ARE WE GOING TO DO ABOUT THE REST OF THE --
DR. ZHANG!
DOC!
WE GOT AN INMATE THAT CAUGHT A BEATING OVER IN THE CANTEEN.
WHAT?
YES, RIGHT.
I-I MEAN, YOU DO?
YES, YES, GET HIM ON THE OPERATING PLATEAU.
I-I'LL GET THE DIAGNOSATRON.
WE GOTTA HURRY. WE'RE GONNA LOSE HIM, DOC.
HE'S LOST A LOT OF er... BLOOD, OR WHATEVER.
YES, I'LL... I'LL GET RIGHT ON IT.
IT'S COOL, BABE, WE'LL GET IT ALL WORKED OUT.
NOME SAYIN'?
O-OKAY, BRING HIM OVER, BRING HIM OVER.
WE'RE GONNA MOVE HIM ON THREE, READY?
I TELL YA, THIS IS WHERE IT ALL ENDS FOR THESE DUMBASS BOOSKAS...
ONE, TWO...
THREE!
HNNF
THEY DON'T KNOW HOW TO LET SLEEPING GIANTS LIE.

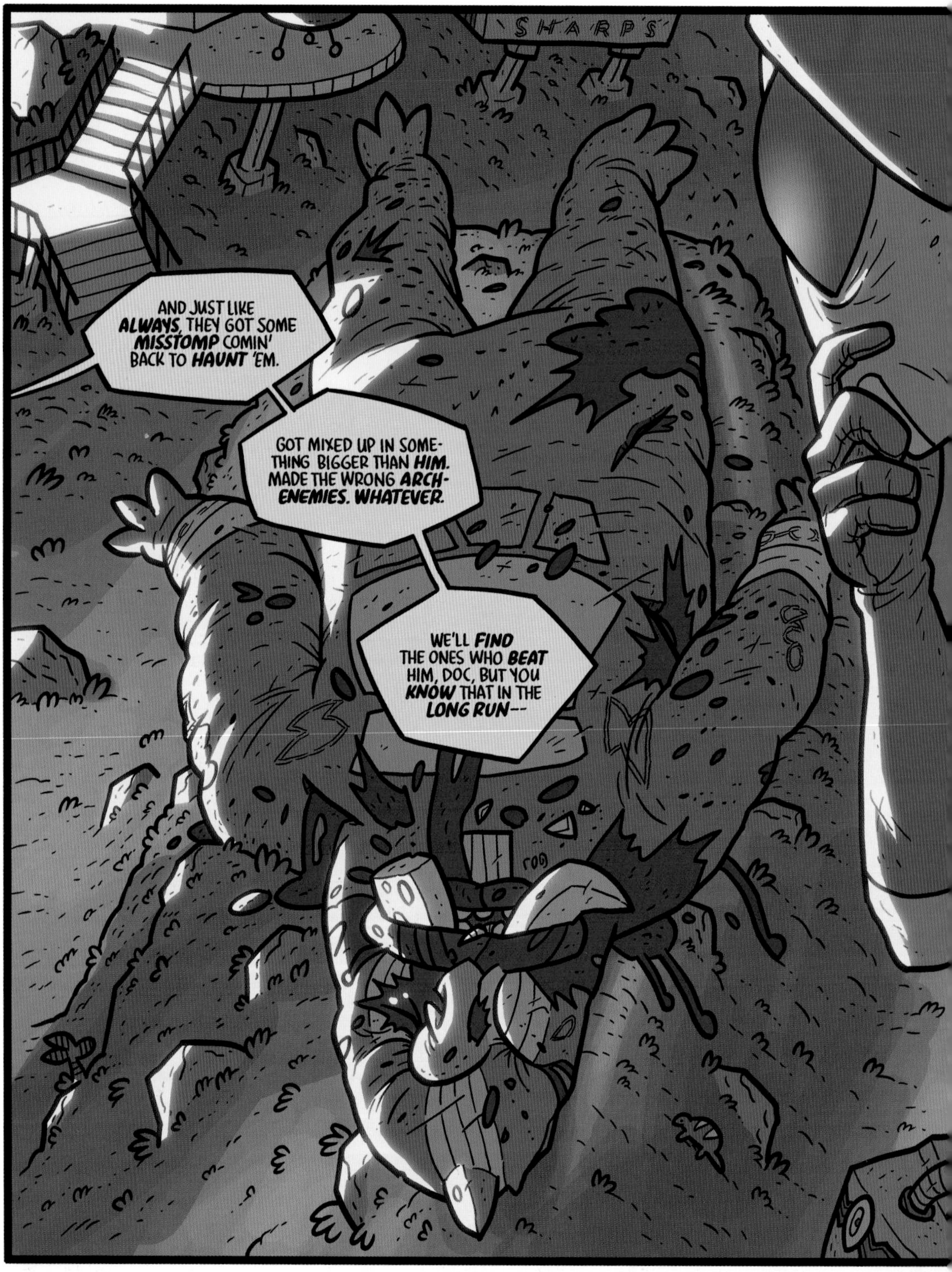
SHARPS
AND JUST LIKE ALWAYS, THEY GOT SOME MISSTOMP COMIN' BACK TO HAUNT 'EM.
GOT MIXED UP IN SOMETHING BIGGER THAN HIM. MADE THE WRONG ARCH-ENEMIES. WHATEVER.
WE'LL FIND THE ONES WHO BEAT HIM, DOC, BUT YOU KNOW THAT IN THE LONG RUN--

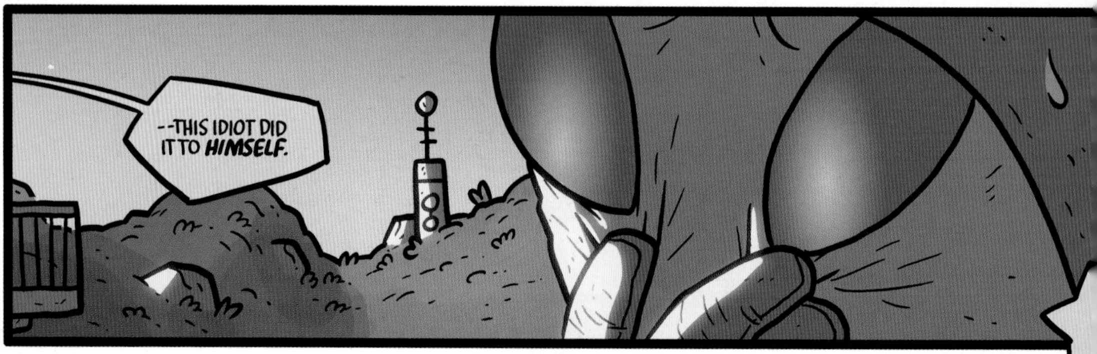
--THIS IDIOT DID IT TO HIMSELF.

EPISODE 3

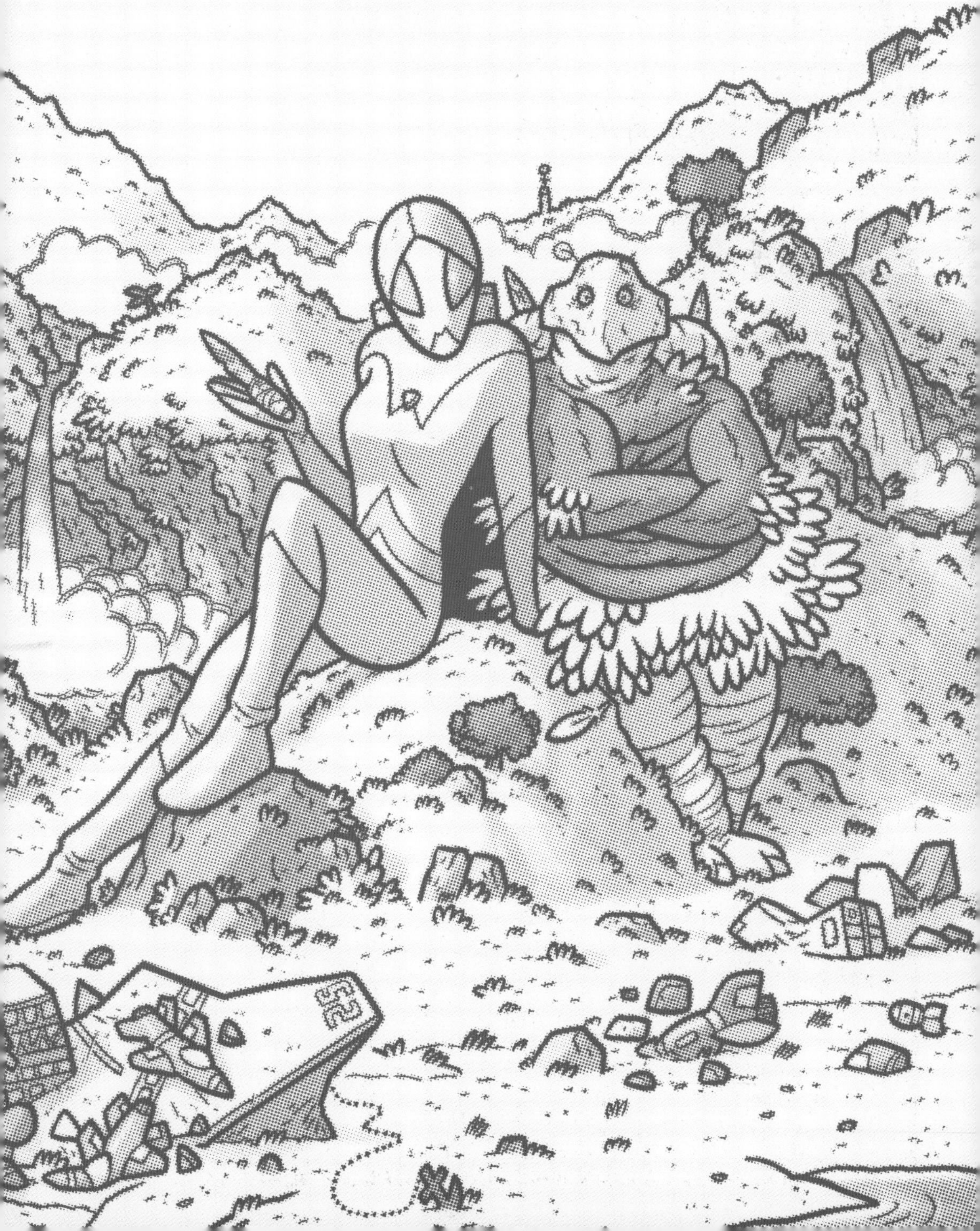

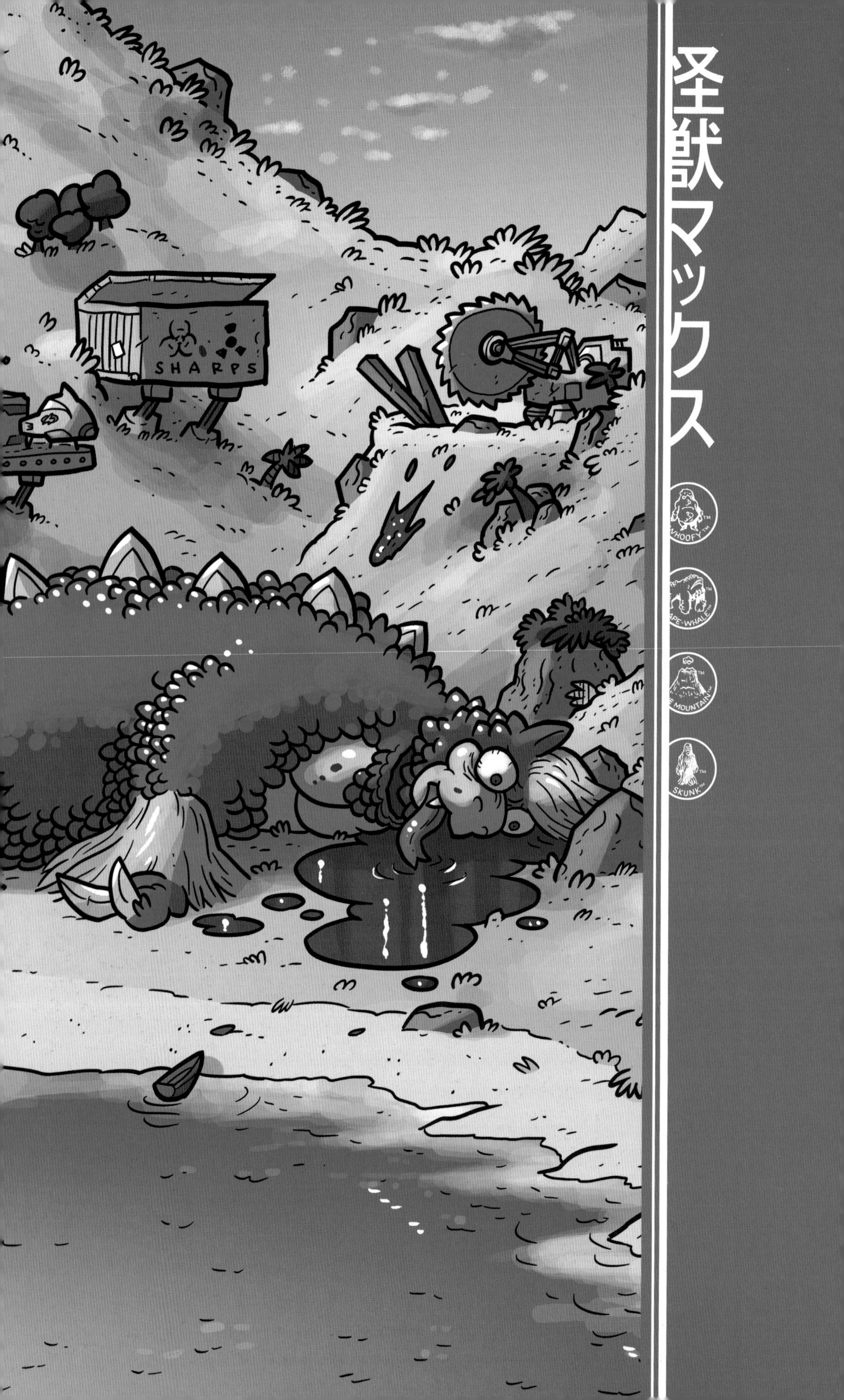
SHARPS
怪獣マックス

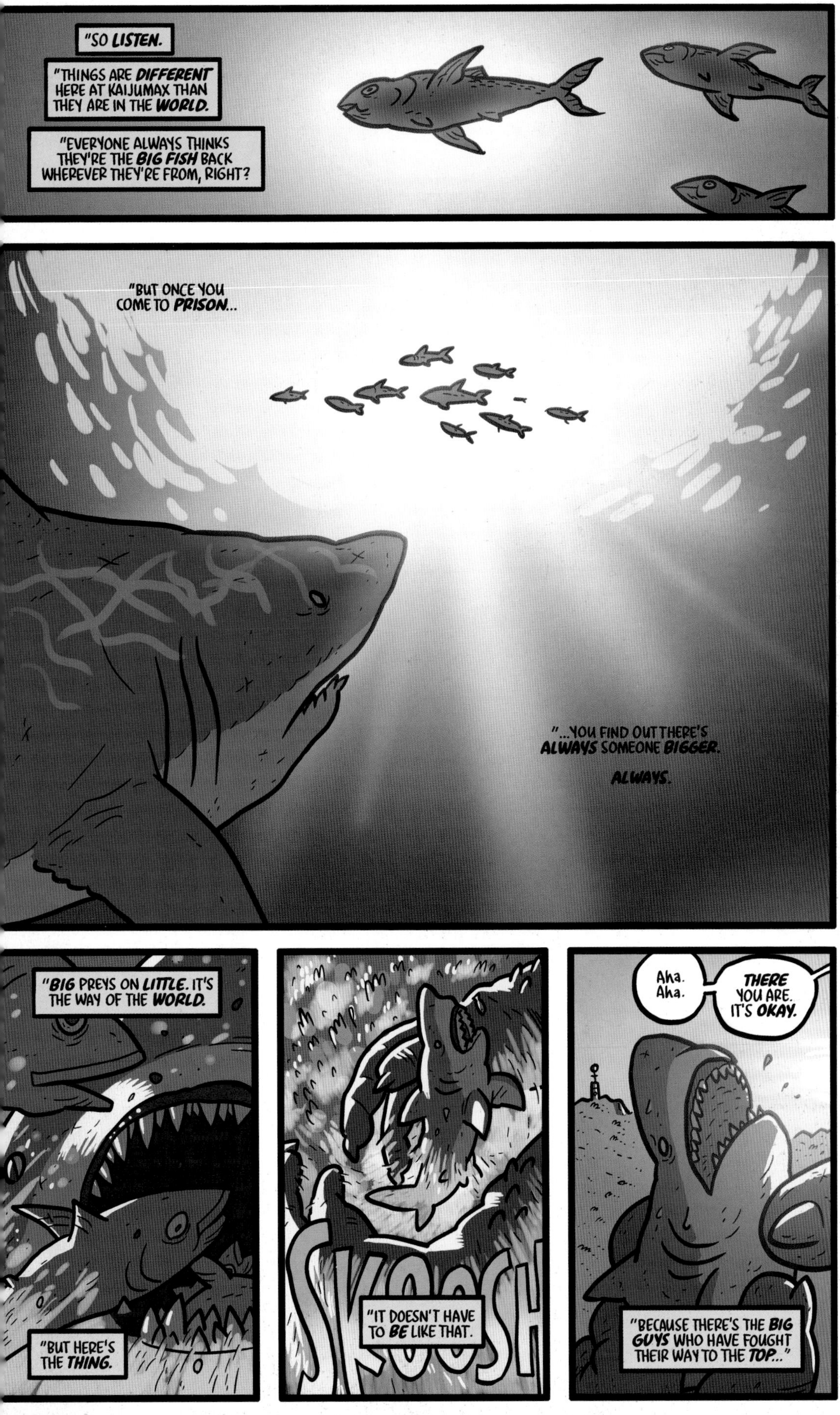
"SO LISTEN.
"THINGS ARE DIFFERENT HERE AT KAIJUMAX THAN THEY ARE IN THE WORLD.
"EVERYONE ALWAYS THINKS THEY'RE THE BIG FISH BACK WHEREVER THEY'RE FROM, RIGHT?
"BUT ONCE YOU COME TO PRISON...
"...YOU FIND OUT THERE'S ALWAYS SOMEONE BIGGER.
ALWAYS.
"BIG PREYS ON LITTLE. IT'S THE WAY OF THE WORLD.
"BUT HERE'S THE THING.
SKOOSH
"IT DOESN'T HAVE TO BE LIKE THAT.
Aha. Aha.
THERE YOU ARE. IT'S OKAY.
"BECAUSE THERE'S THE BIG GUYS WHO HAVE FOUGHT THEIR WAY TO THE TOP..."

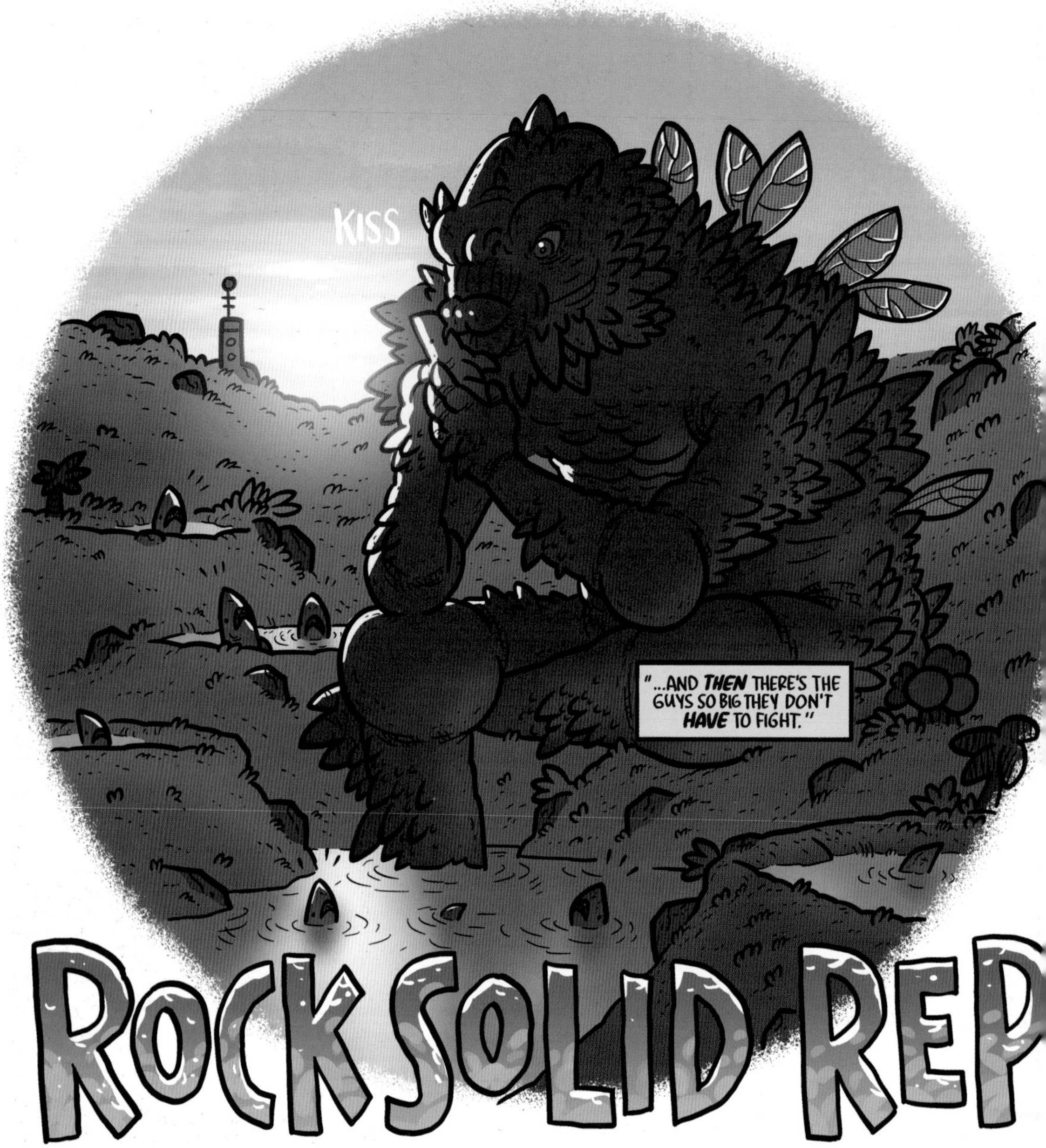
KISS
"...AND THEN THERE'S THE GUYS SO BIG THEY DON'T HAVE TO FIGHT."
ROCK SOLID REP

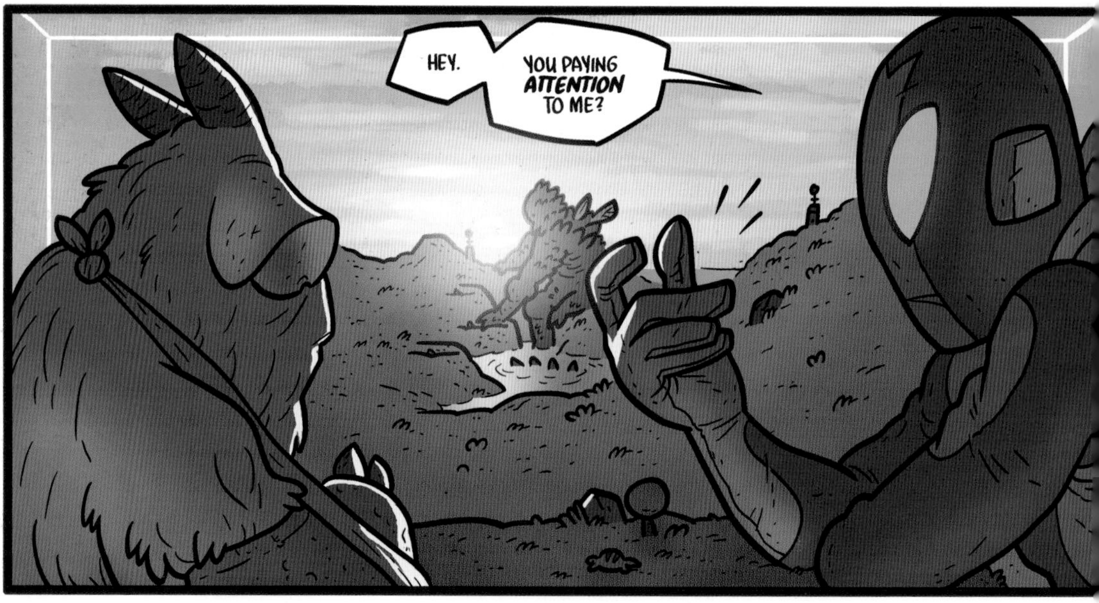
HEY.
YOU PAYING ATTENTION TO ME?

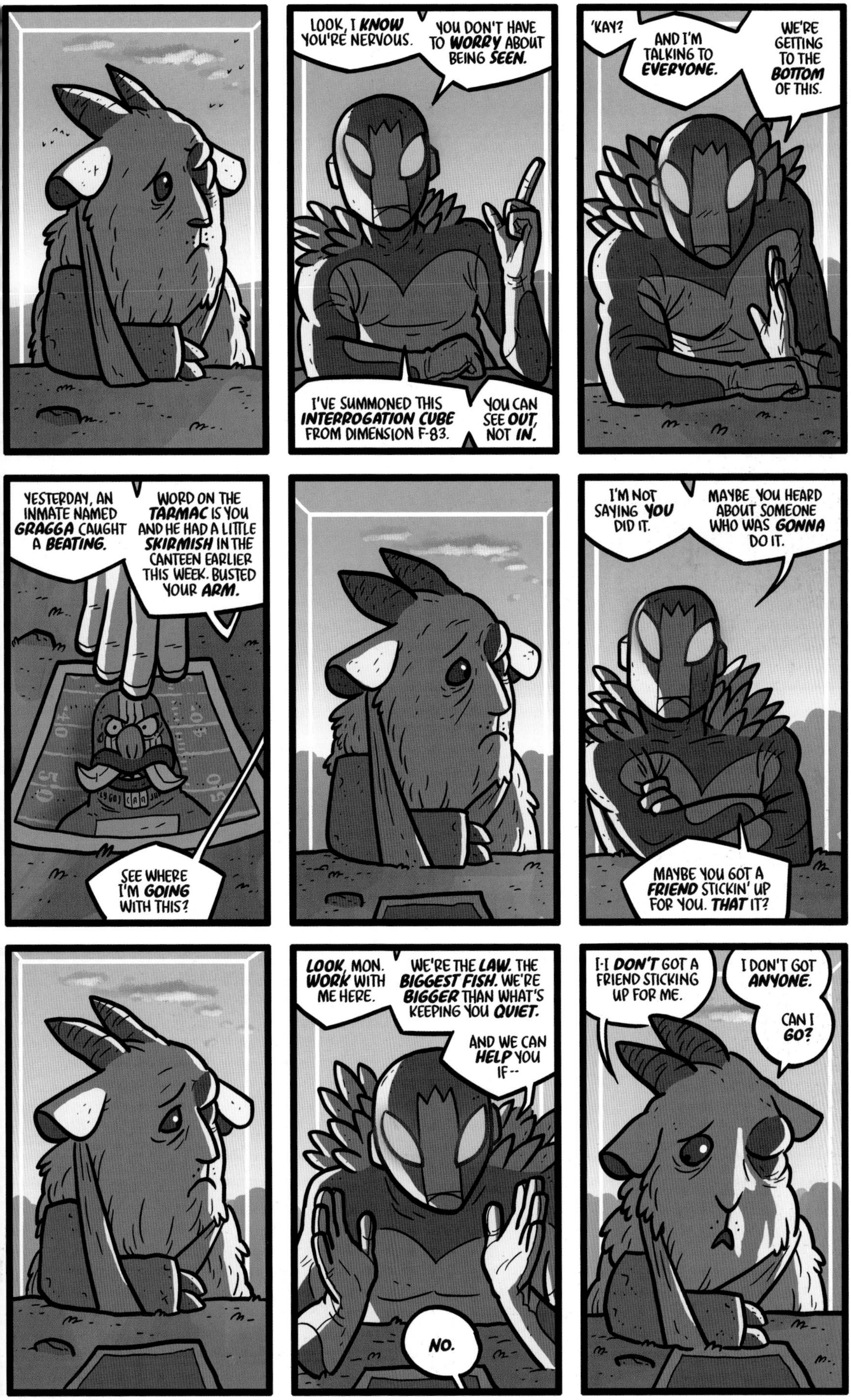

LOOK, I KNOW YOU'RE NERVOUS.
YOU DON'T HAVE TO WORRY ABOUT BEING SEEN.
I'VE SUMMONED THIS INTERROGATION CUBE FROM DIMENSION F-83.
YOU CAN SEE OUT, NOT IN.
'KAY?
AND I'M TALKING TO EVERYONE.
WE'RE GETTING TO THE BOTTOM OF THIS.
YESTERDAY, AN INMATE NAMED GRAGGA CAUGHT A BEATING.
WORD ON THE TARMAC IS YOU AND HE HAD A LITTLE SKIRMISH IN THE CANTEEN EARLIER THIS WEEK. BUSTED YOUR ARM.
SEE WHERE I'M GOING WITH THIS?
I'M NOT SAYING YOU DID IT.
MAYBE YOU HEARD ABOUT SOMEONE WHO WAS GONNA DO IT.
MAYBE YOU GOT A FRIEND STICKIN' UP FOR YOU. THAT IT?
LOOK, MON. WORK WITH ME HERE.
WE'RE THE LAW. THE BIGGEST FISH. WE'RE BIGGER THAN WHAT'S KEEPING YOU QUIET.
AND WE CAN HELP YOU IF--
NO.
I-I DON'T GOT A FRIEND STICKING UP FOR ME.
I DON'T GOT ANYONE.
CAN I GO?

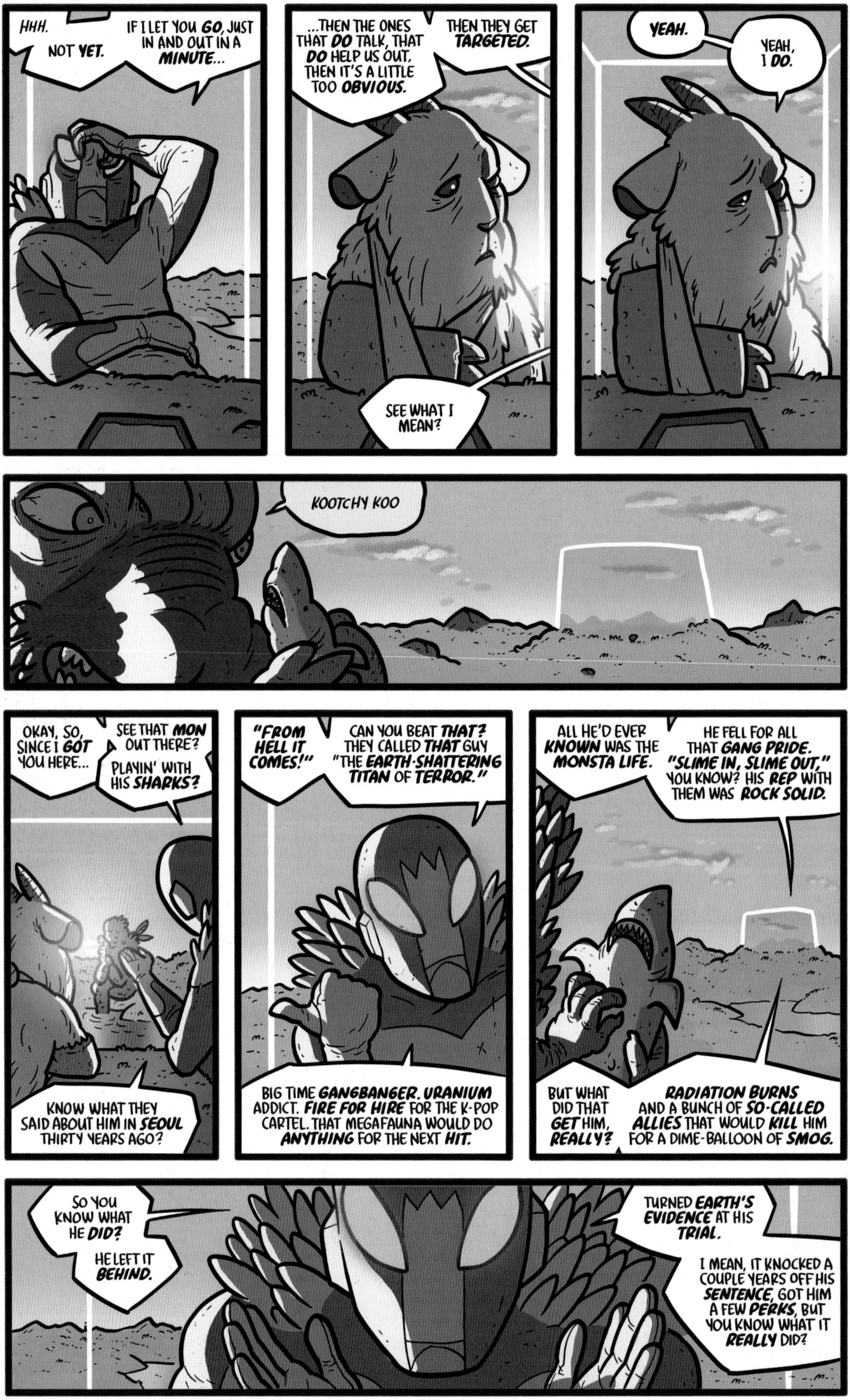
HHH.
NOT YET.
IF I LET YOU GO, JUST IN AND OUT IN A MINUTE...
...THEN THE ONES THAT DO TALK, THAT DO HELP US OUT, THEN IT'S A LITTLE TOO OBVIOUS.
THEN THEY GET TARGETED.
SEE WHAT I MEAN?
YEAH.
YEAH, I DO.
KOOTCHY KOO
OKAY, SO, SINCE I GOT YOU HERE...
SEE THAT MON OUT THERE?
PLAYIN' WITH HIS SHARKS?
KNOW WHAT THEY SAID ABOUT HIM IN SEOUL THIRTY YEARS AGO?
"FROM HELL IT COMES!"
CAN YOU BEAT THAT? THEY CALLED THAT GUY "THE EARTH-SHATTERING TITAN OF TERROR."
BIG TIME GANGBANGER. URANIUM ADDICT. FIRE FOR HIRE FOR THE K-POP CARTEL. THAT MEGAFAUNA WOULD DO ANYTHING FOR THE NEXT HIT.
ALL HE'D EVER KNOWN WAS THE MONSTA LIFE.
HE FELL FOR ALL THAT GANG PRIDE. "SLIME IN, SLIME OUT," YOU KNOW? HIS REP WITH THEM WAS ROCK SOLID.
BUT WHAT DID THAT GET HIM, REALLY?
RADIATION BURNS AND A BUNCH OF SO-CALLED ALLIES THAT WOULD KILL HIM FOR A DIME-BALLOON OF SMOG.
SO YOU KNOW WHAT HE DID?
HE LEFT IT BEHIND.
TURNED EARTH'S EVIDENCE AT HIS TRIAL.
I MEAN, IT KNOCKED A COUPLE YEARS OFF HIS SENTENCE, GOT HIM A FEW PERKS, BUT YOU KNOW WHAT IT REALLY DID?

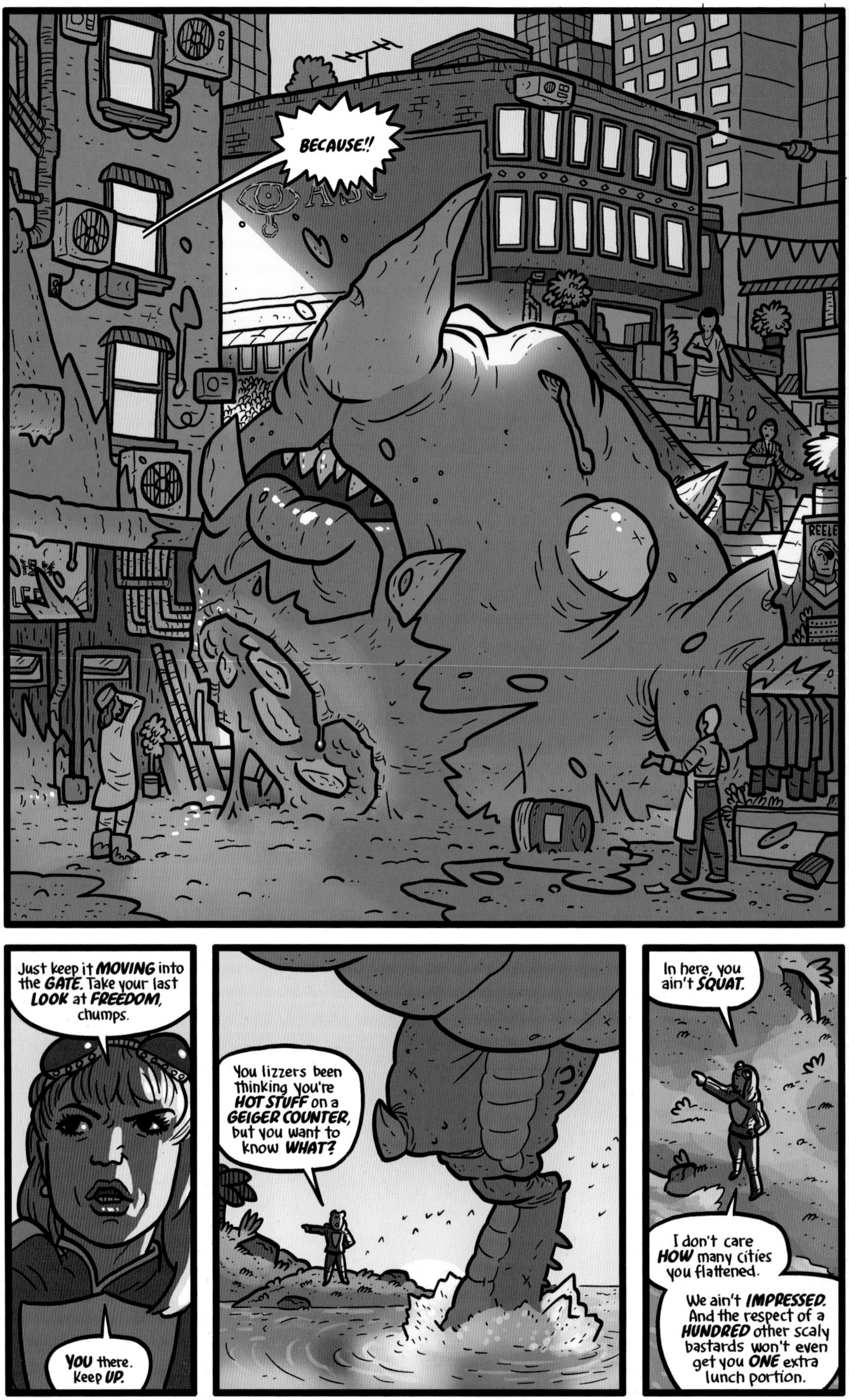
BECAUSE!!
Just keep it MOVING into the GATE. Take your last LOOK at FREEDOM, chumps.
YOU there. Keep UP.
You lizzers been thinking you're HOT STUFF on a GEIGER COUNTER, but you want to know WHAT?
In here, you ain't SQUAT.
I don't care HOW many cities you flattened.
We ain't IMPRESSED. And the respect of a HUNDRED other scaly bastards won't even get you ONE extra lunch portion.

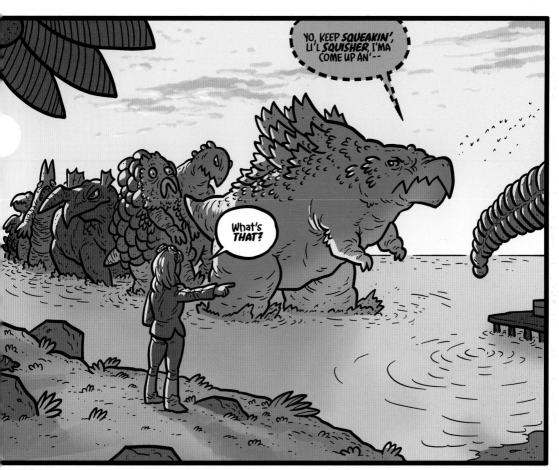

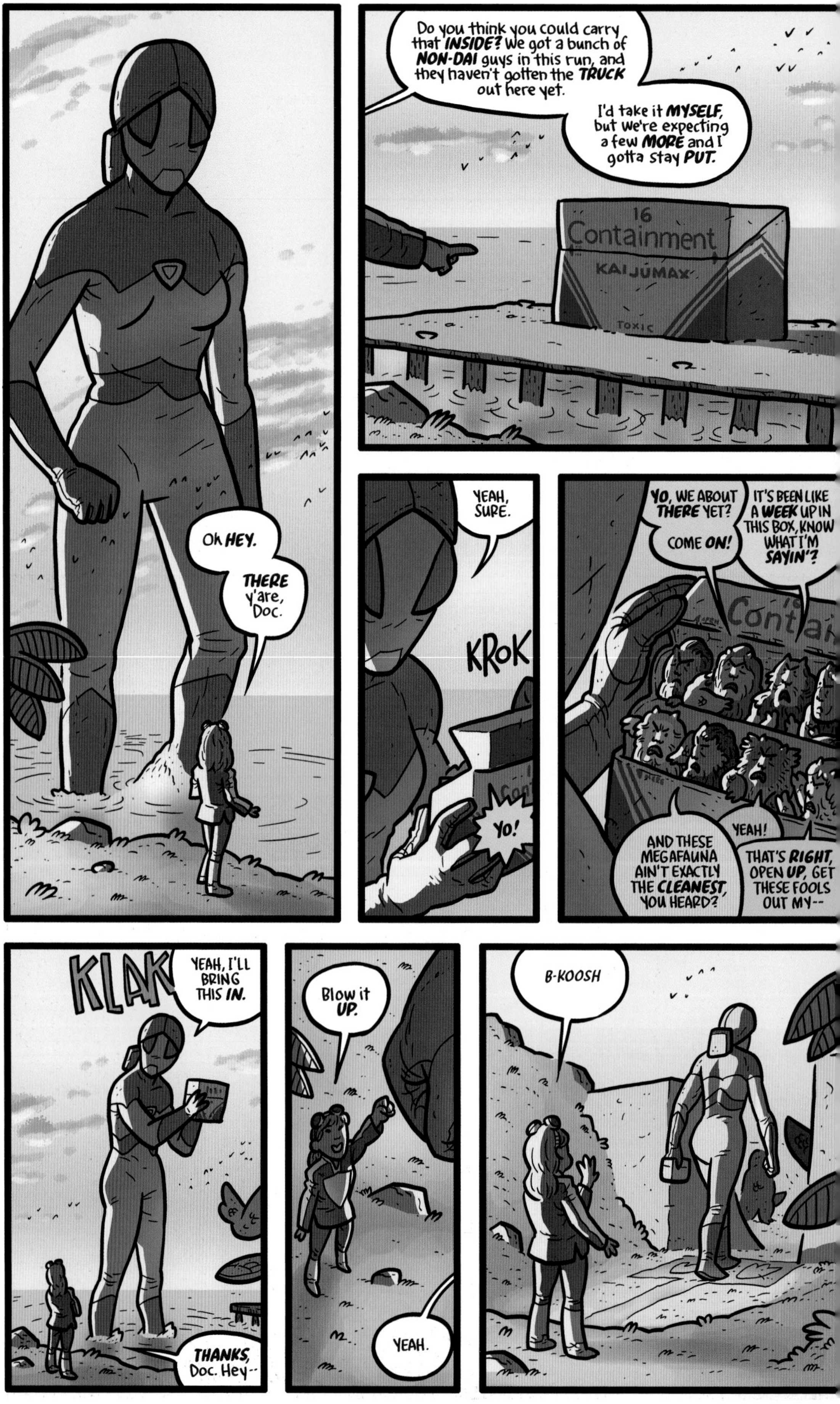
Ok HEY.
THERE y'are, Doc.
Do you think you could carry that INSIDE? We got a bunch of NON-DAI guys in this run, and they haven't gotten the TRUCK out here yet.
I'd take it MYSELF, but we're expecting a few MORE and I gotta stay PUT.
16 Containment
KAIJUMAX
TOXIC
YEAH, SURE.
KROK
YO!
YO, WE ABOUT THERE YET?
COME ON!
IT'S BEEN LIKE A WEEK UP IN THIS BOX, KNOW WHAT I'M SAYIN'?
AND THESE MEGAFAUNA AIN'T EXACTLY THE CLEANEST, YOU HEARD?
YEAH!
THAT'S RIGHT, OPEN UP, GET THESE FOOLS OUT MY--
KLAK
YEAH, I'LL BRING THIS IN.
THANKS, Doc. Hey--
Blow it UP.
YEAH.
B-KOOSH

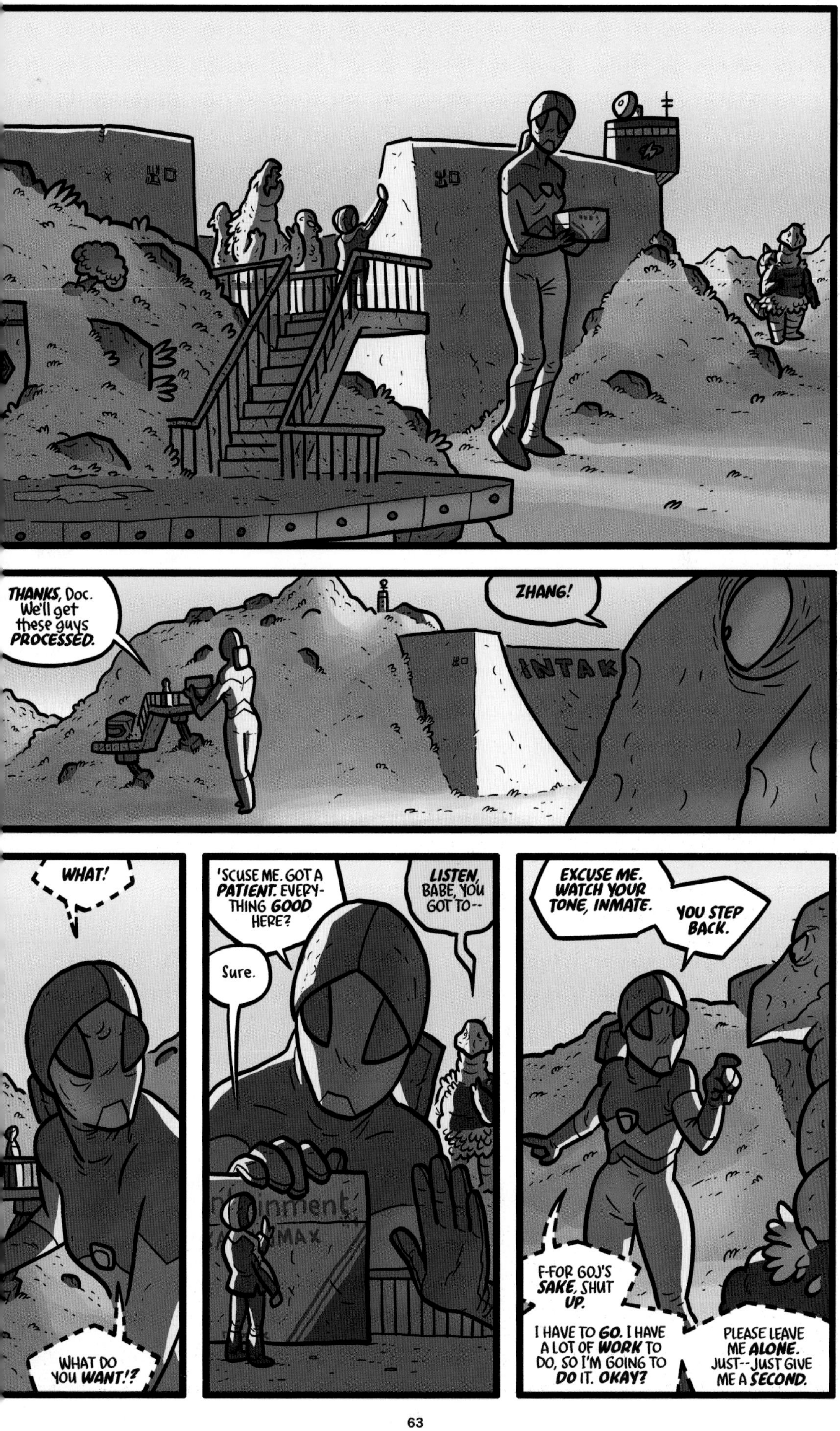

THANKS, Doc. We'll get these guys PROCESSED.
ZHANG!
INTAK
WHAT!
WHAT DO YOU WANT!?
'SCUSE ME. GOT A PATIENT. EVERYTHING GOOD HERE?
Sure.
LISTEN, BABE, YOU GOT TO--
EXCUSE ME. WATCH YOUR TONE, INMATE.
YOU STEP BACK.
F-FOR GOJ'S SAKE, SHUT UP.
I HAVE TO GO. I HAVE A LOT OF WORK TO DO, SO I'M GOING TO DO IT. OKAY?
PLEASE LEAVE ME ALONE. JUST--JUST GIVE ME A SECOND.

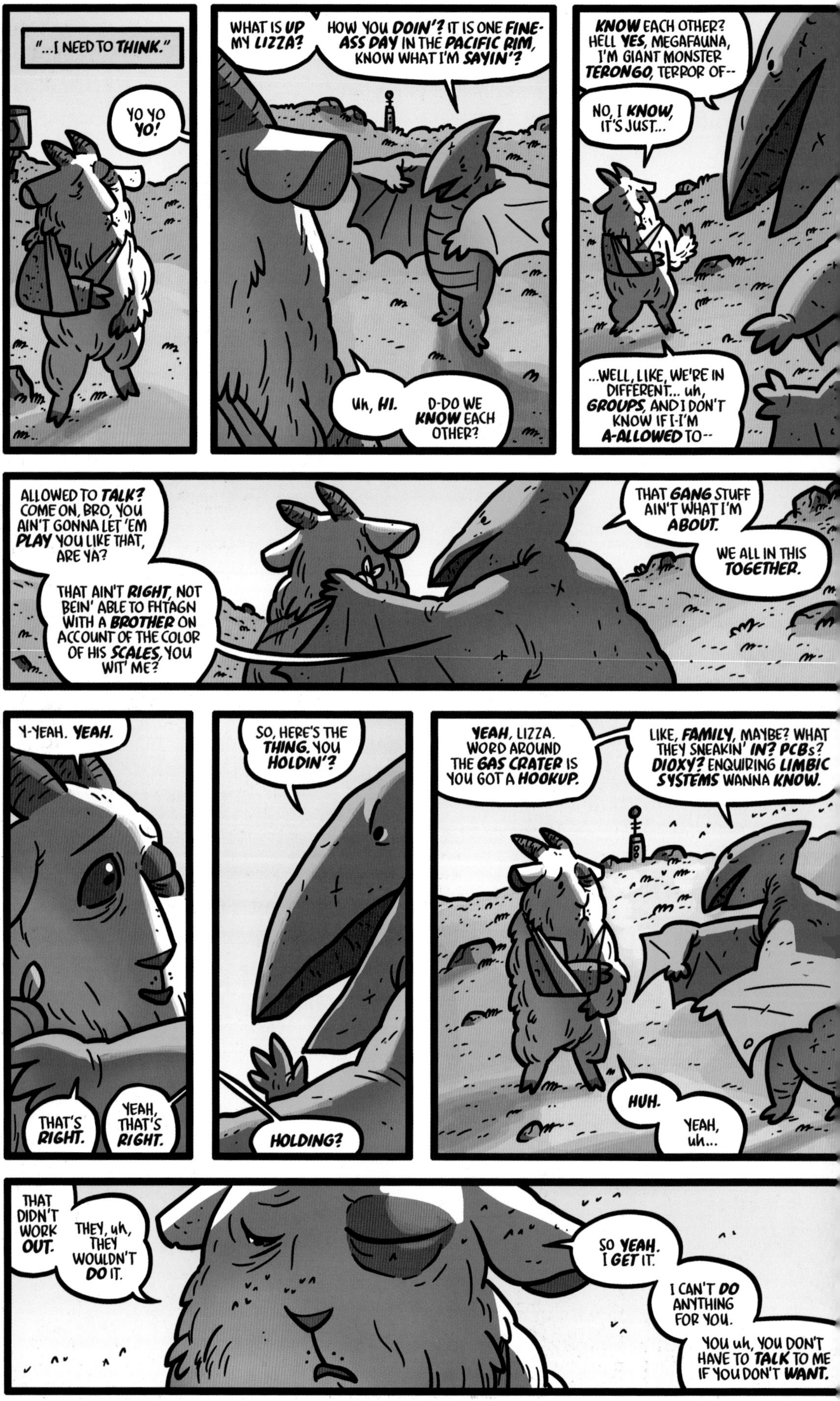
"...I NEED TO THINK."
YO YO YO!
WHAT IS UP MY LIZZA?
HOW YOU DOIN'? IT IS ONE FINE-ASS DAY IN THE PACIFIC RIM, KNOW WHAT I'M SAYIN'?
Uh, HI.
D-DO WE KNOW EACH OTHER?
KNOW EACH OTHER? HELL YES, MEGAFAUNA, I'M GIANT MONSTER TERONGO, TERROR OF--
NO, I KNOW, IT'S JUST...
...WELL, LIKE, WE'RE IN DIFFERENT... uh, GROUPS, AND I DON'T KNOW IF I-I'M A-ALLOWED TO--
ALLOWED TO TALK? COME ON, BRO, YOU AIN'T GONNA LET 'EM PLAY YOU LIKE THAT, ARE YA?
THAT AIN'T RIGHT, NOT BEIN' ABLE TO FHTAGN WITH A BROTHER ON ACCOUNT OF THE COLOR OF HIS SCALES, YOU WIT' ME?
THAT GANG STUFF AIN'T WHAT I'M ABOUT.
WE ALL IN THIS TOGETHER.
Y-YEAH. YEAH.
THAT'S RIGHT.
YEAH, THAT'S RIGHT.
SO, HERE'S THE THING. YOU HOLDIN'?
HOLDING?
YEAH, LIZZA. WORD AROUND THE GAS CRATER IS YOU GOT A HOOKUP.
LIKE, FAMILY, MAYBE? WHAT THEY SNEAKIN' IN? PCBs? DIOXY? ENQUIRING LIMBIC SYSTEMS WANNA KNOW.
HUH.
YEAH, uh...
THAT DIDN'T WORK OUT.
THEY, uh, THEY WOULDN'T DO IT.
SO YEAH. I GET IT.
I CAN'T DO ANYTHING FOR YOU.
YOU uh, YOU DON'T HAVE TO TALK TO ME IF YOU DON'T WANT.

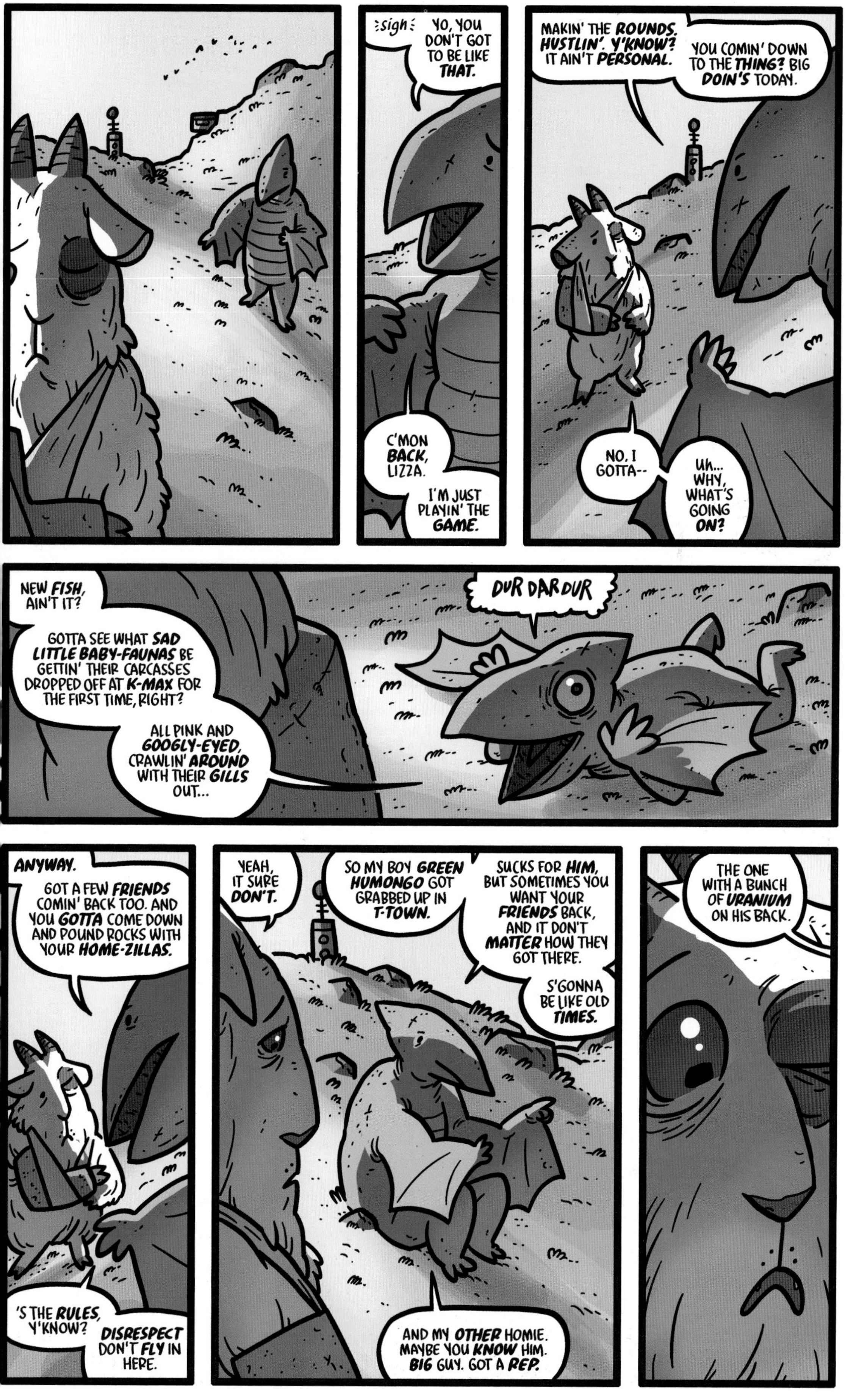

:sigh:
YO, YOU DON'T GOT TO BE LIKE THAT.
C'MON BACK, LIZZA.
I'M JUST PLAYIN' THE GAME.
MAKIN' THE ROUNDS. HUSTLIN'. Y'KNOW? IT AIN'T PERSONAL.
YOU COMIN' DOWN TO THE THING? BIG DOIN'S TODAY.
NO, I GOTTA--
UH... WHY, WHAT'S GOING ON?
NEW FISH, AIN'T IT?
GOTTA SEE WHAT SAD LITTLE BABY-FAUNAS BE GETTIN' THEIR CARCASSES DROPPED OFF AT K-MAX FOR THE FIRST TIME, RIGHT?
ALL PINK AND GOOGLY-EYED, CRAWLIN' AROUND WITH THEIR GILLS OUT...
DUR DAR DUR
ANYWAY.
GOT A FEW FRIENDS COMIN' BACK TOO. AND YOU GOTTA COME DOWN AND POUND ROCKS WITH YOUR HOME-ZILLAS.
'S THE RULES, Y'KNOW?
DISRESPECT DON'T FLY IN HERE.
YEAH, IT SURE DON'T.
SO MY BOY GREEN HUMONGO GOT GRABBED UP IN T-TOWN.
SUCKS FOR HIM, BUT SOMETIMES YOU WANT YOUR FRIENDS BACK, AND IT DON'T MATTER HOW THEY GOT THERE.
S'GONNA BE LIKE OLD TIMES.
AND MY OTHER HOMIE. MAYBE YOU KNOW HIM. BIG GUY. GOT A REP.
THE ONE WITH A BUNCH OF URANIUM ON HIS BACK.

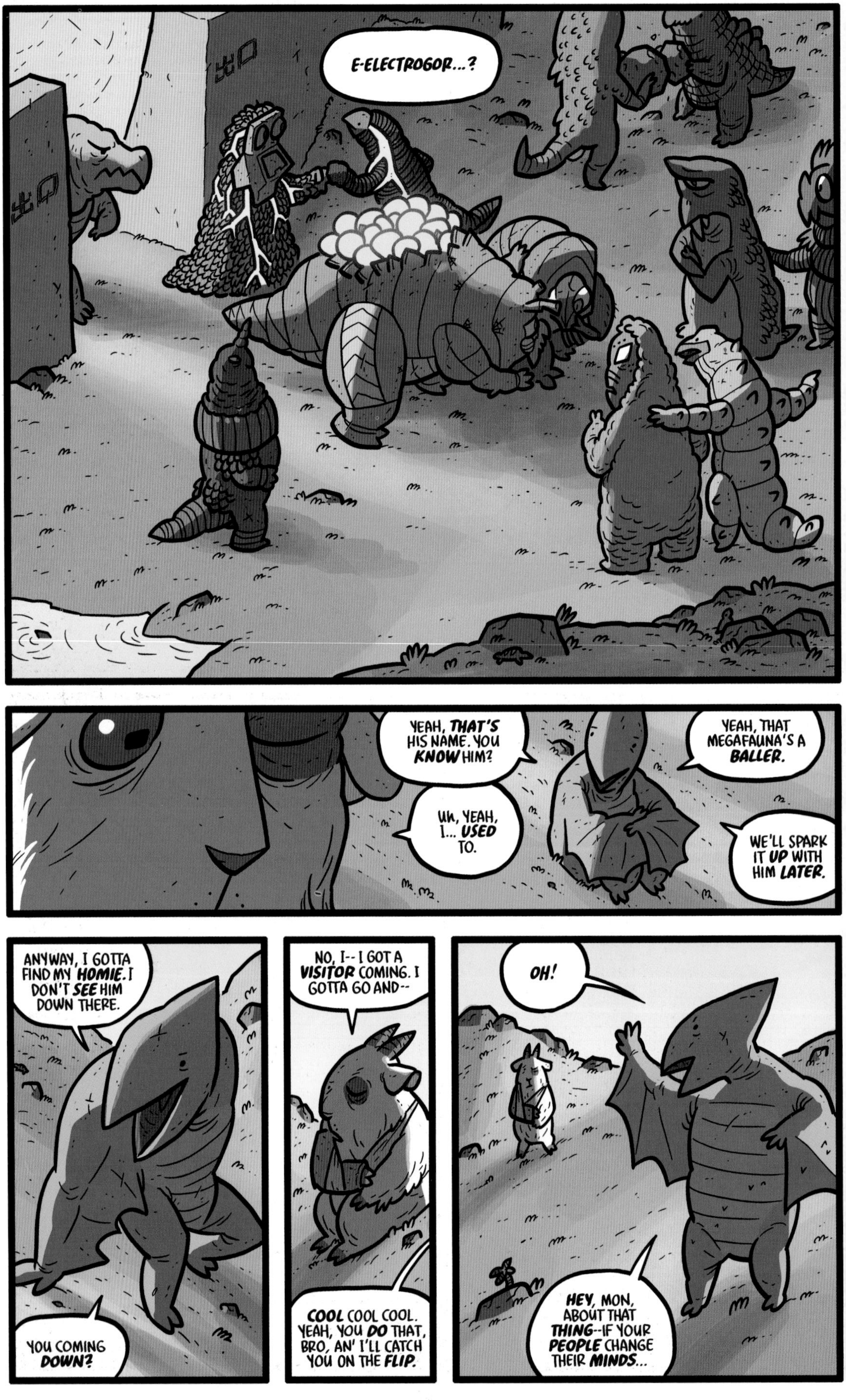
E-ELECTROGOR...?
YEAH, THAT'S HIS NAME. YOU KNOW HIM?
UH, YEAH, I... USED TO.
YEAH, THAT MEGAFAUNA'S A BALLER.
WE'LL SPARK IT UP WITH HIM LATER.
ANYWAY, I GOTTA FIND MY HOMIE. I DON'T SEE HIM DOWN THERE.
YOU COMING DOWN?
NO, I-- I GOT A VISITOR COMING. I GOTTA GO AND--
COOL COOL COOL. YEAH, YOU DO THAT, BRO, AN' I'LL CATCH YOU ON THE FLIP.
OH!
HEY, MON, ABOUT THAT THING--IF YOUR PEOPLE CHANGE THEIR MINDS...

"...DON'T FORGET TO SHARE THE *LOVE*, huh?"

VISITORS

VORP

?

OH! Hello, ma'am. *SORRY*, I didn't hear a *PLANE* land. Here for a *VISIT*, then?

Yes. Good *MORROW* to you. My name on your rolls would be *MERCY GOODWIN.*

Right, I have you down for *ONE O'CLOCK* with... mm, yes, the *CREATURE FROM DEVIL'S CREEK.*

CREATURE from DEVIL'S CREEK

That... that is his *PENNY-DREADFUL* name, *YES.*

But *I* call my son *DANIEL*, an' it please you, sir.

Sure. Pardon *ME*, ma'am. And I'm afraid I'll need to *FRISK* you before you go *IN. APOLOGIES* if it's *INTRUSIVE.*

Not at *ALL.* As the book *SAYS:* "Thrice cursed are the *WEAK*, whose insecurity makes them *VILE.*"

Okay.

I'll need to see into your *PURSE* as well.

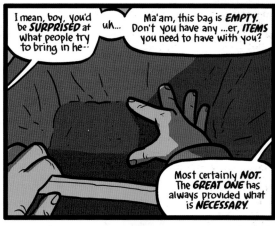

I mean, boy, you'd be *SURPRISED* at what people try to bring in he--

uh...

Ma'am, this bag is *EMPTY.* Don't you have any ...er, *ITEMS* you need to have with you?

Most certainly *NOT.* The *GREAT ONE* has always provided what is *NECESSARY.*

Uh, all right, Ma'am, that's *FINE.* Have a nice *VISIT*, then.

YES.

And may the *LORD* keep you.

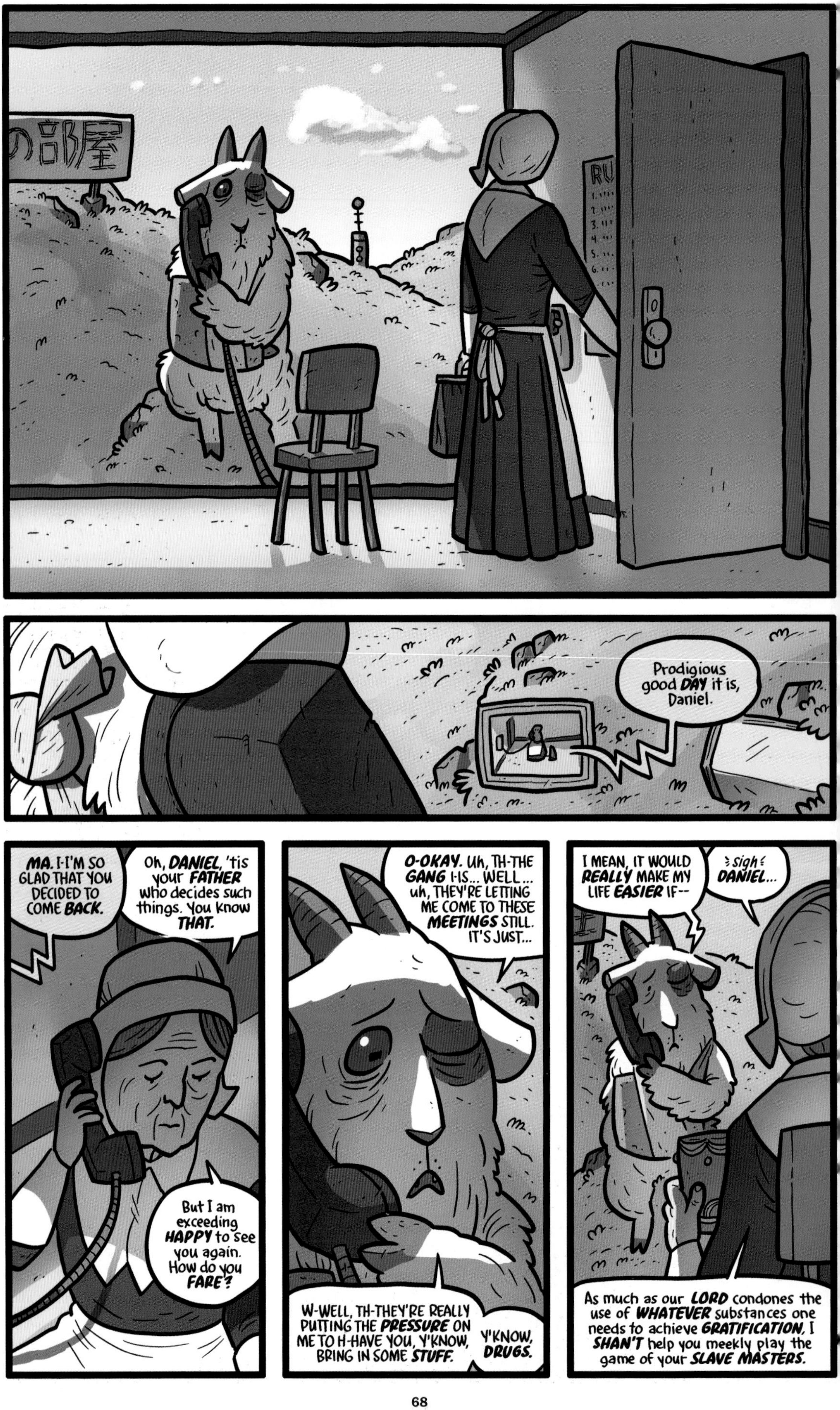

の部屋
RU
1.
2.
3.
4.
5.
6.
Prodigious good DAY it is, Daniel.
MA. I-I'M SO GLAD THAT YOU DECIDED TO COME BACK.
Oh, DANIEL, 'tis your FATHER who decides such things. You know THAT.
But I am exceeding HAPPY to see you again. How do you FARE?
O-OKAY. Uh, TH-THE GANG I-IS... WELL... uh, THEY'RE LETTING ME COME TO THESE MEETINGS STILL. IT'S JUST...
W-WELL, TH-THEY'RE REALLY PUTTING THE PRESSURE ON ME TO H-HAVE YOU, Y'KNOW, BRING IN SOME STUFF.
Y'KNOW, DRUGS.
I MEAN, IT WOULD REALLY MAKE MY LIFE EASIER IF--
sigh DANIEL...
As much as our LORD condones the use of WHATEVER substances one needs to achieve GRATIFICATION, I SHAN'T help you meekly play the game of your SLAVE MASTERS.

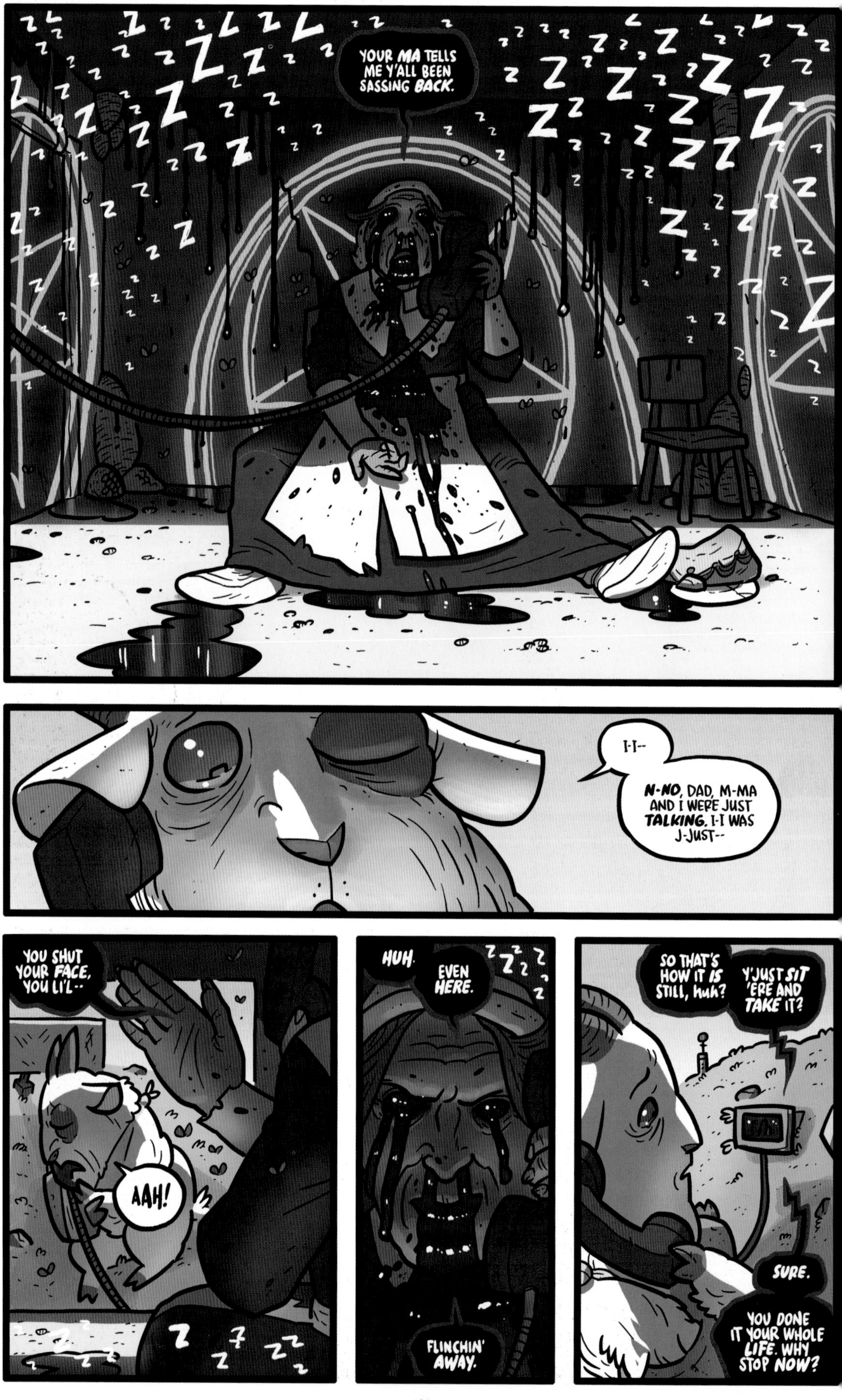
YOUR MA TELLS ME Y'ALL BEEN SASSING BACK.
I-I--
N-NO, DAD, M-MA AND I WERE JUST TALKING. I-I WAS J-JUST--
YOU SHUT YOUR FACE, YOU LI'L--
AAH!
HUH.
EVEN HERE.
FLINCHIN' AWAY.
SO THAT'S HOW IT IS STILL, huh?
Y'JUST SIT 'ERE AND TAKE IT?
SURE.
YOU DONE IT YOUR WHOLE LIFE. WHY STOP NOW?

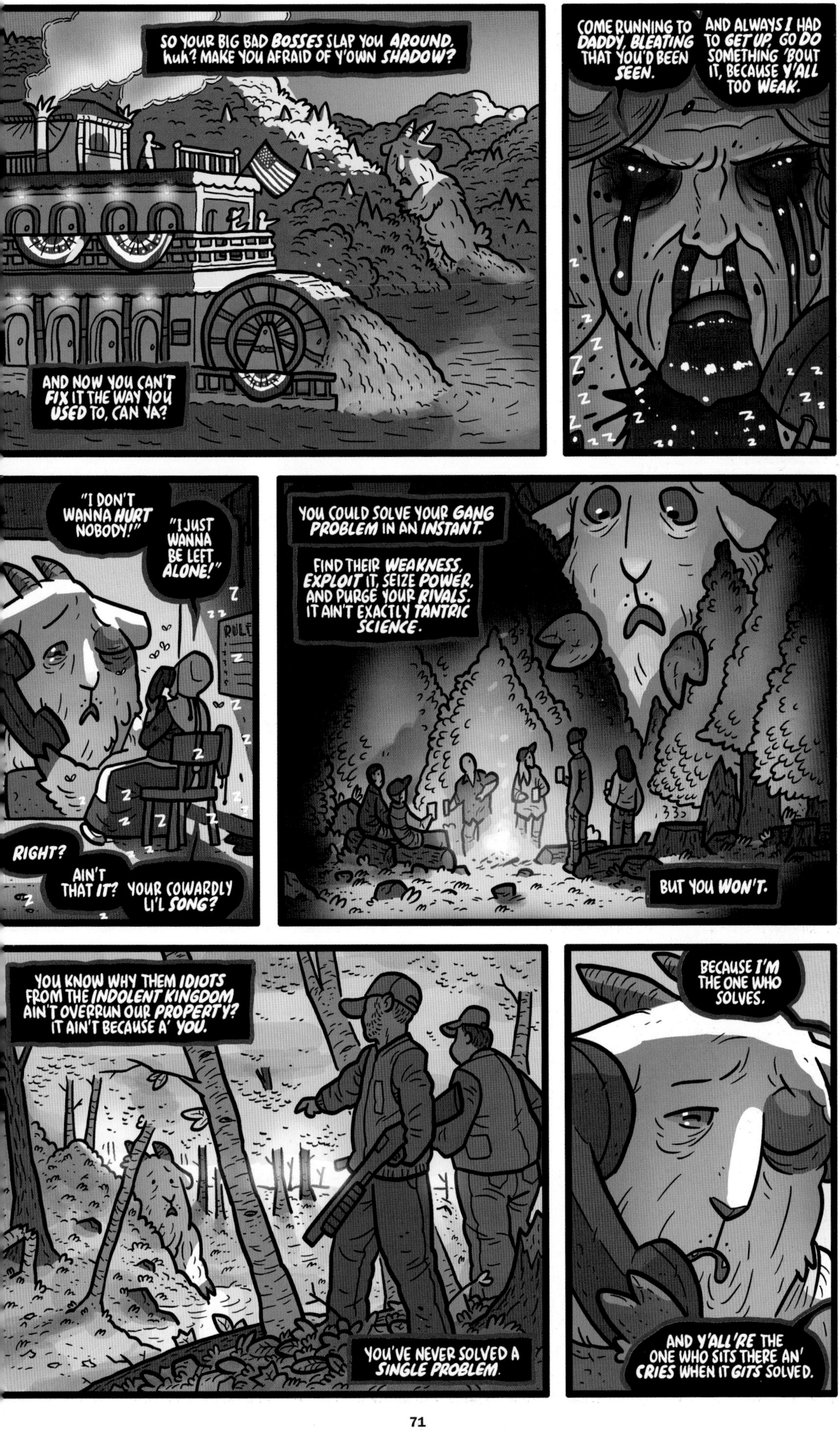
SO YOUR BIG BAD BOSSES SLAP YOU AROUND, huh? MAKE YOU AFRAID OF Y'OWN SHADOW?
AND NOW YOU CAN'T FIX IT THE WAY YOU USED TO, CAN YA?
COME RUNNING TO DADDY, BLEATING THAT YOU'D BEEN SEEN.
AND ALWAYS I HAD TO GET UP, GO DO SOMETHING 'BOUT IT, BECAUSE Y'ALL TOO WEAK.
"I DON'T WANNA HURT NOBODY!"
"I JUST WANNA BE LEFT ALONE!"
RIGHT?
AIN'T THAT IT?
YOUR COWARDLY LI'L SONG?
YOU COULD SOLVE YOUR GANG PROBLEM IN AN INSTANT.
FIND THEIR WEAKNESS, EXPLOIT IT, SEIZE POWER, AND PURGE YOUR RIVALS. IT AIN'T EXACTLY TANTRIC SCIENCE.
BUT YOU WON'T.
YOU KNOW WHY THEM IDIOTS FROM THE INDOLENT KINGDOM AIN'T OVERRUN OUR PROPERTY? IT AIN'T BECAUSE A' YOU.
YOU'VE NEVER SOLVED A SINGLE PROBLEM.
BECAUSE I'M THE ONE WHO SOLVES.
AND Y'ALL'RE THE ONE WHO SITS THERE AN' CRIES WHEN IT GITS SOLVED.

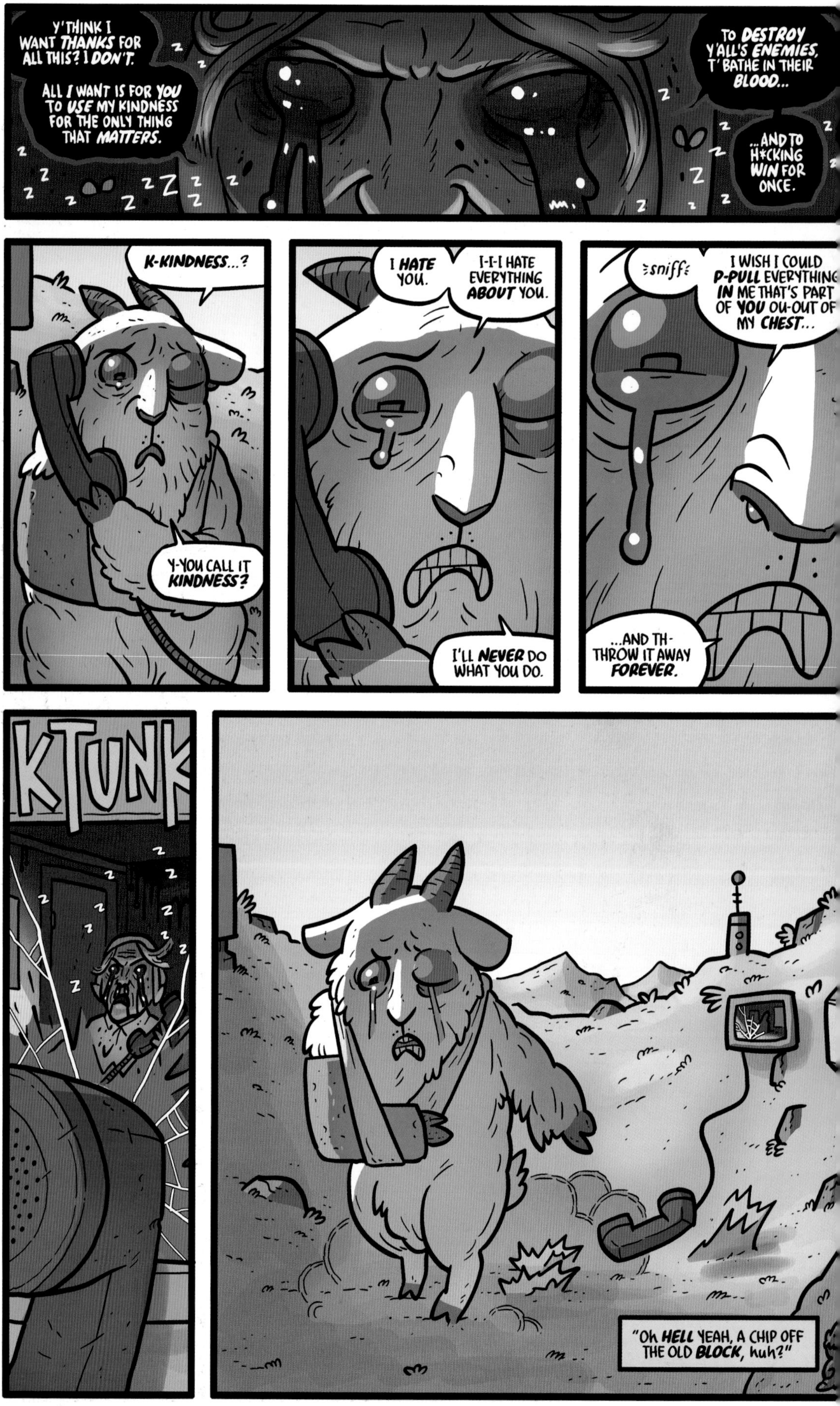
Y'THINK I WANT THANKS FOR ALL THIS? I DON'T.
ALL I WANT IS FOR YOU TO USE MY KINDNESS FOR THE ONLY THING THAT MATTERS.
TO DESTROY Y'ALL'S ENEMIES, T' BATHE IN THEIR BLOOD...
...AND TO H*CKING WIN FOR ONCE.
K-KINDNESS...?
Y-YOU CALL IT KINDNESS?
I HATE YOU.
I-I-I HATE EVERYTHING ABOUT YOU.
I'LL NEVER DO WHAT YOU DO.
sniff
I WISH I COULD P-PULL EVERYTHING IN ME THAT'S PART OF YOU OU-OUT OF MY CHEST...
...AND TH-THROW IT AWAY FOREVER.
KTUNK
"Oh HELL YEAH, A CHIP OFF THE OLD BLOCK, huh?"

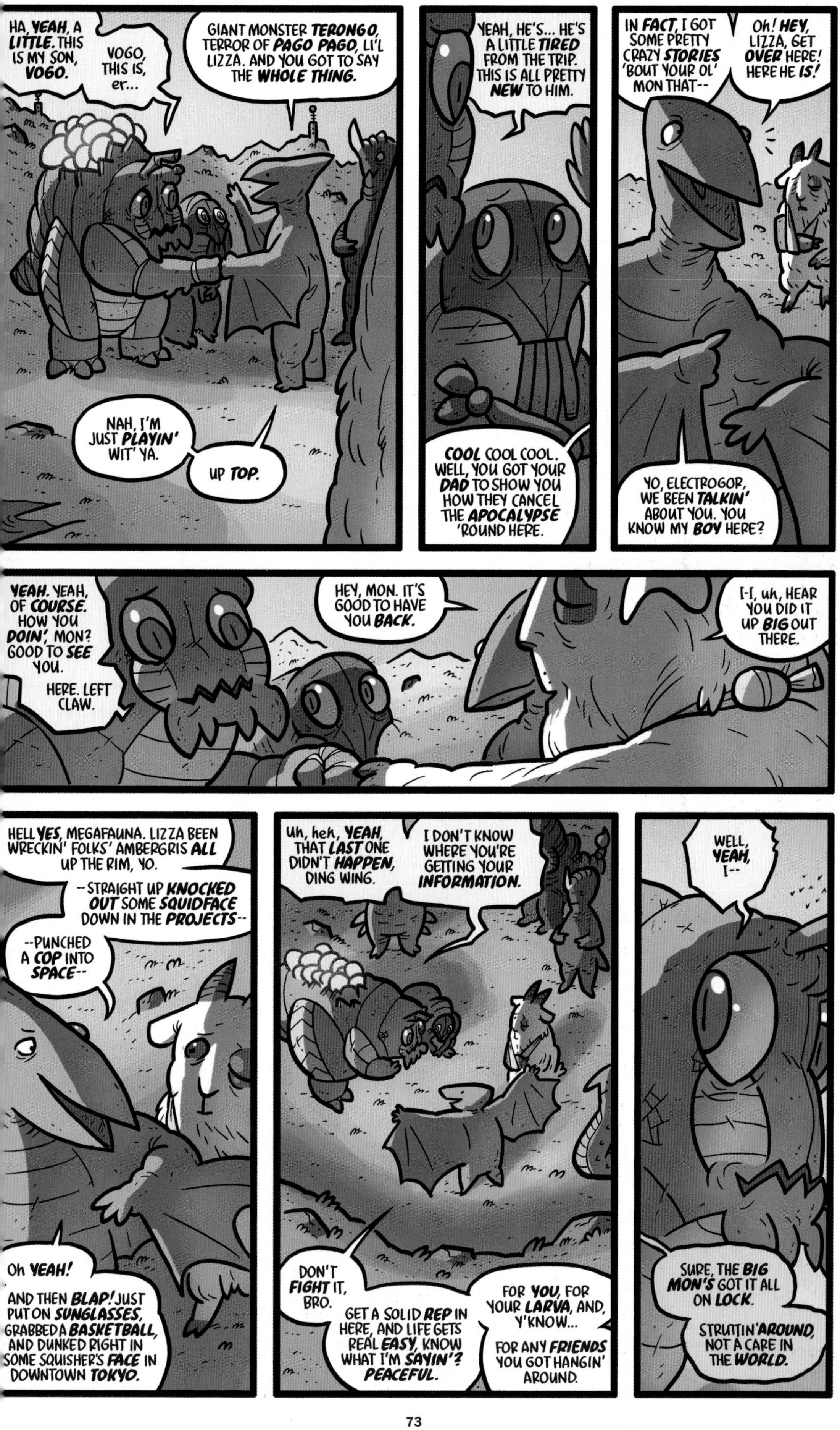
HA, YEAH, A LITTLE. THIS IS MY SON, VOGO.
VOGO, THIS IS, er...
GIANT MONSTER TERONGO, TERROR OF PAGO PAGO, LI'L LIZZA. AND YOU GOT TO SAY THE WHOLE THING.
NAH, I'M JUST PLAYIN' WIT' YA.
UP TOP.
YEAH, HE'S... HE'S A LITTLE TIRED FROM THE TRIP. THIS IS ALL PRETTY NEW TO HIM.
COOL COOL COOL. WELL, YOU GOT YOUR DAD TO SHOW YOU HOW THEY CANCEL THE APOCALYPSE 'ROUND HERE.
IN FACT, I GOT SOME PRETTY CRAZY STORIES 'BOUT YOUR OL' MON THAT--
Oh! HEY, LIZZA, GET OVER HERE! HERE HE IS!
YO, ELECTROGOR, WE BEEN TALKIN' ABOUT YOU. YOU KNOW MY BOY HERE?
YEAH. YEAH, OF COURSE. HOW YOU DOIN', MON? GOOD TO SEE YOU.
HERE. LEFT CLAW.
HEY, MON. IT'S GOOD TO HAVE YOU BACK.
I-I, uh, HEAR YOU DID IT UP BIG OUT THERE.
HELL YES, MEGAFAUNA. LIZZA BEEN WRECKIN' FOLKS' AMBERGRIS ALL UP THE RIM, YO.
--STRAIGHT UP KNOCKED OUT SOME SQUIDFACE DOWN IN THE PROJECTS--
--PUNCHED A COP INTO SPACE--
Oh YEAH!
AND THEN BLAP! JUST PUT ON SUNGLASSES, GRABBED A BASKETBALL, AND DUNKED RIGHT IN SOME SQUISHER'S FACE IN DOWNTOWN TOKYO.
Uh, heh, YEAH, THAT LAST ONE DIDN'T HAPPEN, DING WING.
I DON'T KNOW WHERE YOU'RE GETTING YOUR INFORMATION.
DON'T FIGHT IT, BRO.
GET A SOLID REP IN HERE, AND LIFE GETS REAL EASY, KNOW WHAT I'M SAYIN'? PEACEFUL.
FOR YOU, FOR YOUR LARVA, AND, Y'KNOW...
FOR ANY FRIENDS YOU GOT HANGIN' AROUND.
WELL, YEAH, I--
SURE, THE BIG MON'S GOT IT ALL ON LOCK.
STRUTTIN' AROUND, NOT A CARE IN THE WORLD.

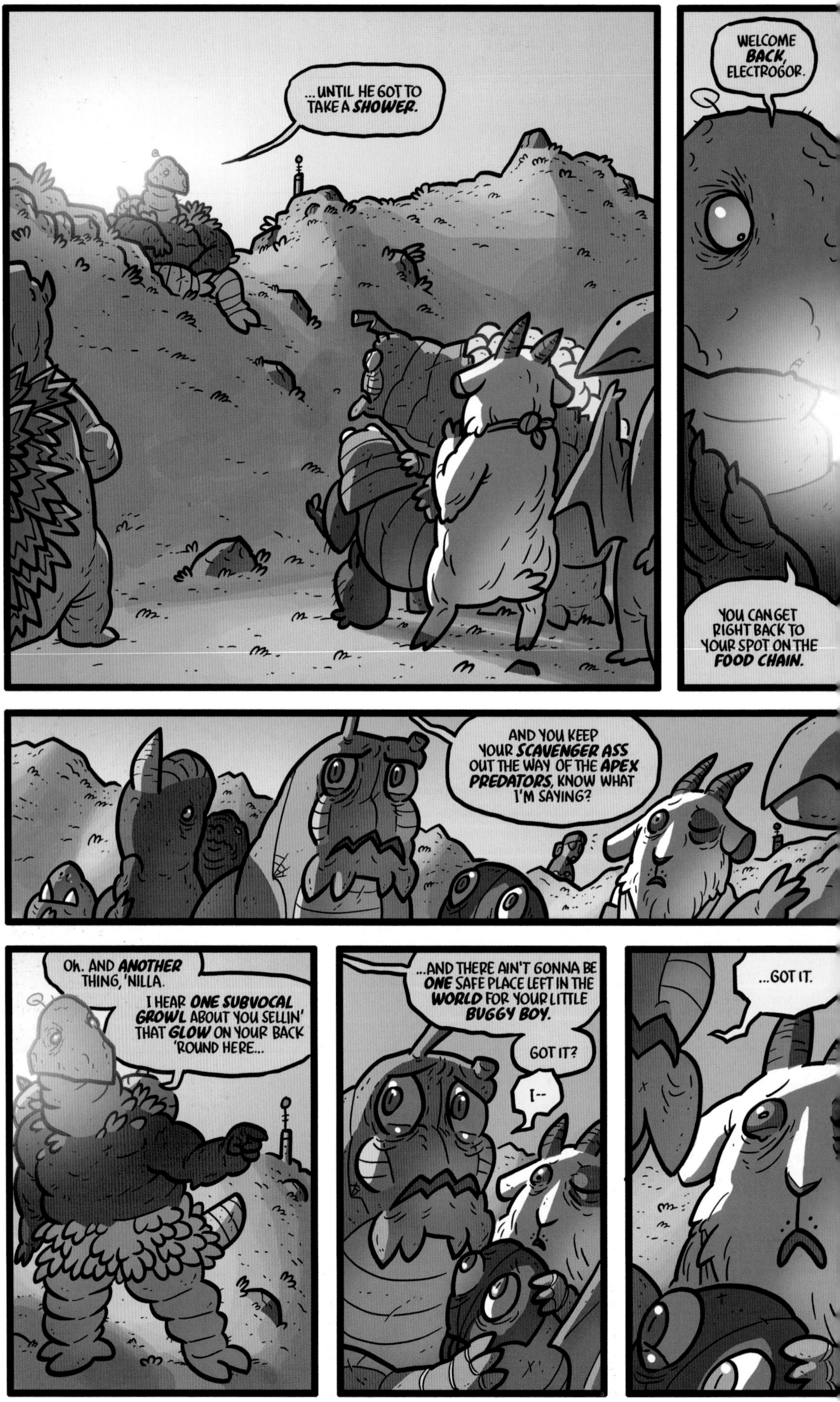

...UNTIL HE GOT TO TAKE A SHOWER.
WELCOME BACK, ELECTROGOR.
YOU CAN GET RIGHT BACK TO YOUR SPOT ON THE FOOD CHAIN.
AND YOU KEEP YOUR SCAVENGER ASS OUT THE WAY OF THE APEX PREDATORS, KNOW WHAT I'M SAYING?
Oh. AND ANOTHER THING, 'NILLA.
I HEAR ONE SUBVOCAL GROWL ABOUT YOU SELLIN' THAT GLOW ON YOUR BACK 'ROUND HERE...
...AND THERE AIN'T GONNA BE ONE SAFE PLACE LEFT IN THE WORLD FOR YOUR LITTLE BUGGY BOY.
GOT IT?
I--
...GOT IT.

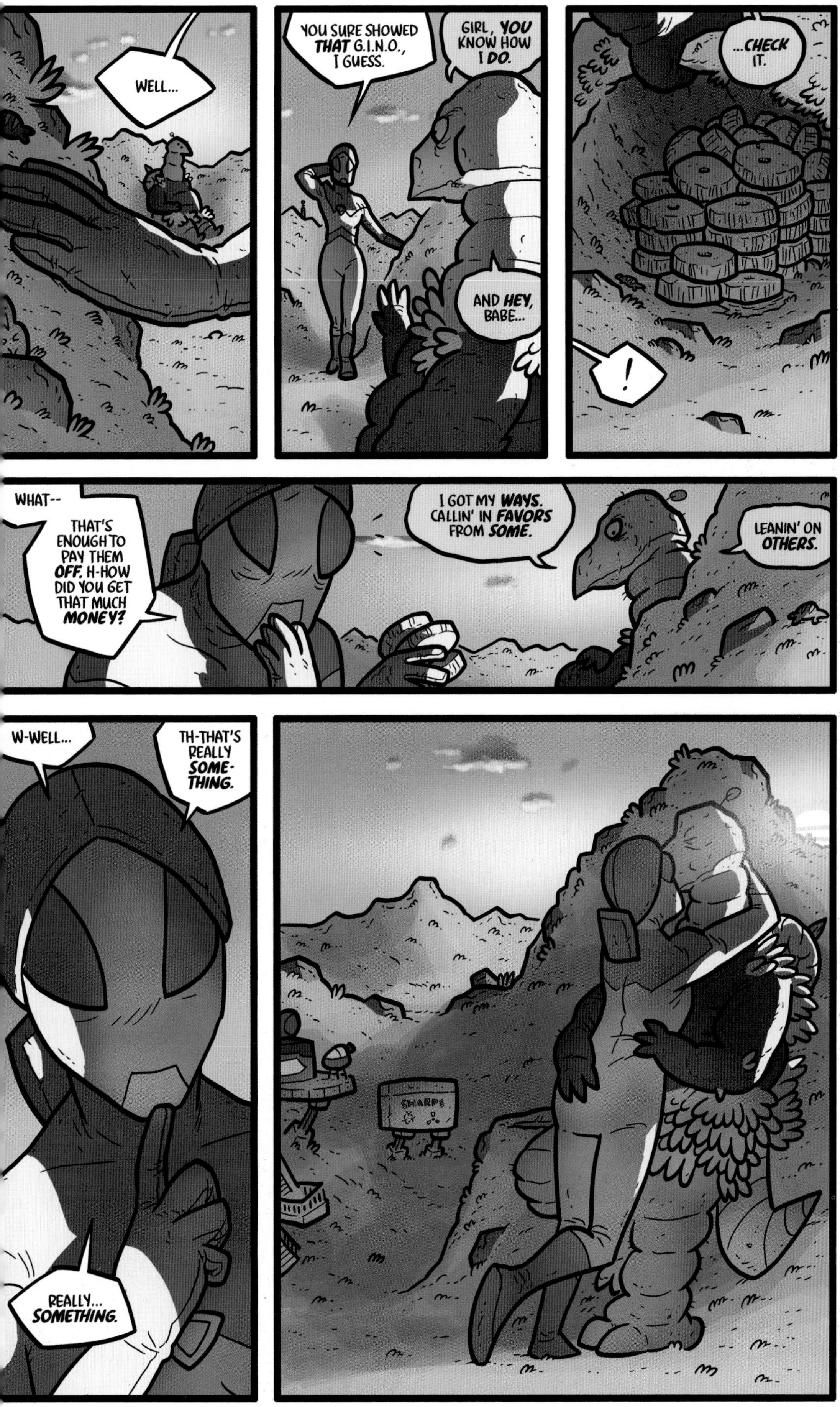
WELL...
YOU SURE SHOWED THAT G.I.N.O., I GUESS.
GIRL, YOU KNOW HOW I DO.
AND HEY, BABE...
...CHECK IT.
!
WHAT--
THAT'S ENOUGH TO PAY THEM OFF. H-HOW DID YOU GET THAT MUCH MONEY?
I GOT MY WAYS. CALLIN' IN FAVORS FROM SOME.
LEANIN' ON OTHERS.
W-WELL...
TH-THAT'S REALLY SOME-THING.
REALLY... SOMETHING.
SHARPS

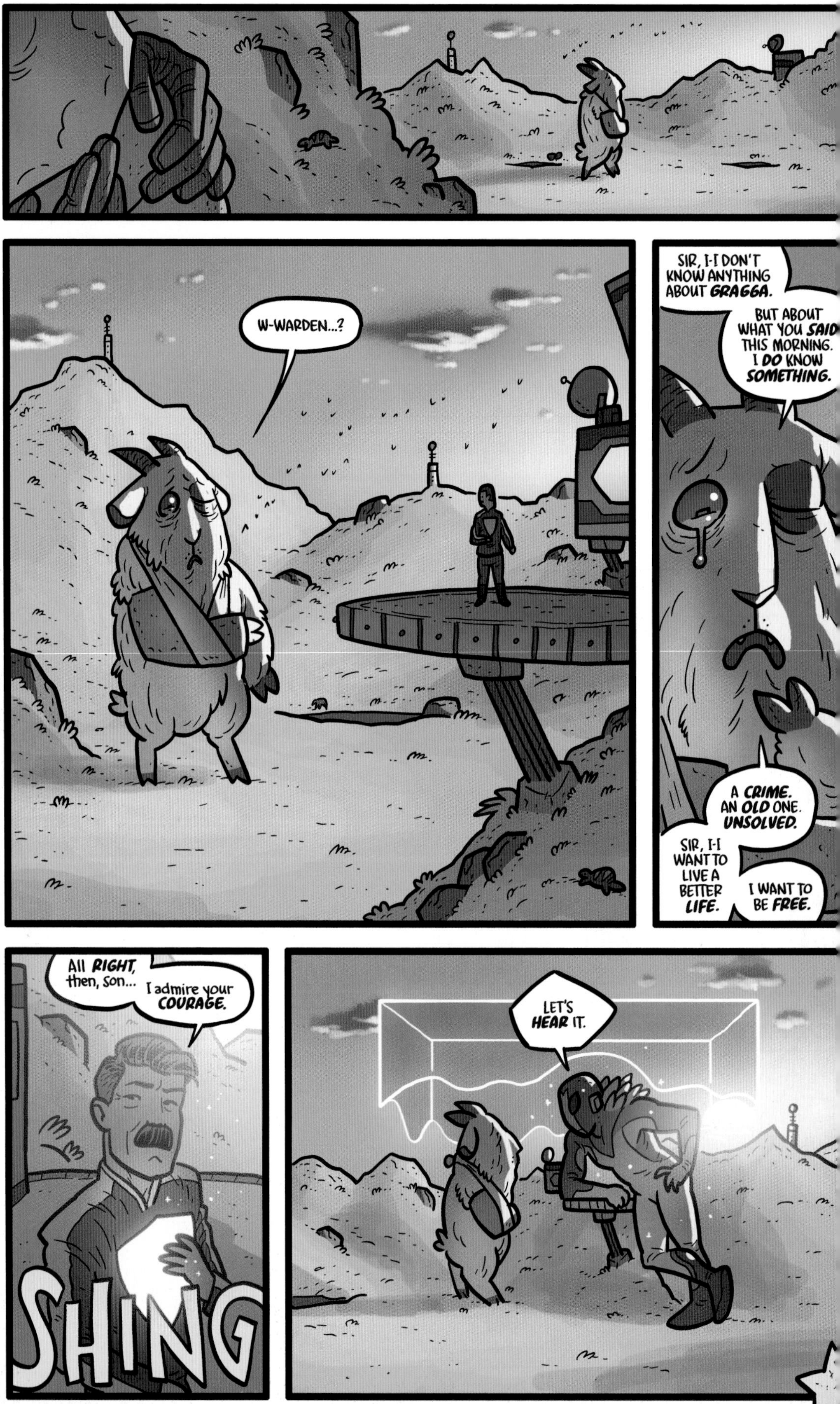

W-WARDEN...?
SIR, I-I DON'T KNOW ANYTHING ABOUT GRAGGA.
BUT ABOUT WHAT YOU SAID THIS MORNING. I DO KNOW SOMETHING.
A CRIME. AN OLD ONE. UNSOLVED.
SIR, I-I WANT TO LIVE A BETTER LIFE.
I WANT TO BE FREE.
All RIGHT, then, son...
I admire your COURAGE.
SHING
LET'S HEAR IT.

EPISODE 4

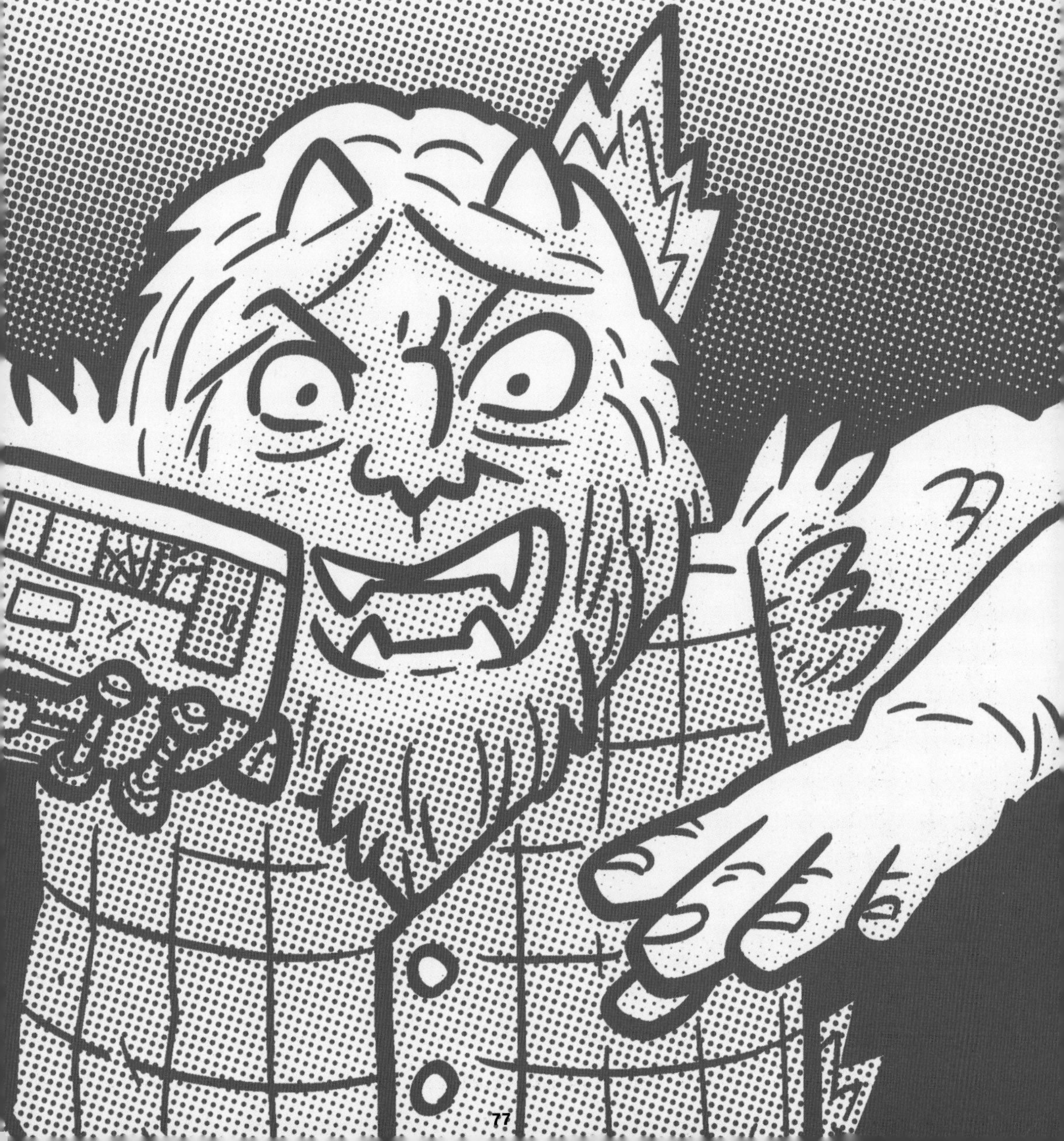

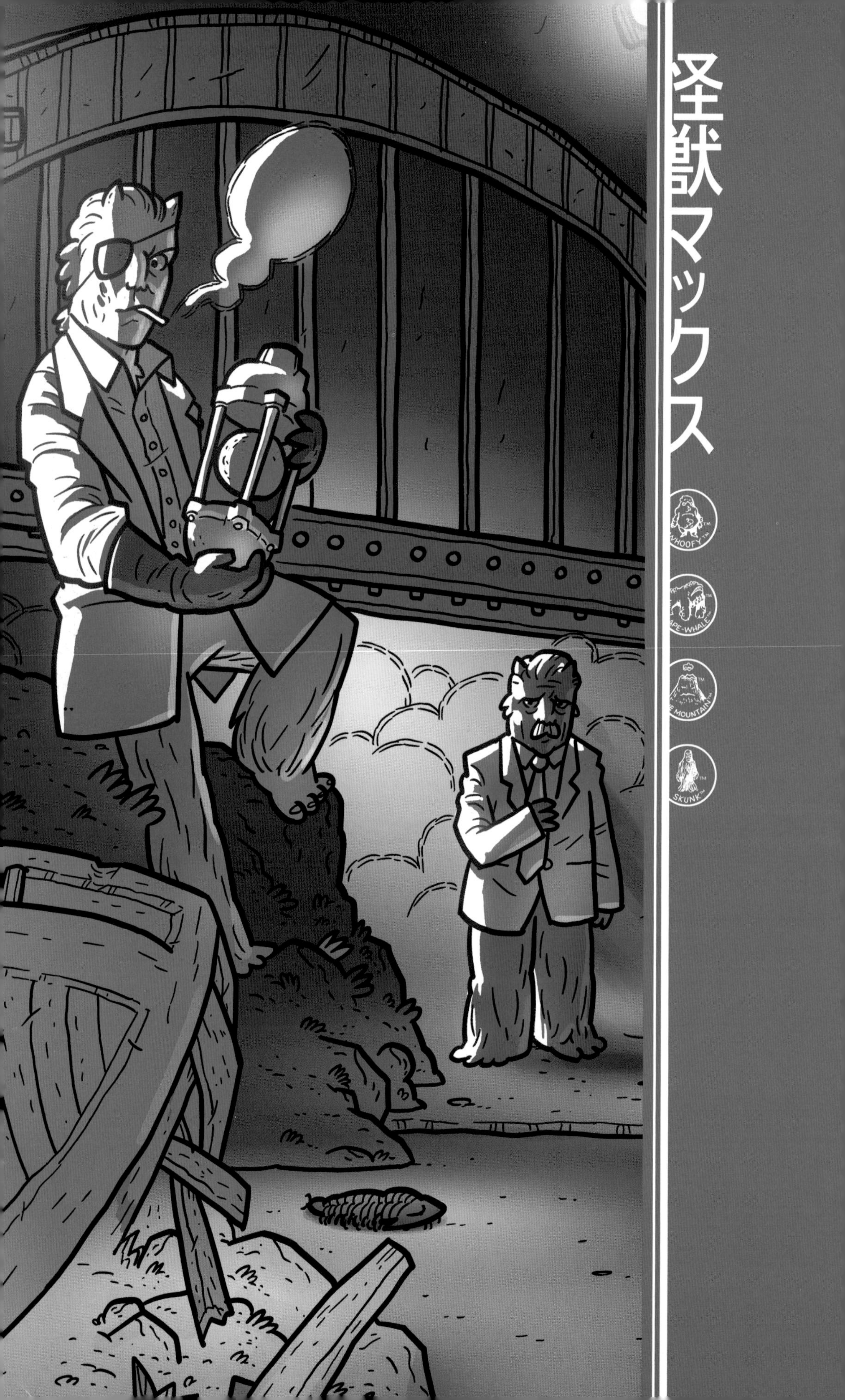
怪獣マックス
WHOOFY™
APE-WHALE™
E MOUNTAIN™
SKUNK™

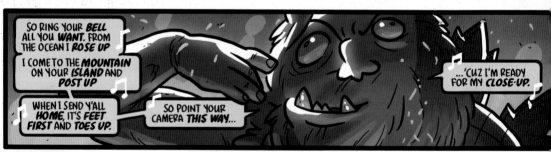

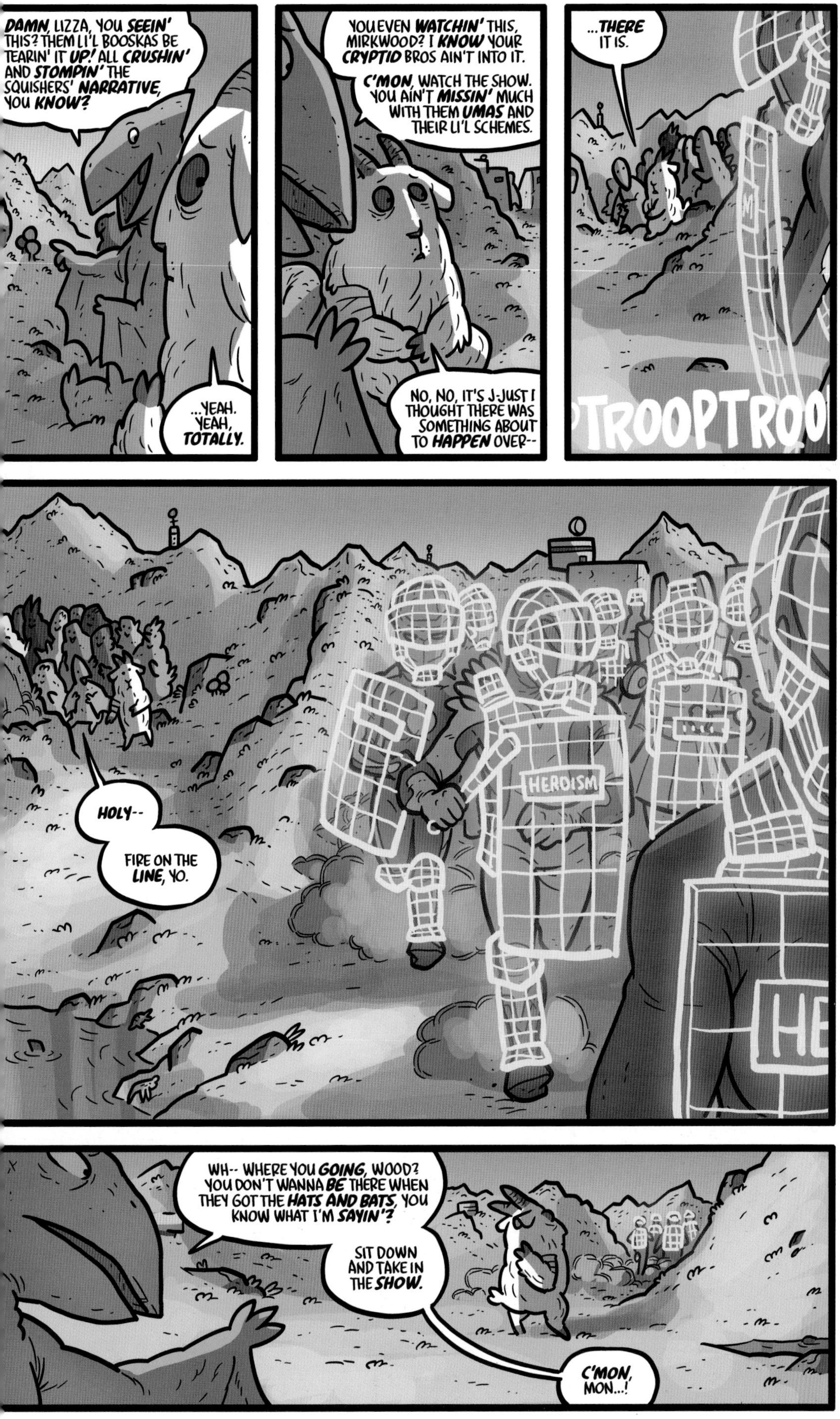

DAMN, LIZZA, YOU SEEIN' THIS? THEM LI'L BOOSKAS BE TEARIN' IT UP! ALL CRUSHIN' AND STOMPIN' THE SQUISHERS' NARRATIVE, YOU KNOW?
...YEAH. YEAH, TOTALLY.
YOU EVEN WATCHIN' THIS, MIRKWOOD? I KNOW YOUR CRYPTID BROS AIN'T INTO IT.
C'MON, WATCH THE SHOW. YOU AIN'T MISSIN' MUCH WITH THEM UMAS AND THEIR LI'L SCHEMES.
NO, NO, IT'S J-JUST I THOUGHT THERE WAS SOMETHING ABOUT TO HAPPEN OVER--
...THERE IT IS.
TROOPTROO
HOLY--
FIRE ON THE LINE, YO.
HEROISM
WH-- WHERE YOU GOING, WOOD? YOU DON'T WANNA BE THERE WHEN THEY GOT THE HATS AND BATS, YOU KNOW WHAT I'M SAYIN'?
SIT DOWN AND TAKE IN THE SHOW.
C'MON, MON...!

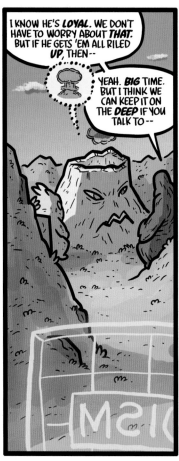

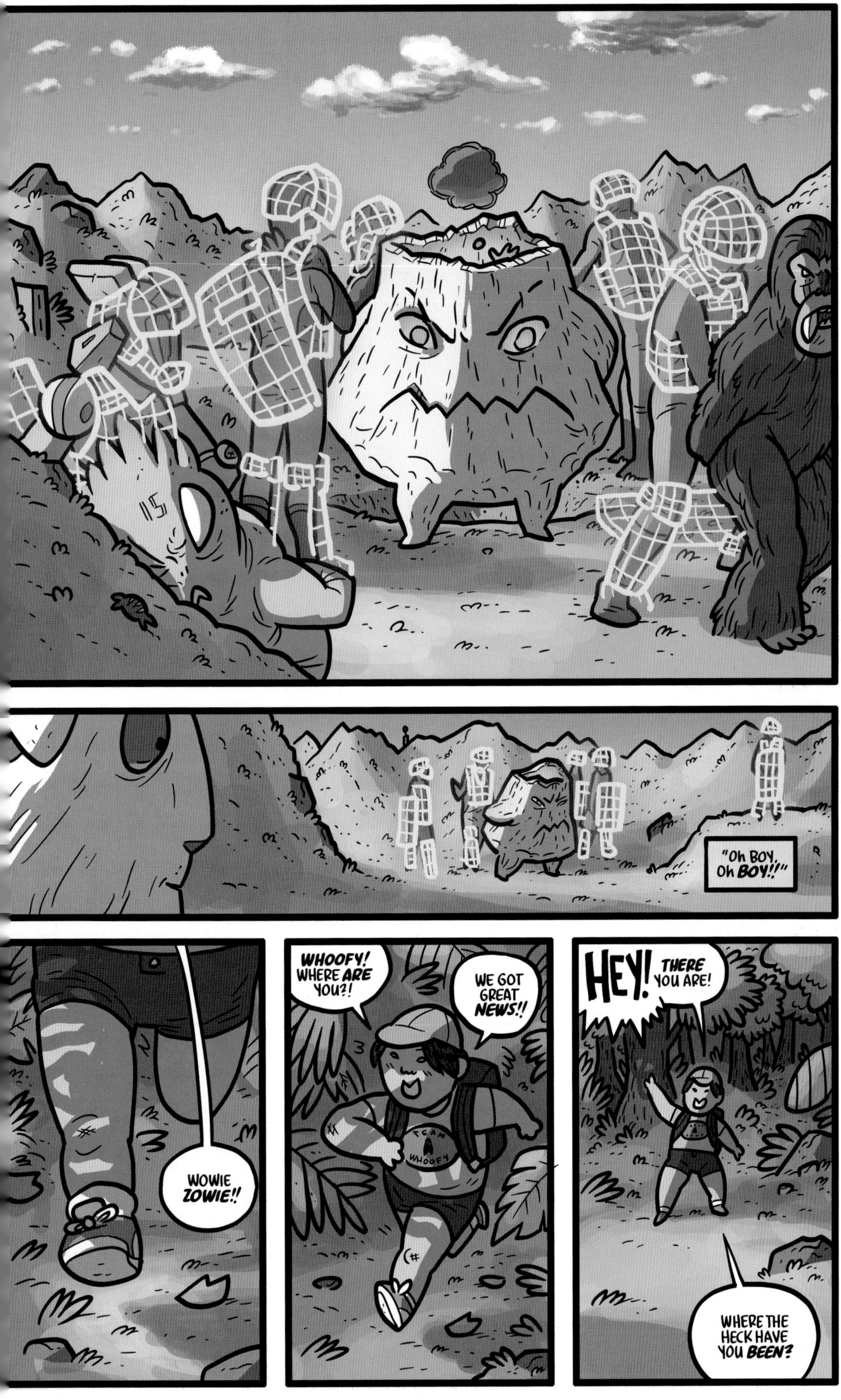
15
"Oh BOY, Oh BOY!!"
WOWIE ZOWIE!!
WHOOFY! WHERE ARE YOU?!
WE GOT GREAT NEWS!!
TEAM WHOOFY
HEY!
THERE YOU ARE!
WHERE THE HECK HAVE YOU BEEN?

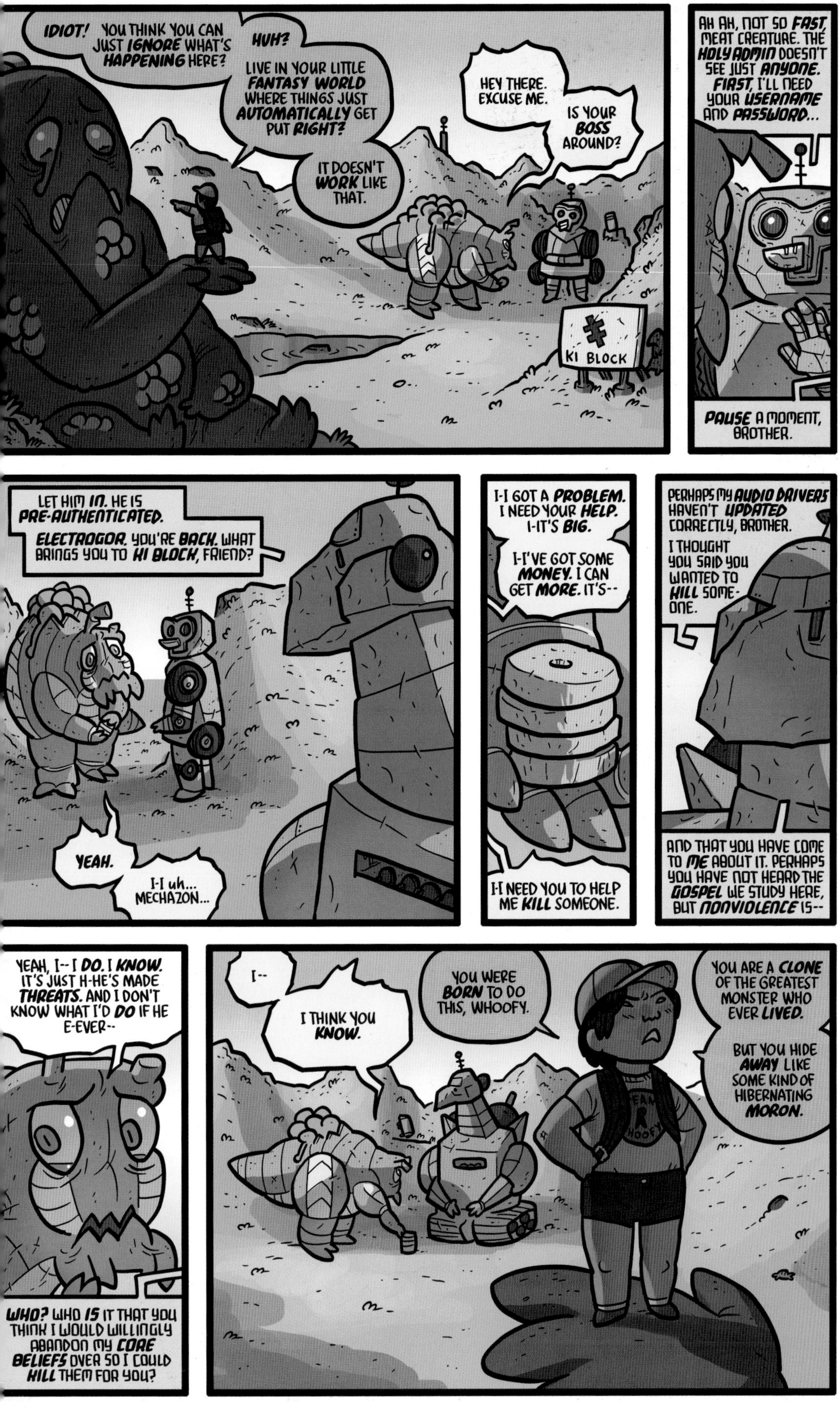
IDIOT! YOU THINK YOU CAN JUST IGNORE WHAT'S HAPPENING HERE?
HUH?
LIVE IN YOUR LITTLE FANTASY WORLD WHERE THINGS JUST AUTOMATICALLY GET PUT RIGHT?
IT DOESN'T WORK LIKE THAT.
HEY THERE. EXCUSE ME.
IS YOUR BOSS AROUND?
KI BLOCK
AH AH, NOT SO FAST, MEAT CREATURE. THE HOLY ADMIN DOESN'T SEE JUST ANYONE. FIRST, I'LL NEED YOUR USERNAME AND PASSWORD...
PAUSE A MOMENT, BROTHER.
LET HIM IN. HE IS PRE-AUTHENTICATED.
ELECTROGOR. YOU'RE BACK. WHAT BRINGS YOU TO KI BLOCK, FRIEND?
YEAH.
I-I uh... MECHAZON...
I-I GOT A PROBLEM. I NEED YOUR HELP. I-IT'S BIG.
I-I'VE GOT SOME MONEY. I CAN GET MORE. IT'S--
I-I NEED YOU TO HELP ME KILL SOMEONE.
PERHAPS MY AUDIO DRIVERS HAVEN'T UPDATED CORRECTLY, BROTHER.
I THOUGHT YOU SAID YOU WANTED TO KILL SOME-ONE.
AND THAT YOU HAVE COME TO ME ABOUT IT. PERHAPS YOU HAVE NOT HEARD THE GOSPEL WE STUDY HERE, BUT NONVIOLENCE IS--
YEAH, I-- I DO. I KNOW. IT'S JUST H-HE'S MADE THREATS. AND I DON'T KNOW WHAT I'D DO IF HE E-EVER--
WHO? WHO IS IT THAT YOU THINK I WOULD WILLINGLY ABANDON MY CORE BELIEFS OVER SO I COULD KILL THEM FOR YOU?
I--
I THINK YOU KNOW.
YOU WERE BORN TO DO THIS, WHOOFY.
YOU ARE A CLONE OF THE GREATEST MONSTER WHO EVER LIVED.
BUT YOU HIDE AWAY LIKE SOME KIND OF HIBERNATING MORON.

YOU SEE THIS OPPORTUNITY RIGHT IN *FRONT* OF YOU, DON'T YOU? BUT YOU WON'T *TAKE* IT.

LIKE YOU'RE IN SOME KIND OF *TRANCE.*

YO.

MM.

I'M HERE WITH YOUR *FIX*, JUNKIE.

FINEST *YELLOW-CAKE*. STRAIGHT FROM THE *MOON*.

LIKED THAT YESTERDAY, *DIDN'T* YA?

WELL, HERE'S *MORE*. BUT THE *COST* WENT UP.

I SAID *YO!*

SNXF?!

Z-ZONN? H-HEY, NO, M'*GOOD*. I'M OKAY.

UH HUH.

I CAN *SEE* THAT.

KEEPIN' YOURSELF PRETTY *DOPED*.

DON'T EVEN GOT TIME TO FEED YOUR *SHARKS*.

SO I GOT ONE *QUESTION*.

THAP

WHY DO YOU THINK I *GAVE* YOU THE *SAMPLE*, MEGAFAUNA?!

SO YOU COULD GO AND TAKE YOUR BUSINESS ACROSS THE *MOUNTAIN RANGE* TO SOME *OTHER* PUSHER? HUH?

WHAT YOU *GAVE* ME-- S-SO *STRONG*, MON. I-I WAS *FIENDIN'*. I N-*NEEDED* IT. AN' *HE* COME BY AN'-- I-I JUST GAVE HIM TH-THE R-REST A' MY *MONEY*--

"HE?" WHO'S--

OK.

YEAH, I THINK I *KNOW*.

YOU CAN SEE WHERE *THIS* IS GOING.

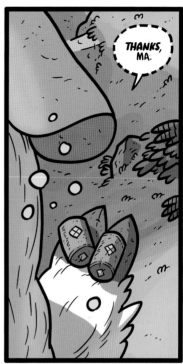

"OKAY, YOU GOTTA BE **THOROUGH** HERE.

MAKE SURE YOU GET ALL THE **LEAVES** AND **BRANCHES** OFF OF THERE. **FISH**, TOO.

THEN HOLD THEM **UP**, AND SUMMON THE STERILE **FIELD**.

THAT'S RIGHT.

THANKS, DOC. BOY, THIS **SURGERY**, huh? PRETTY **CRAZY**.

I DON'T KNOW HOW YOU CAN BE SO **CALM** ABOUT IT.

WELL, I'VE BEEN **DOING** IT A WHILE. YOU HAVE TO LET **GO** OF SOME OF THE **EMOTIONS**.

AND THIS ONE'S PRETTY **STRAIGHTFORWARD**. JUST REMOVING A **FOREIGN BODY**.

YEAH.

STILL SEEMS **INTENSE**.

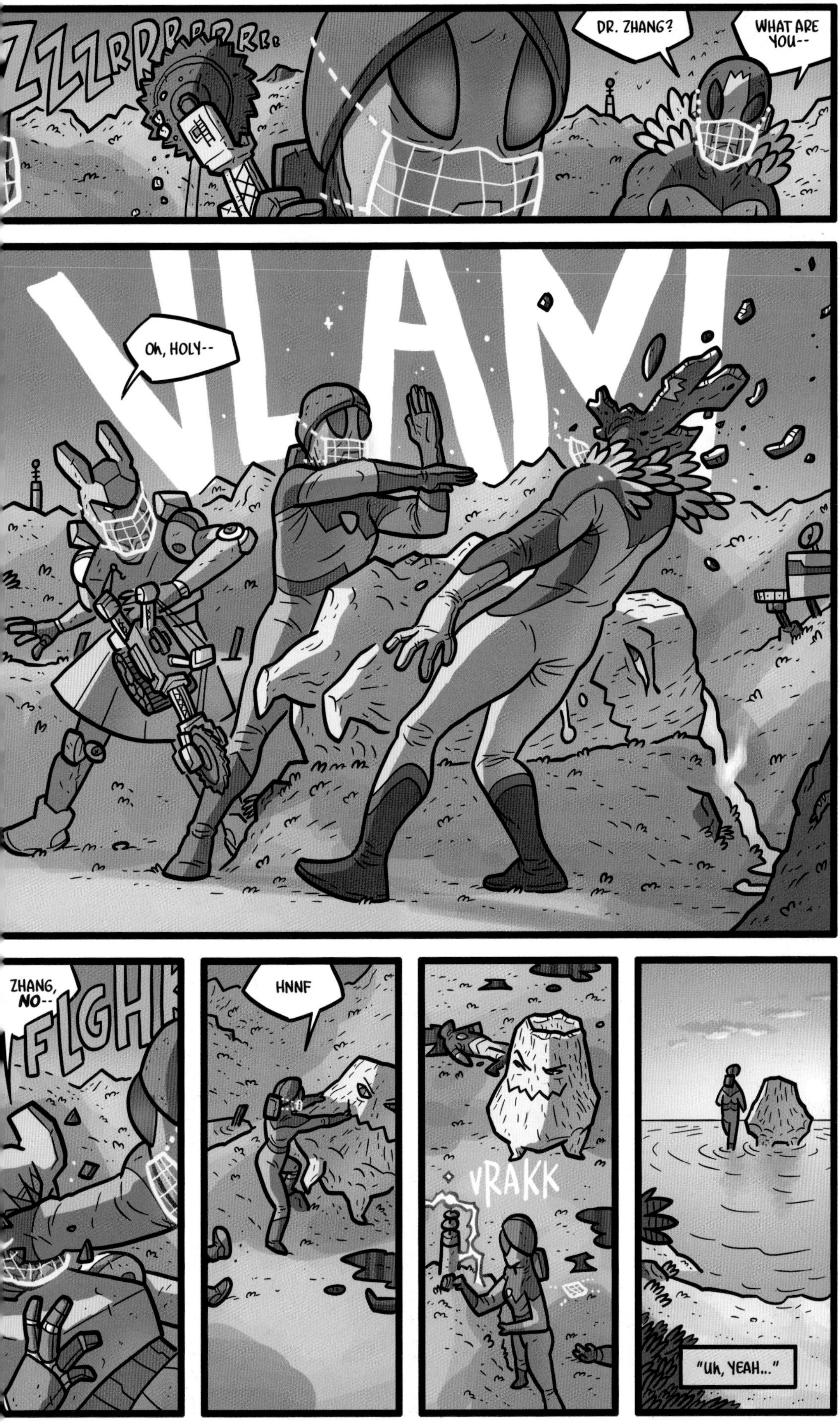
ZZZRRRRRRRR
DR. ZHANG?
WHAT ARE YOU--
VLAM!
Oh, HOLY--
ZHANG, NO--
FLGH
HNNF
VRAKK
"Uh, YEAH..."

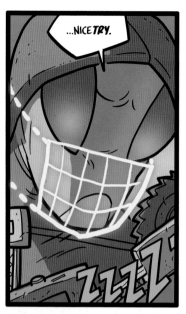

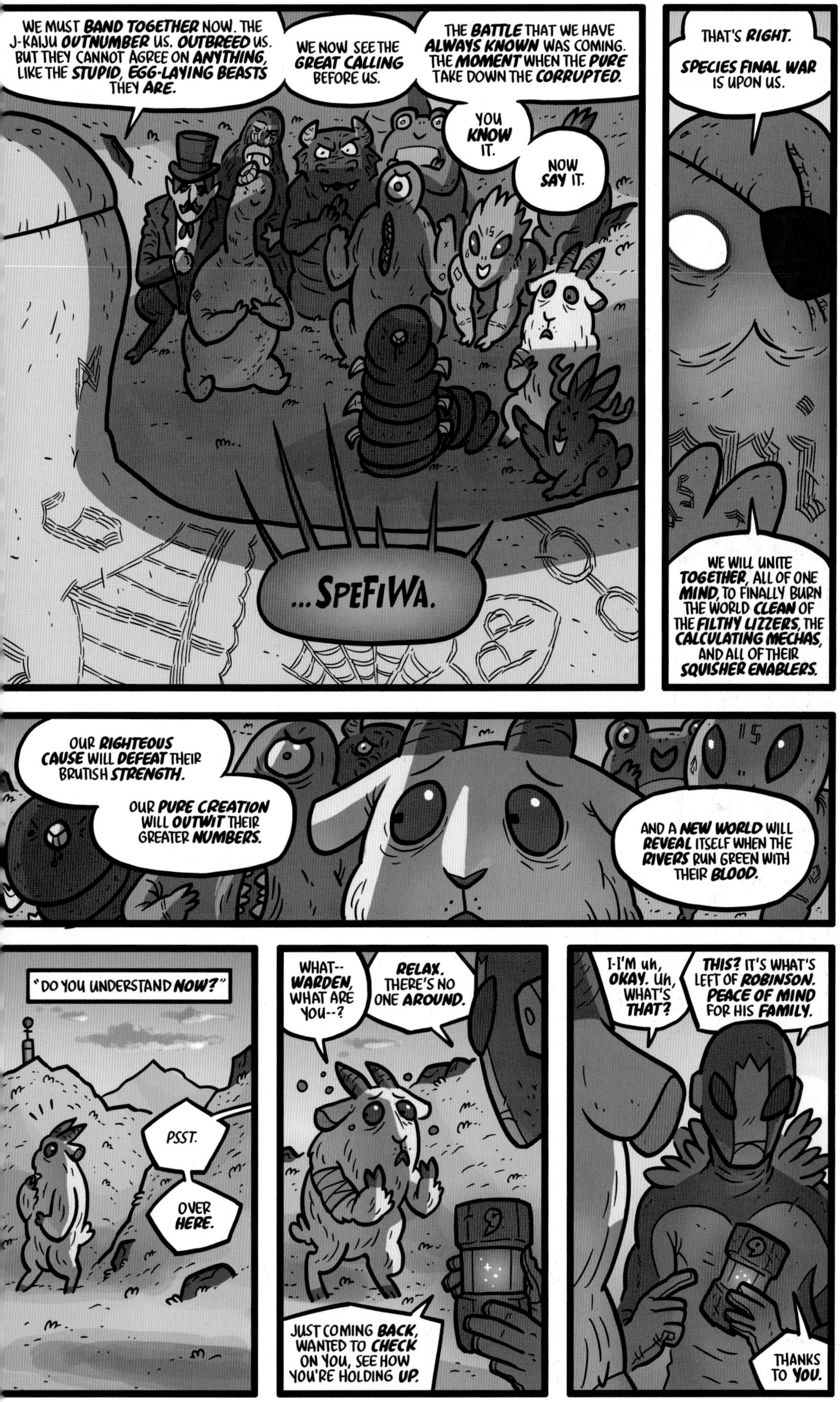
WE MUST BAND TOGETHER NOW. THE J-KAIJU OUTNUMBER US. OUTBREED US. BUT THEY CANNOT AGREE ON ANYTHING, LIKE THE STUPID, EGG-LAYING BEASTS THEY ARE.
WE NOW SEE THE GREAT CALLING BEFORE US.
THE BATTLE THAT WE HAVE ALWAYS KNOWN WAS COMING. THE MOMENT WHEN THE PURE TAKE DOWN THE CORRUPTED.
YOU KNOW IT.
NOW SAY IT.
...SPEFIWA.
THAT'S RIGHT.
SPECIES FINAL WAR IS UPON US.
WE WILL UNITE TOGETHER, ALL OF ONE MIND, TO FINALLY BURN THE WORLD CLEAN OF THE FILTHY LIZZERS, THE CALCULATING MECHAS, AND ALL OF THEIR SQUISHER ENABLERS.
OUR RIGHTEOUS CAUSE WILL DEFEAT THEIR BRUTISH STRENGTH.
OUR PURE CREATION WILL OUTWIT THEIR GREATER NUMBERS.
AND A NEW WORLD WILL REVEAL ITSELF WHEN THE RIVERS RUN GREEN WITH THEIR BLOOD.
"DO YOU UNDERSTAND NOW?"
PSST.
OVER HERE.
WHAT-- WARDEN, WHAT ARE YOU--?
RELAX. THERE'S NO ONE AROUND.
JUST COMING BACK, WANTED TO CHECK ON YOU, SEE HOW YOU'RE HOLDING UP.
I-I'M uh, OKAY. Uh, WHAT'S THAT?
THIS? IT'S WHAT'S LEFT OF ROBINSON. PEACE OF MIND FOR HIS FAMILY.
THANKS TO YOU.

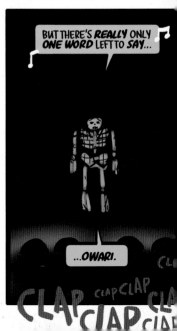

EPISODE 5

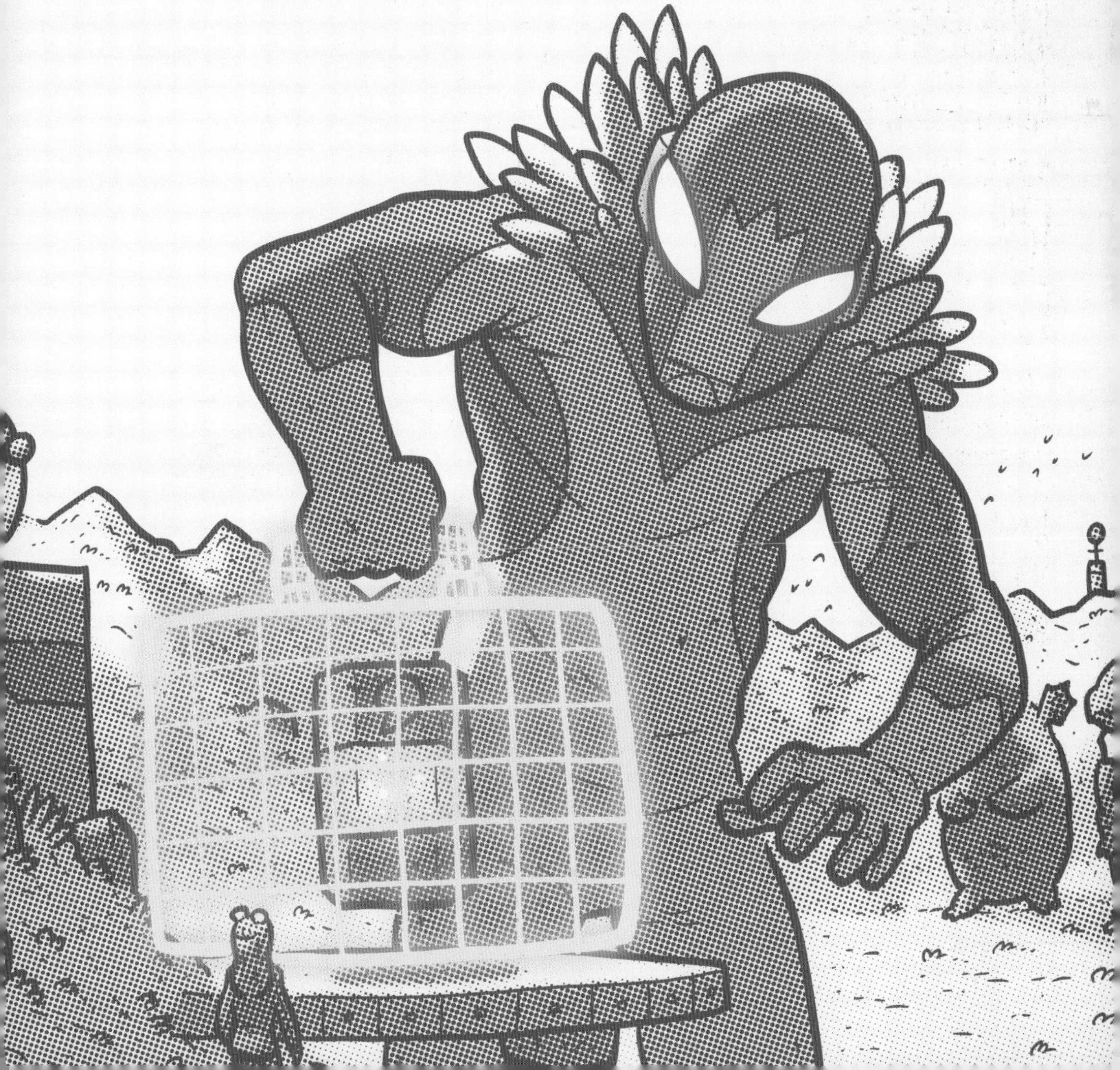

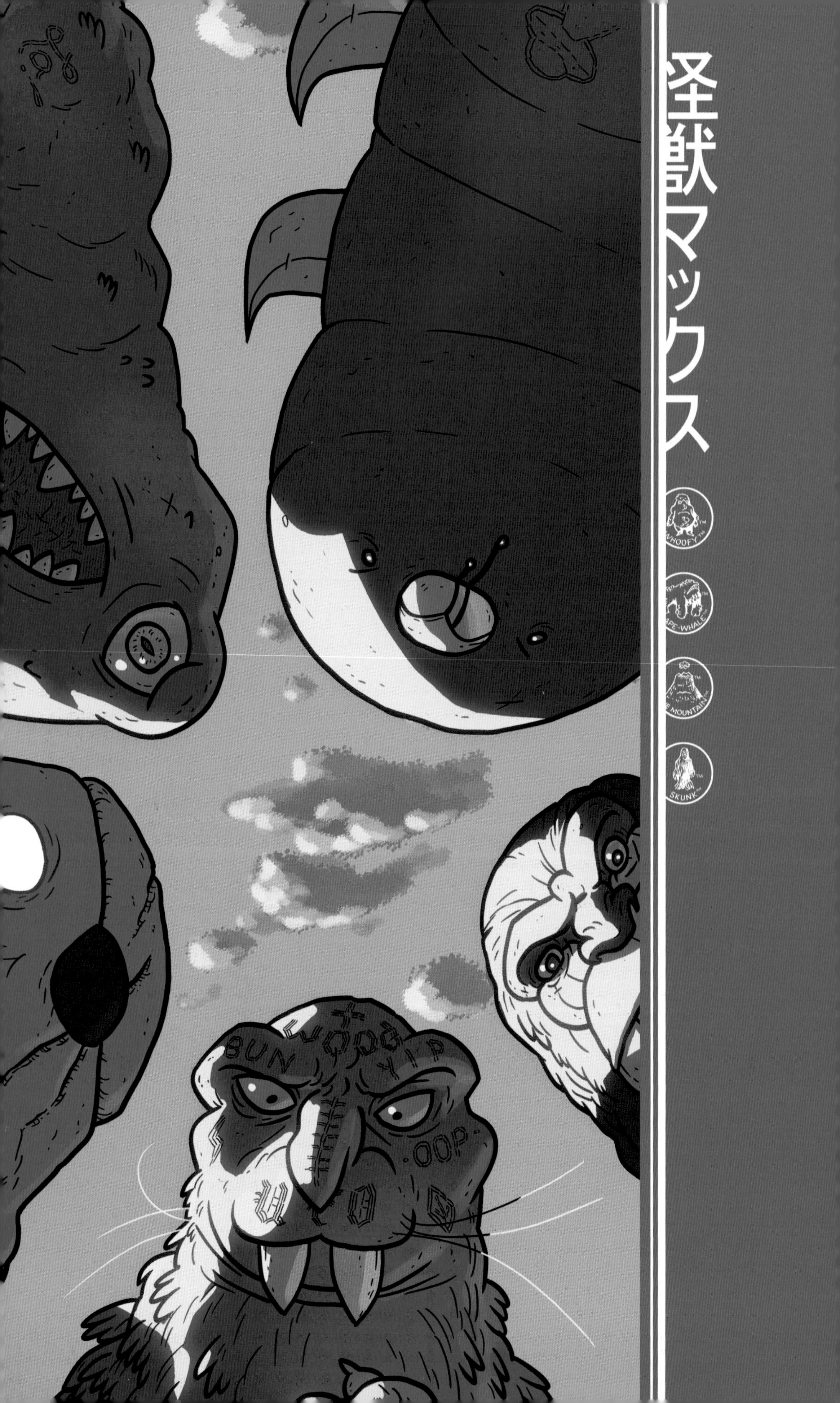

怪獣マックス
WHOOFY™
APE-WHALE™
MOUNTAIN™
SKUNK™
BUN
OOP

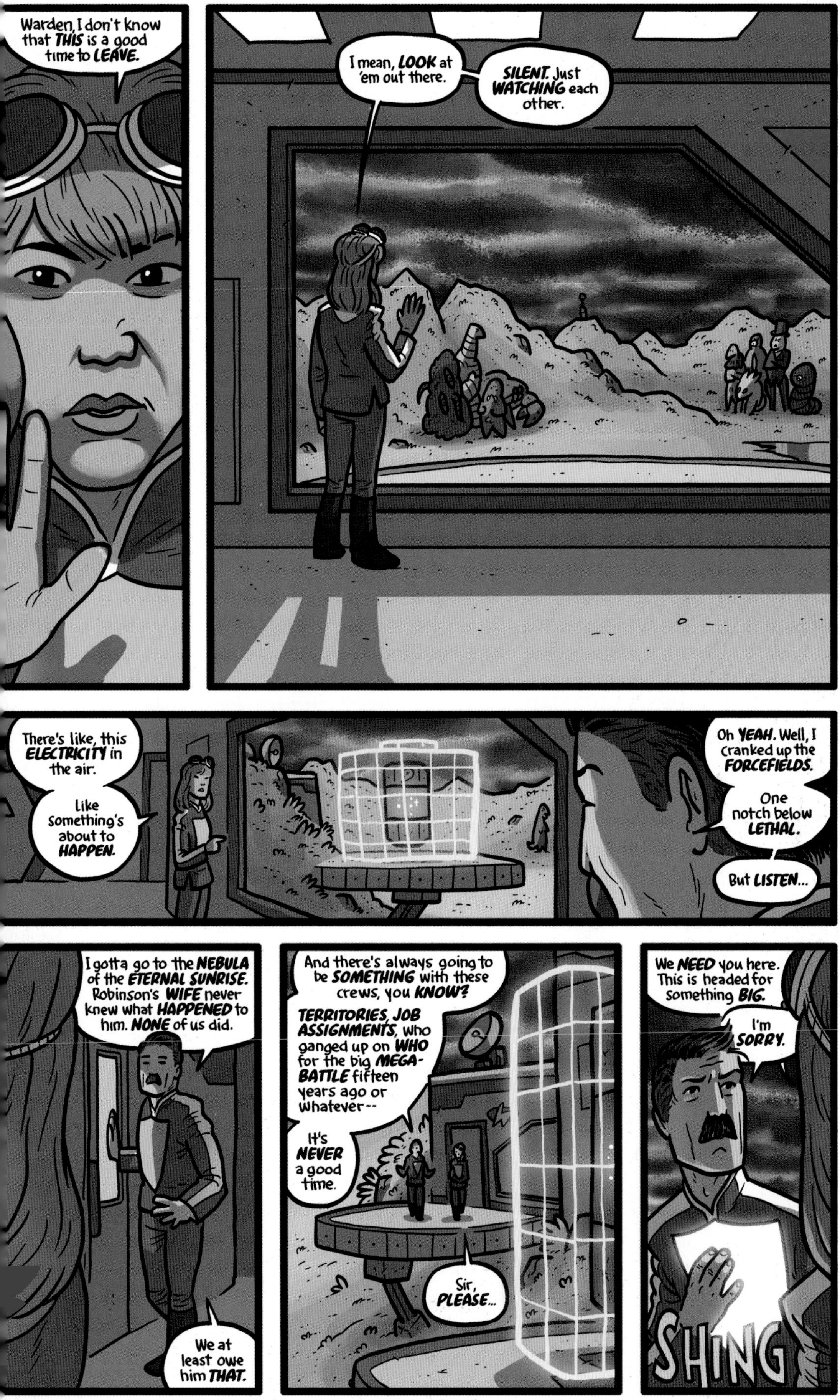

Warden, I don't know that THIS is a good time to LEAVE.
I mean, LOOK at 'em out there.
SILENT. Just WATCHING each other.
There's like, this ELECTRICITY in the air.
Like something's about to HAPPEN.
Oh YEAH. Well, I cranked up the FORCEFIELDS.
One notch below LETHAL.
But LISTEN...
I gotta go to the NEBULA of the ETERNAL SUNRISE. Robinson's WIFE never knew what HAPPENED to him. NONE of us did.
We at least owe him THAT.
And there's always going to be SOMETHING with these crews, you KNOW?
TERRITORIES, JOB ASSIGNMENTS, who ganged up on WHO for the big MEGA-BATTLE fifteen years ago or whatever--
It's NEVER a good time.
Sir, PLEASE...
We NEED you here. This is headed for something BIG.
I'm SORRY.
SHING

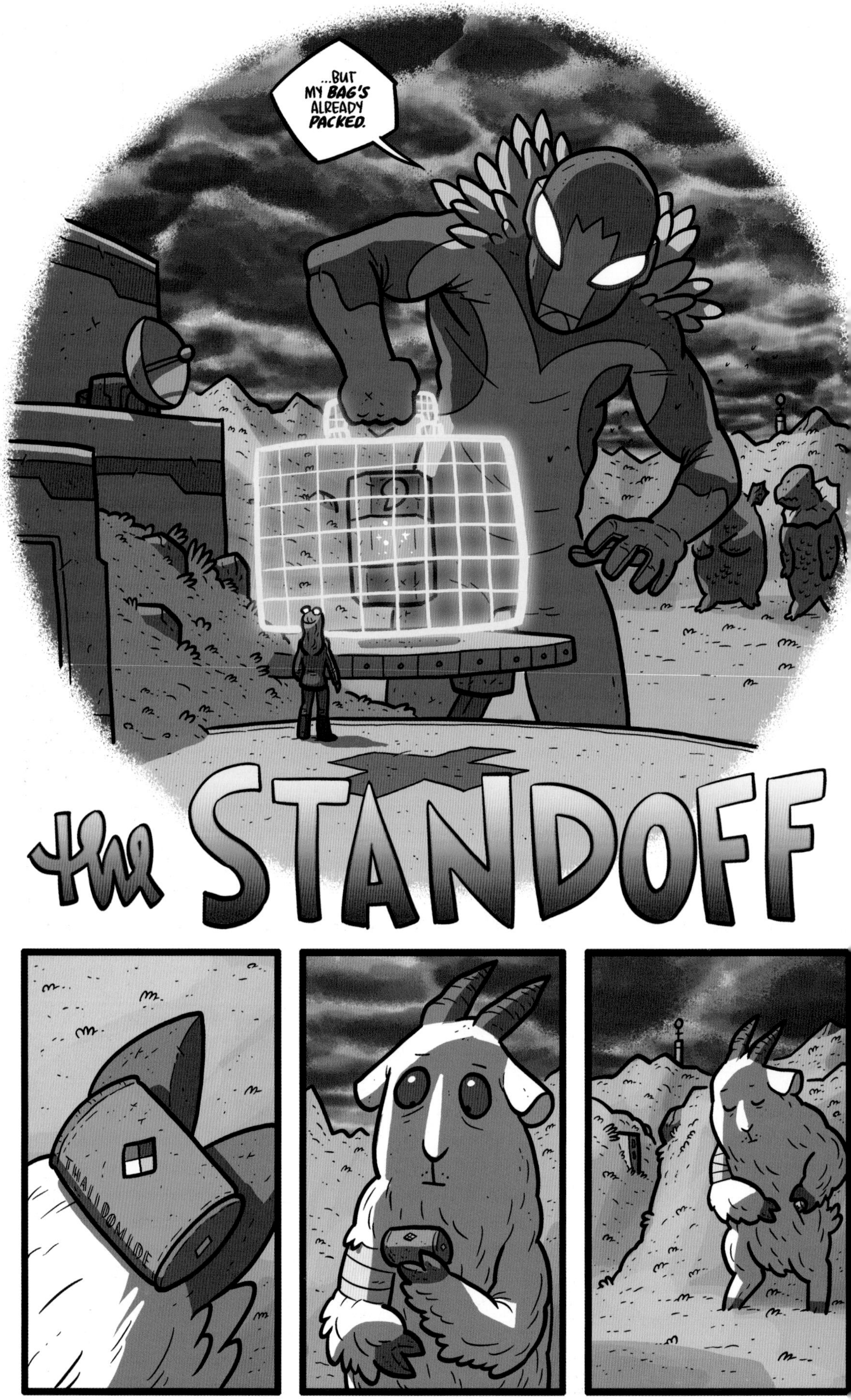
...BUT MY BAG'S ALREADY PACKED.
the STANDOFF

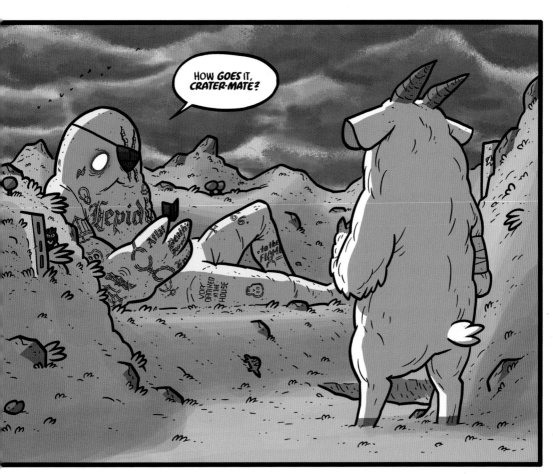

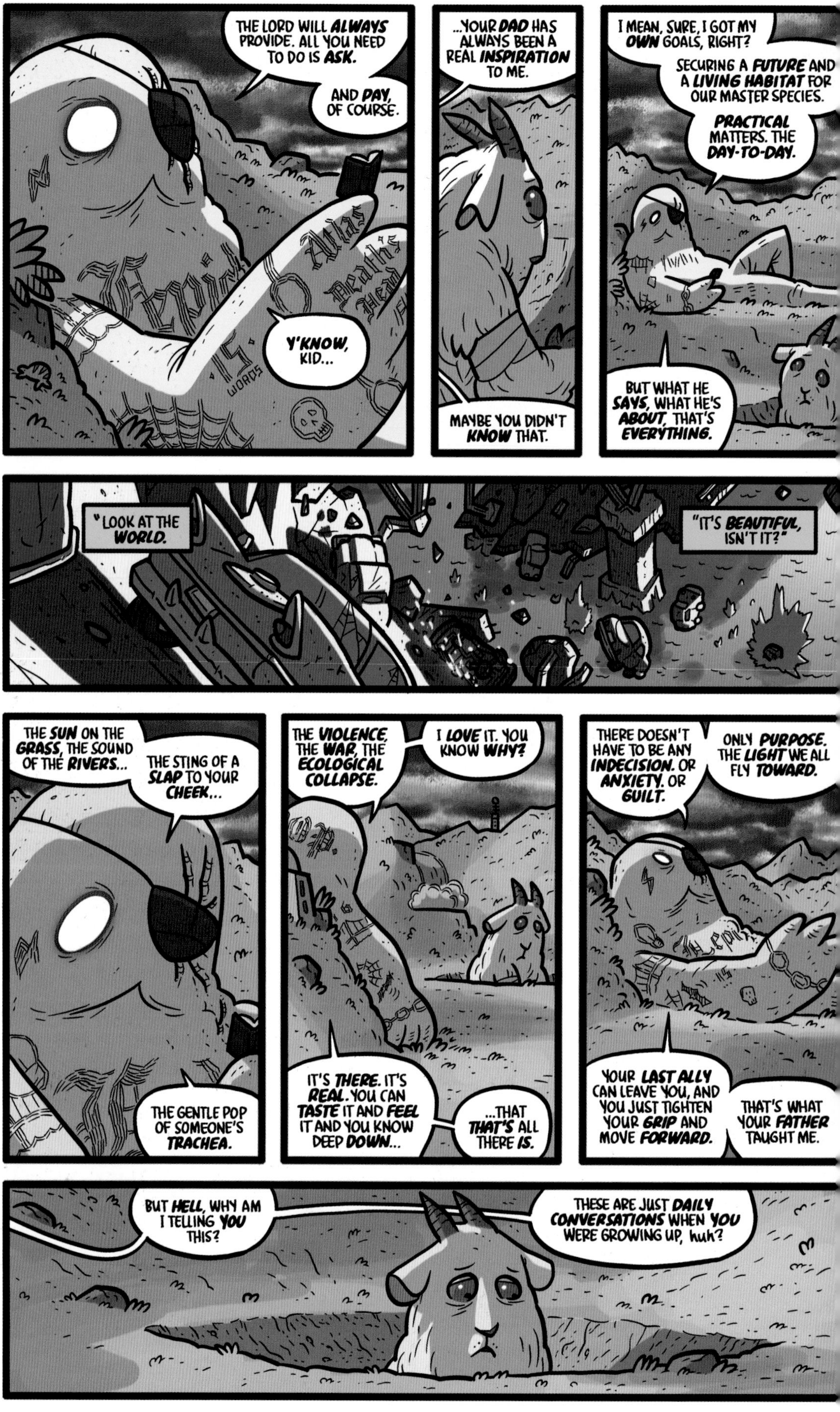
THE LORD WILL ALWAYS PROVIDE. ALL YOU NEED TO DO IS ASK.
AND PAY, OF COURSE.
Y'KNOW, KID...
...YOUR DAD HAS ALWAYS BEEN A REAL INSPIRATION TO ME.
MAYBE YOU DIDN'T KNOW THAT.
I MEAN, SURE, I GOT MY OWN GOALS, RIGHT?
SECURING A FUTURE AND A LIVING HABITAT FOR OUR MASTER SPECIES.
PRACTICAL MATTERS. THE DAY-TO-DAY.
BUT WHAT HE SAYS, WHAT HE'S ABOUT, THAT'S EVERYTHING.
"LOOK AT THE WORLD.
"IT'S BEAUTIFUL, ISN'T IT?"
THE SUN ON THE GRASS, THE SOUND OF THE RIVERS...
THE STING OF A SLAP TO YOUR CHEEK...
THE GENTLE POP OF SOMEONE'S TRACHEA.
THE VIOLENCE, THE WAR, THE ECOLOGICAL COLLAPSE.
I LOVE IT. YOU KNOW WHY?
IT'S THERE. IT'S REAL. YOU CAN TASTE IT AND FEEL IT AND YOU KNOW DEEP DOWN...
...THAT THAT'S ALL THERE IS.
THERE DOESN'T HAVE TO BE ANY INDECISION. OR ANXIETY. OR GUILT.
ONLY PURPOSE. THE LIGHT WE ALL FLY TOWARD.
YOUR LAST ALLY CAN LEAVE YOU, AND YOU JUST TIGHTEN YOUR GRIP AND MOVE FORWARD.
THAT'S WHAT YOUR FATHER TAUGHT ME.
BUT HELL, WHY AM I TELLING YOU THIS?
THESE ARE JUST DAILY CONVERSATIONS WHEN YOU WERE GROWING UP, huh?

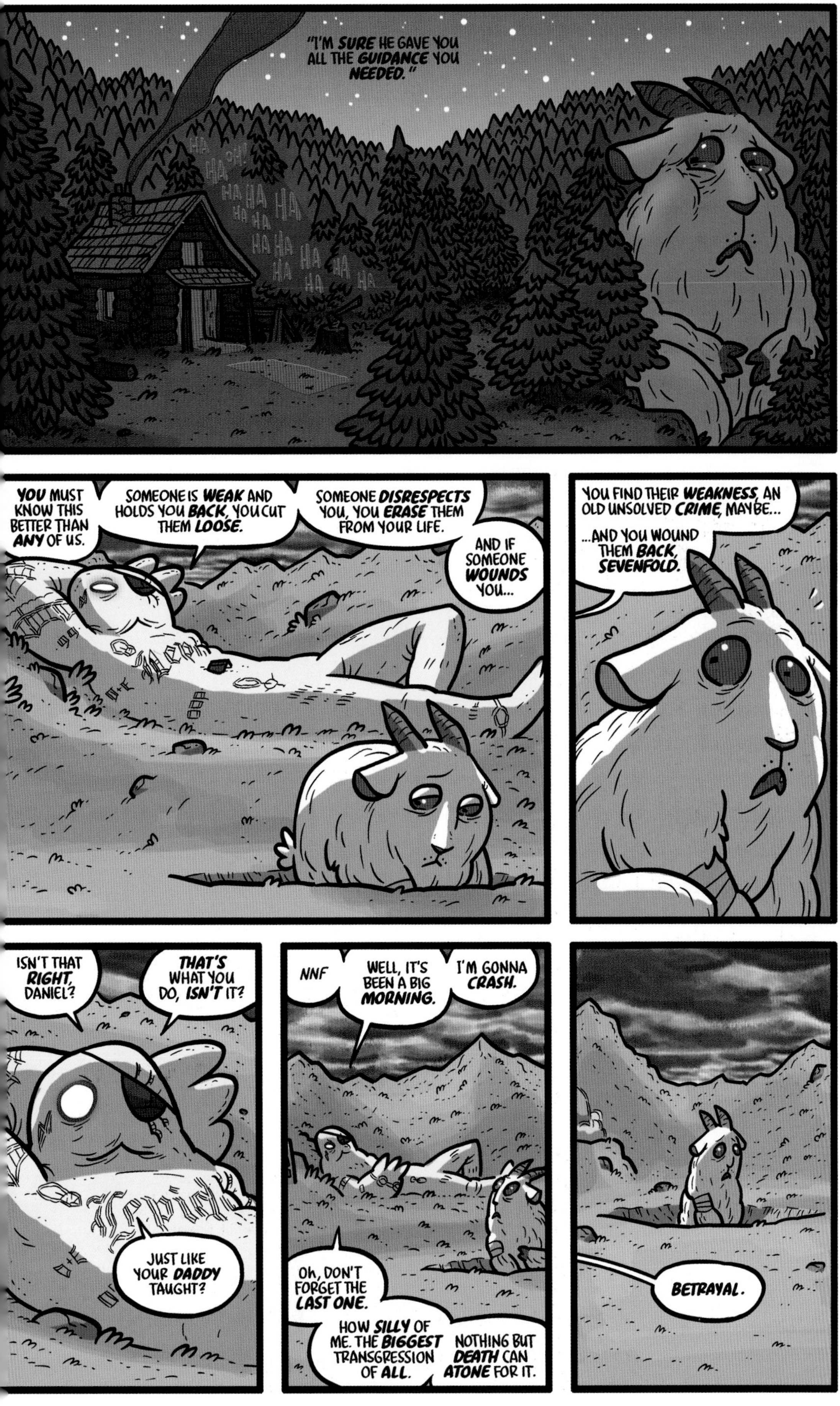
"I'M SURE HE GAVE YOU ALL THE GUIDANCE YOU NEEDED."
HA HA OH! HA HA HA HA HA HA HA HA HA HA HA
YOU MUST KNOW THIS BETTER THAN ANY OF US.
SOMEONE IS WEAK AND HOLDS YOU BACK, YOU CUT THEM LOOSE.
SOMEONE DISRESPECTS YOU, YOU ERASE THEM FROM YOUR LIFE.
AND IF SOMEONE WOUNDS YOU...
YOU FIND THEIR WEAKNESS, AN OLD UNSOLVED CRIME, MAYBE...
...AND YOU WOUND THEM BACK, SEVENFOLD.
ISN'T THAT RIGHT, DANIEL?
THAT'S WHAT YOU DO, ISN'T IT?
JUST LIKE YOUR DADDY TAUGHT?
NNF
WELL, IT'S BEEN A BIG MORNING.
I'M GONNA CRASH.
Oh, DON'T FORGET THE LAST ONE.
HOW SILLY OF ME. THE BIGGEST TRANSGRESSION OF ALL.
NOTHING BUT DEATH CAN ATONE FOR IT.
BETRAYAL.

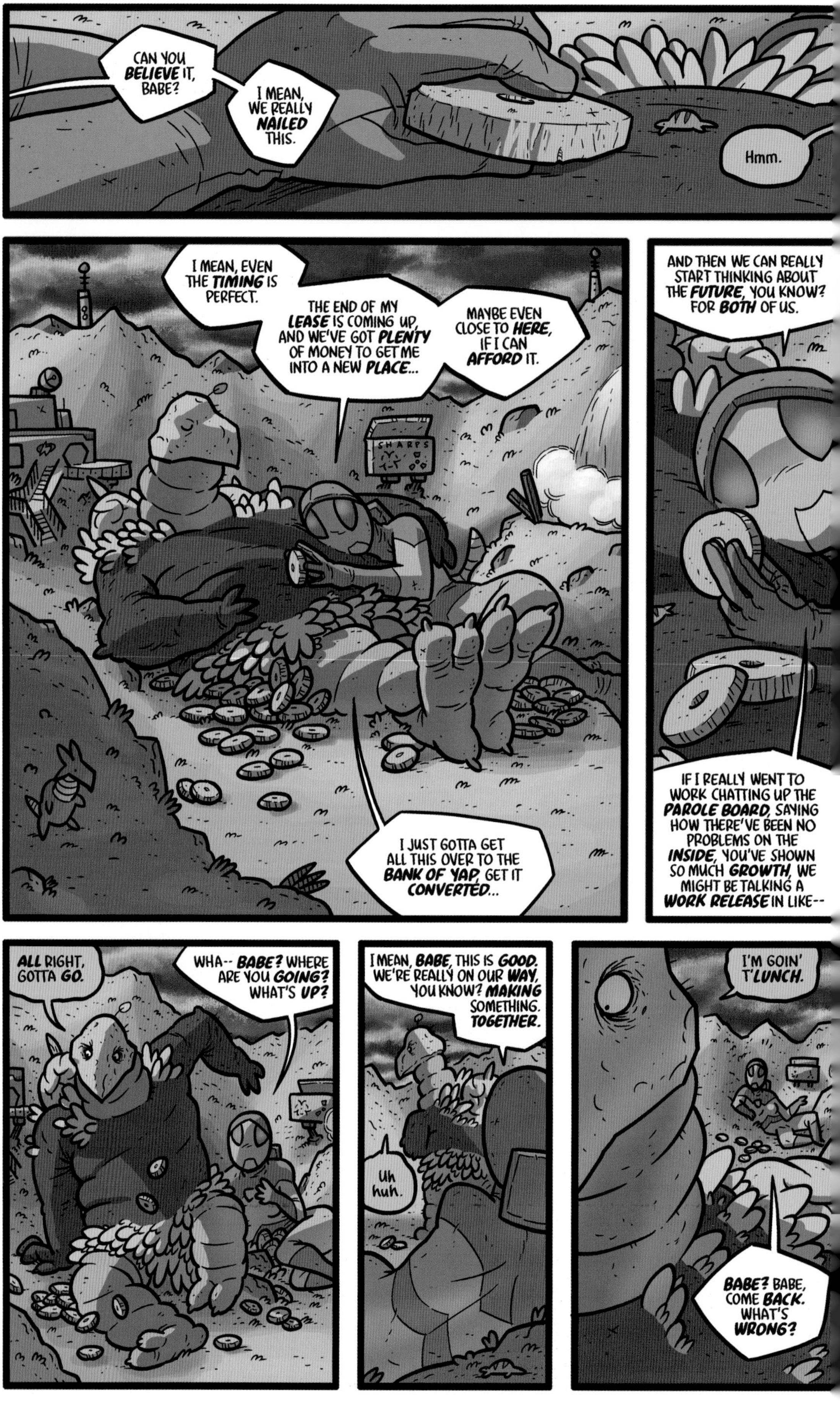
CAN YOU BELIEVE IT, BABE?
I MEAN, WE REALLY NAILED THIS.
Hmm.
I MEAN, EVEN THE TIMING IS PERFECT.
THE END OF MY LEASE IS COMING UP, AND WE'VE GOT PLENTY OF MONEY TO GET ME INTO A NEW PLACE...
MAYBE EVEN CLOSE TO HERE, IF I CAN AFFORD IT.
SHARPS
I JUST GOTTA GET ALL THIS OVER TO THE BANK OF YAP, GET IT CONVERTED...
AND THEN WE CAN REALLY START THINKING ABOUT THE FUTURE, YOU KNOW? FOR BOTH OF US.
IF I REALLY WENT TO WORK CHATTING UP THE PAROLE BOARD, SAYING HOW THERE'VE BEEN NO PROBLEMS ON THE INSIDE, YOU'VE SHOWN SO MUCH GROWTH, WE MIGHT BE TALKING A WORK RELEASE IN LIKE--
ALL RIGHT, GOTTA GO.
WHA-- BABE? WHERE ARE YOU GOING? WHAT'S UP?
I MEAN, BABE, THIS IS GOOD. WE'RE REALLY ON OUR WAY, YOU KNOW? MAKING SOMETHING. TOGETHER.
Uh huh.
I'M GOIN' T'LUNCH.
BABE? BABE, COME BACK. WHAT'S WRONG?

"DID I *OFFEND* YOU?"

I CAN'T UNDERSTAND *WHY* YOU WOULD EVEN *ASK* THE HOLY ADMIN SUCH A THING!

I MEAN, *HILL?!*

SHH! SH!

DO YOU REALLY THINK THE *LEADER* OF OUR *PACIFIST GROUP*--SWORN TO AN ETHOS OF *NONVIOLENCE*-- WOULD *EVER* HILL FOR *ANY* REASON...

...MUCH *LESS* ON BEHALF OF *YOU* MEAT SACKS?

MECHAZON HAS DEVOTED HIS ENTIRE *EXISTENCE* TO THIS. DO YOU REALLY THINK HE IS SOME KIND OF *NESTOR* THAT WOULD THROW THAT ALL *AWAY* JUST FOR YOU AND YOUR... *SUBPROCESS?*

CHILD.

BUT YES, I *KNOW.*

I WOULD *NEVER* ASK IF I WEREN'T *DESPERATE.*

THAT MAY *BE,* BUT IT'S OUT OF THE *QUESTION.*

COME ON, ADMIN, LET'S WASTE NO MORE *CYCLES* WITH THESE *SAVAGES.*

V.O.T.O.M., THANK YOU. YOU HAVE DEFENDED ME *ELOQUENTLY...*

BUT CAN YOU *LEAVE* US FOR A MOMENT?

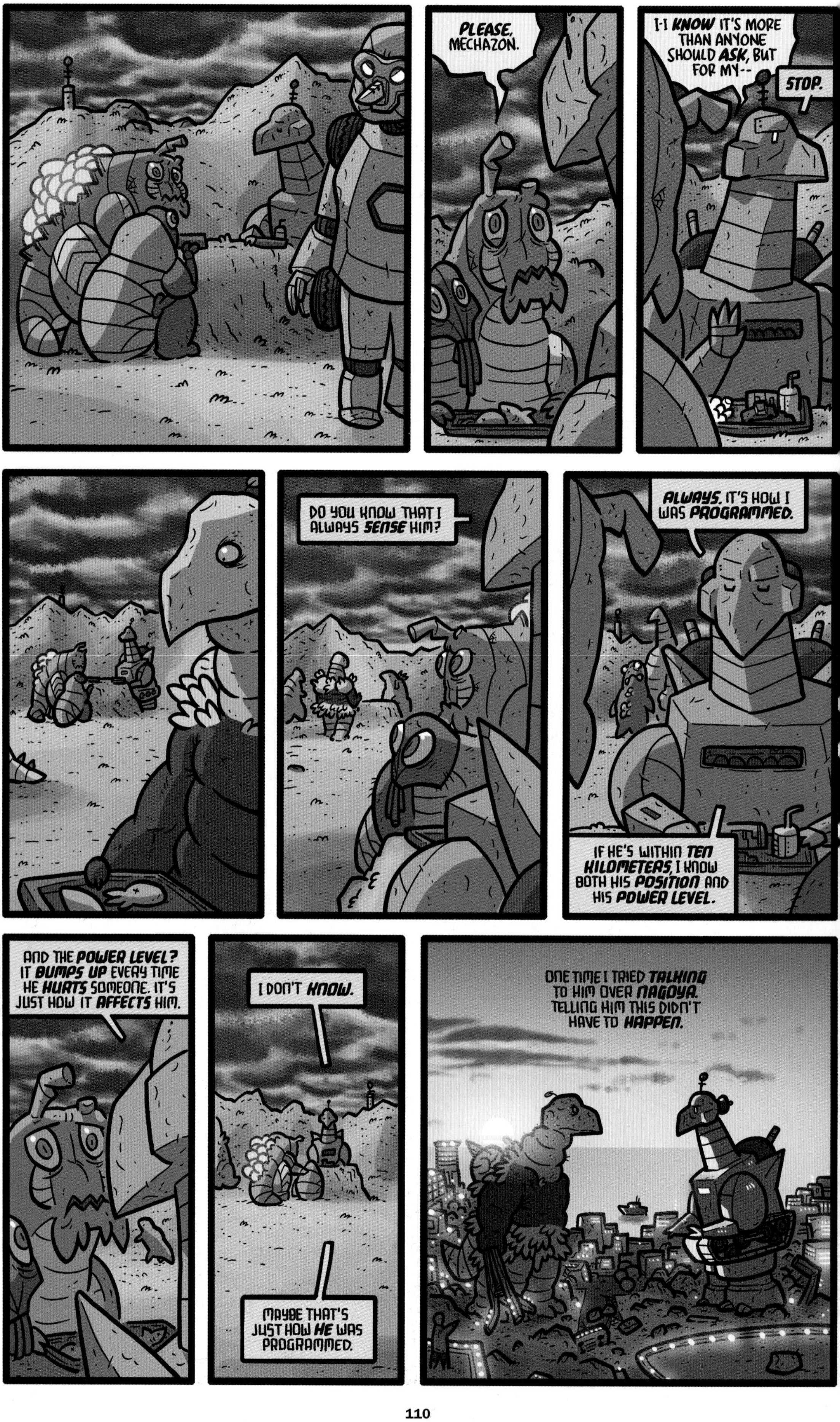

PLEASE, MECHAZON.
I-I KNOW IT'S MORE THAN ANYONE SHOULD ASK, BUT FOR MY--
STOP.
DO YOU KNOW THAT I ALWAYS SENSE HIM?
ALWAYS. IT'S HOW I WAS PROGRAMMED.
IF HE'S WITHIN TEN KILOMETERS, I KNOW BOTH HIS POSITION AND HIS POWER LEVEL.
AND THE POWER LEVEL? IT BUMPS UP EVERY TIME HE HURTS SOMEONE. IT'S JUST HOW IT AFFECTS HIM.
I DON'T KNOW.
MAYBE THAT'S JUST HOW HE WAS PROGRAMMED.
ONE TIME I TRIED TALKING TO HIM OVER NAGOYA. TELLING HIM THIS DIDN'T HAVE TO HAPPEN.

HE ATE A *CITY BUS* IN *FRONT* OF ME.

LITTLE *BUMP*.

THEN A *TOUR BOAT*. LITTLE *BUMP*.

I *BELIEVE* IN NONVIOLENCE. I LIVE IT EVERY *DAY*.

BUT I LIVE *THIS* EVERY DAY *TOO*.

EVERY *HOUR*. LITTLE *BUMPS*.

MECHAZON--

I'M NOT AS *GOOD* AS YOU *THINK* I AM.

HE CAN'T BE *TALKED* TO. HE CAN'T BE *NEGOTIATED* WITH.

AND I WANT IT TO *STOP*.

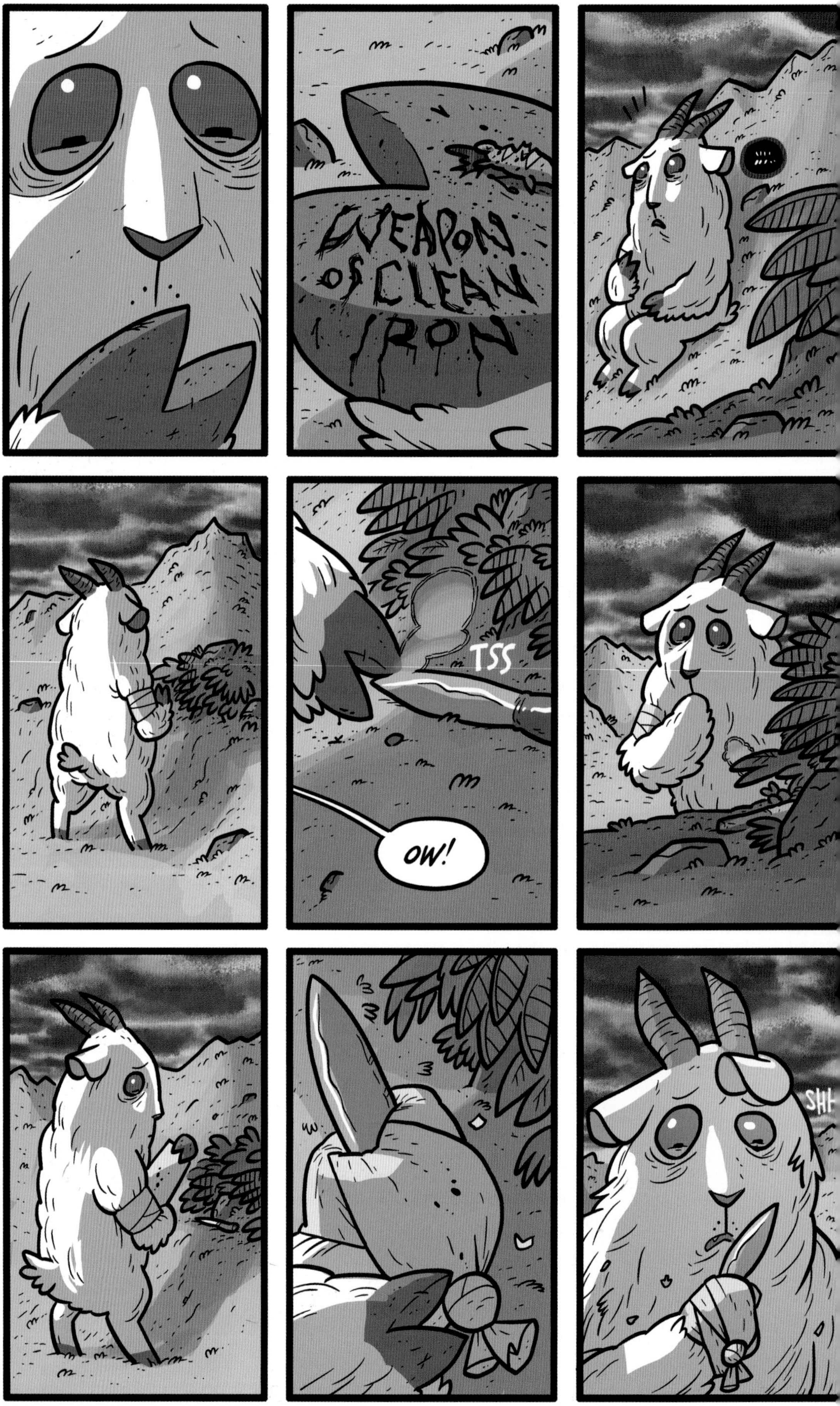
WEAPON OF CLEAN IRON
TSS
OW!
SHI

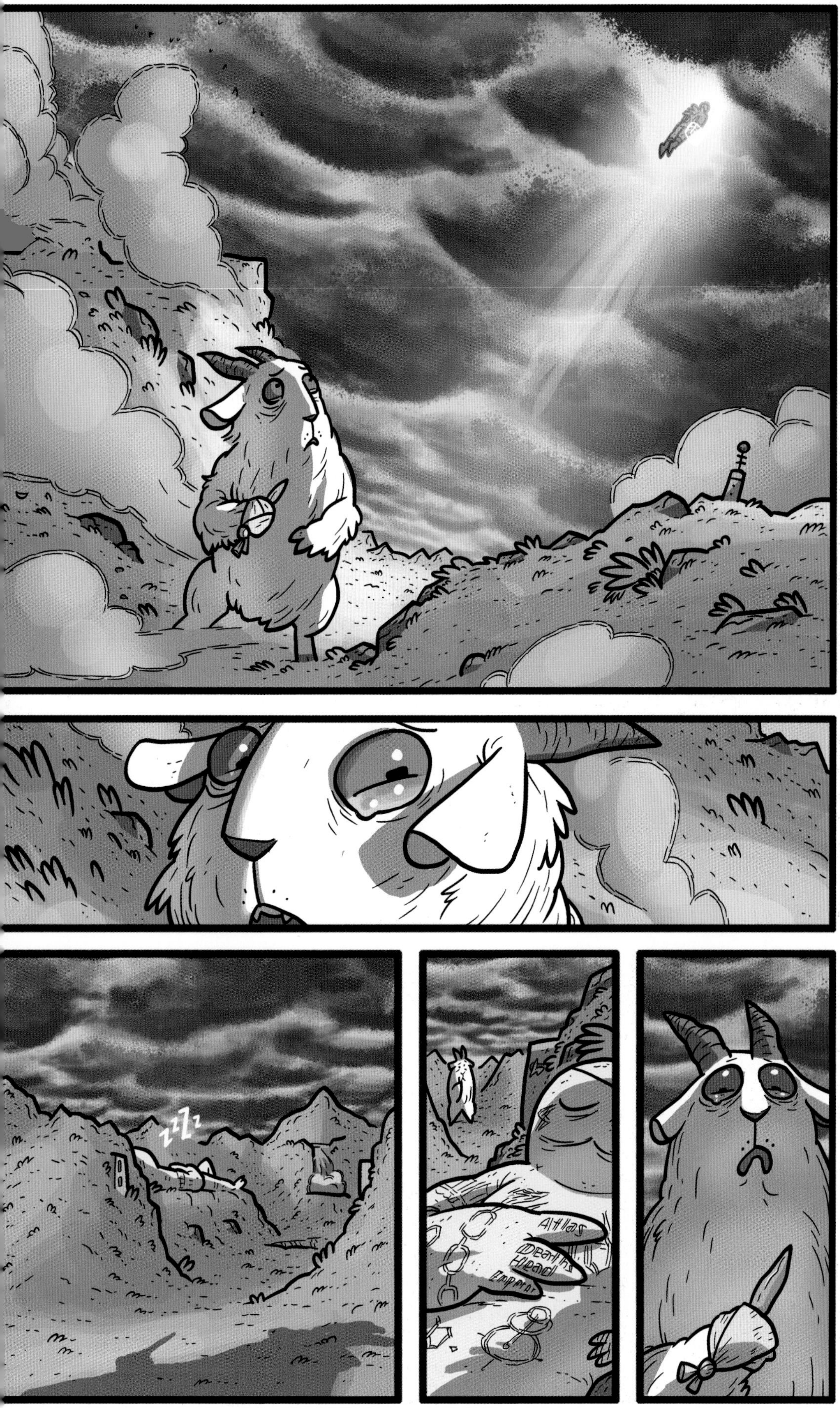
zZZz
Atlas
Deaths Head
Emperor

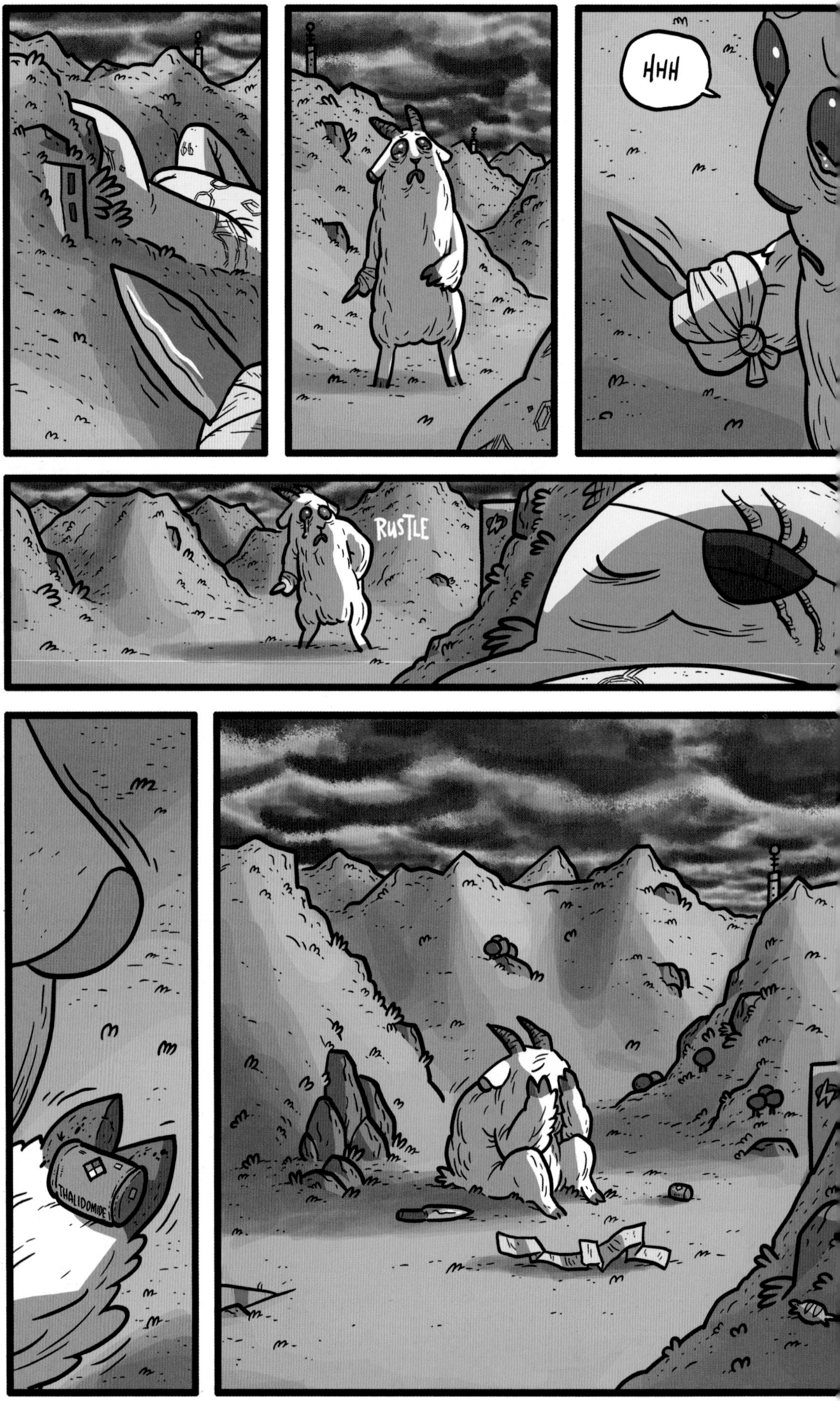
HHH
RUSTLE
THALIDOMIDE

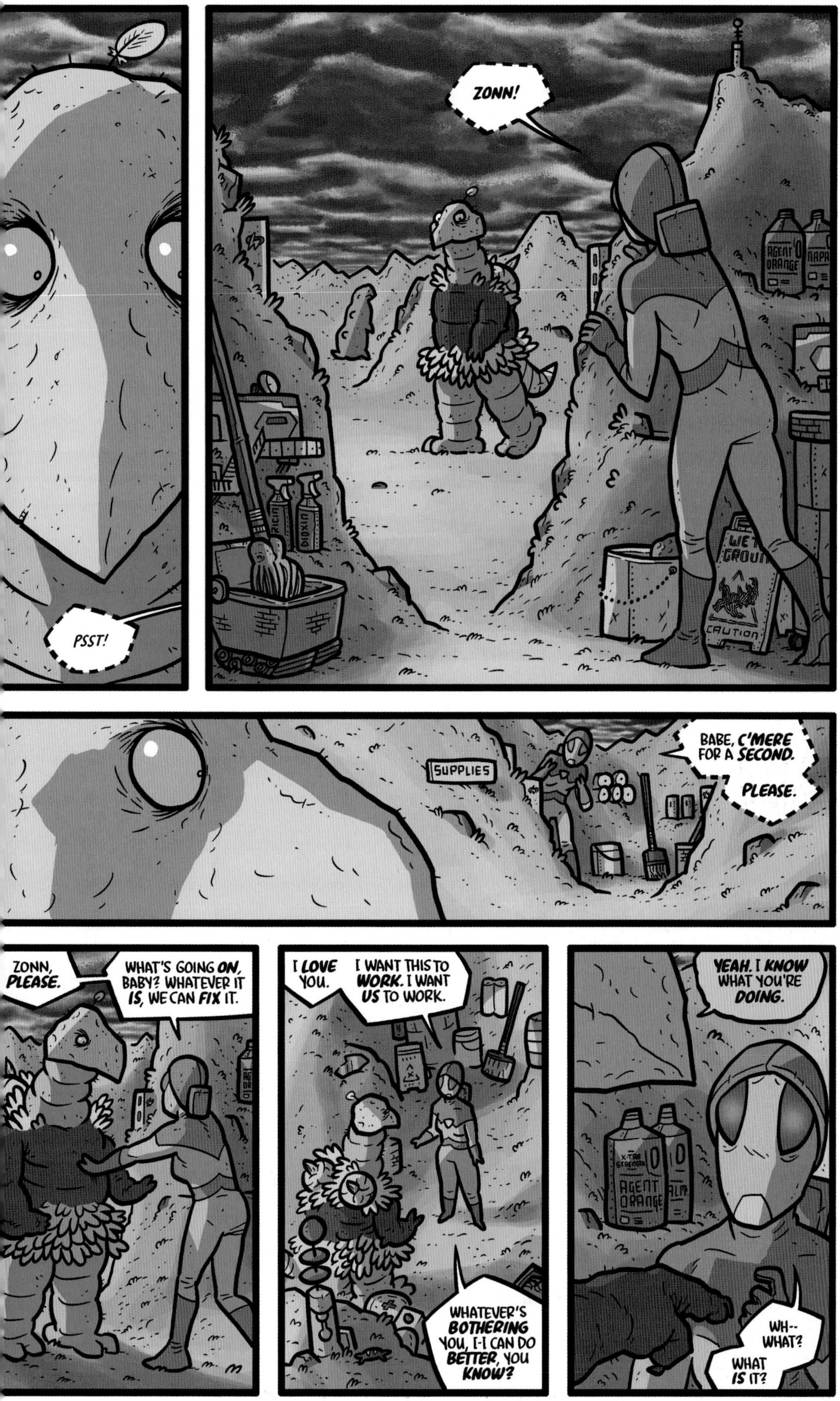
ZONN!
PSST!
AGENT ORANGE
NAPA
RICIN
DIOXIN
WET GROUND
CAUTION
SUPPLIES
BABE, C'MERE FOR A SECOND.
PLEASE.
ZONN, PLEASE.
WHAT'S GOING ON, BABY? WHATEVER IT IS, WE CAN FIX IT.
I LOVE YOU.
I WANT THIS TO WORK. I WANT US TO WORK.
WHATEVER'S BOTHERING YOU, I-I CAN DO BETTER, YOU KNOW?
YEAH. I KNOW WHAT YOU'RE DOING.
X-TRA STRENGTH
AGENT ORANGE
WH-- WHAT?
WHAT IS IT?

YEAH.

YOU THINK I CAN'T *SEE* THAT YOU WANT *OUT?*

OUT? NO, BABE, I--

CHANGING *APARTMENTS?* CAN'T LEAVE YOUR *MONEY* HERE? YOU WANT TO TAKE THIS GIG SOMEWHERE *ELSE,* DON'T YOU? YOU THINK I'M *WORTHLESS.*

WHAT? BABE, *WHAT* ARE YOU--

YOU *SAID* IT. "*WORTHLESS.*" SOON AS I ANSWERED THE *PHONE.*

I...

COME ON, BABE, I WAS *S-STRESSED,* YOU KNOW?

TH-THERE WAS A LOT OF STUFF GOING *ON* THEN, AND...

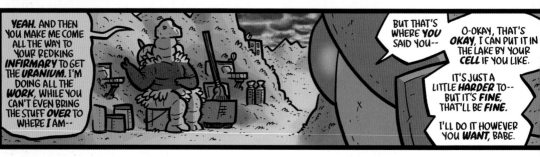

YEAH. AND THEN YOU MAKE ME COME ALL THE WAY TO YOUR REDKING *INFIRMARY* TO GET THE *URANIUM.* I'M DOING ALL THE *WORK,* WHILE YOU CAN'T EVEN BRING THE STUFF *OVER* TO WHERE *I* AM--

BUT THAT'S WHERE *YOU* SAID YOU--

O-OKAY, THAT'S *OKAY,* I CAN PUT IT IN THE LAKE BY YOUR *CELL* IF YOU LIKE.

IT'S JUST A LITTLE *HARDER* TO-- BUT IT'S *FINE,* THAT'LL BE *FINE.*

I'LL DO IT HOWEVER YOU *WANT,* BABE.

HMMH.

WELL.

JUST THAT *THEN* THERE'S THAT *SHRIMP-ASS MEGAFAUNA,* TOO, CUTTIN' INTO OUR *BUSINESS.*

SHRIMP-A...? Y-YOU MEAN... *ELECTROGOR?*

OH, BABE, DON'T *WORRY* ABOUT THAT WEAK *DAIEI-BRAND URANIUM* HE'S GOT.

IT HAS *NOTHING* ON THE STUFF WE GET FROM THE *MOON...!*

UH HUH. YOU *WOULD* DEFEND HIM, WITH THE WAY YOU *LOOK* AT HIM SOMETIMES...

WHAT--

BABE, *NO,* COME *ON,* ARE YOU *KIDDING* ME? THAT *CRYBABY* LITTLE *RARE-BEAST?*

I GOT HIM SENT TO THE *HOLE* FOR *TALKING* ABOUT YOU, *REMEMBER?*

YOU ARE THE *ONE,* BABY.

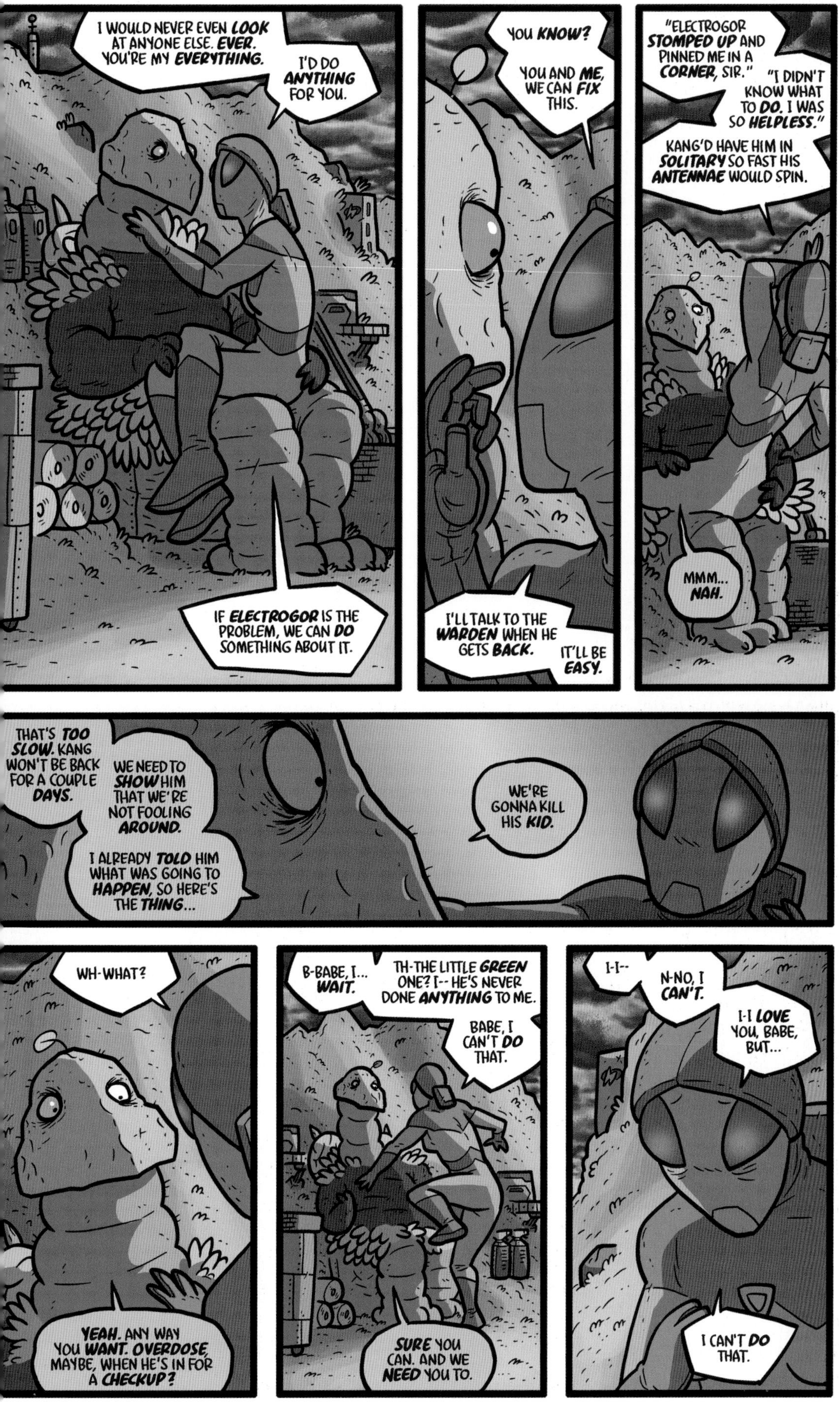

I WOULD NEVER EVEN LOOK AT ANYONE ELSE. EVER. YOU'RE MY EVERYTHING.
I'D DO ANYTHING FOR YOU.
IF ELECTROGOR IS THE PROBLEM, WE CAN DO SOMETHING ABOUT IT.
YOU KNOW?
YOU AND ME, WE CAN FIX THIS.
I'LL TALK TO THE WARDEN WHEN HE GETS BACK.
IT'LL BE EASY.
"ELECTROGOR STOMPED UP AND PINNED ME IN A CORNER, SIR."
"I DIDN'T KNOW WHAT TO DO. I WAS SO HELPLESS."
KANG'D HAVE HIM IN SOLITARY SO FAST HIS ANTENNAE WOULD SPIN.
MMM... NAH.
THAT'S TOO SLOW. KANG WON'T BE BACK FOR A COUPLE DAYS.
WE NEED TO SHOW HIM THAT WE'RE NOT FOOLING AROUND.
I ALREADY TOLD HIM WHAT WAS GOING TO HAPPEN, SO HERE'S THE THING...
WE'RE GONNA KILL HIS KID.
WH-WHAT?
YEAH. ANY WAY YOU WANT. OVERDOSE, MAYBE, WHEN HE'S IN FOR A CHECKUP?
B-BABE, I... WAIT.
TH-THE LITTLE GREEN ONE? I-- HE'S NEVER DONE ANYTHING TO ME.
BABE, I CAN'T DO THAT.
SURE YOU CAN. AND WE NEED YOU TO.
I-I--
N-NO, I CAN'T.
I-I LOVE YOU, BABE, BUT...
I CAN'T DO THAT.

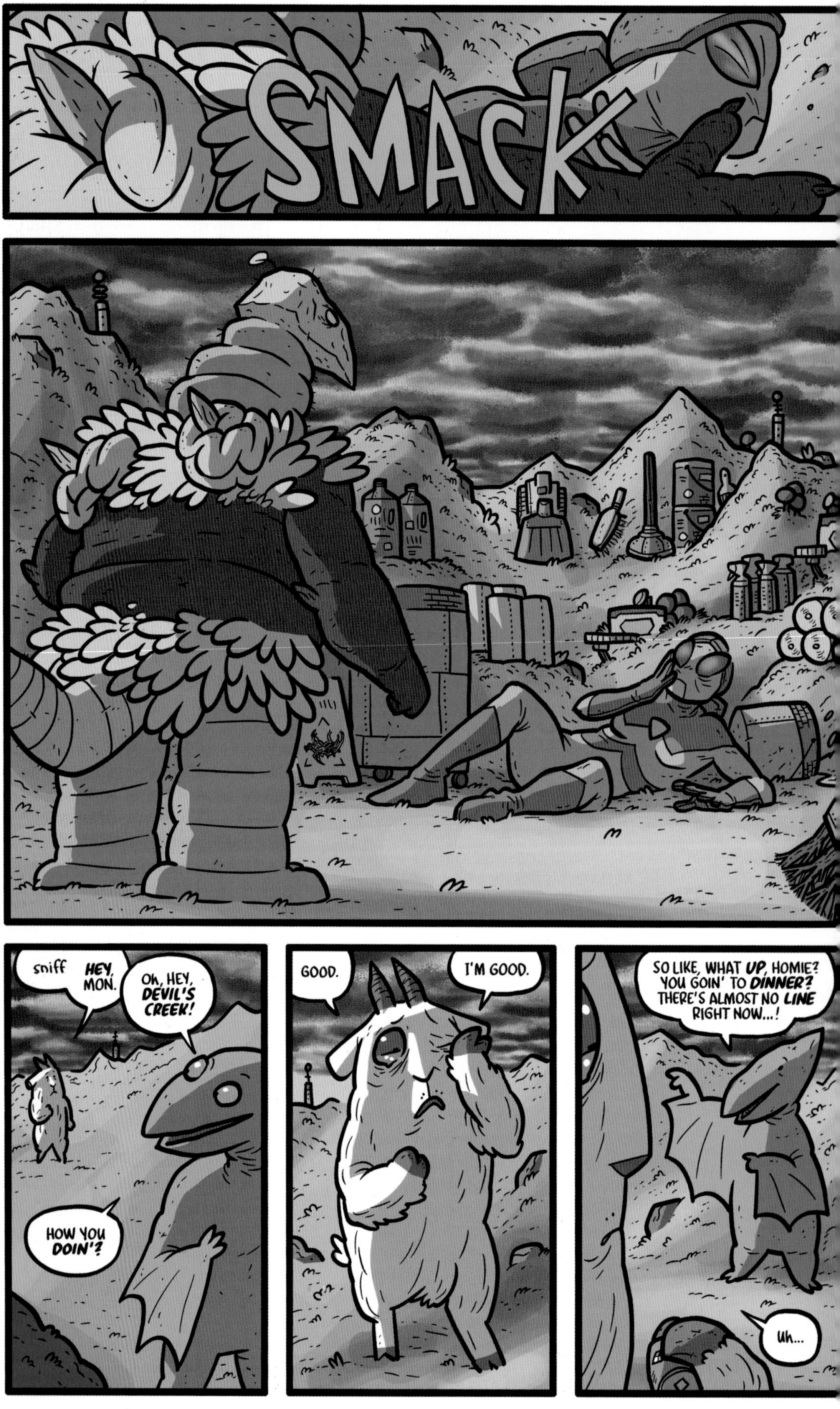
SMACK
sniff HEY, MON.
Oh, HEY, DEVIL'S CREEK!
HOW YOU DOIN'?
GOOD.
I'M GOOD.
SO LIKE, WHAT UP, HOMIE? YOU GOIN' TO DINNER? THERE'S ALMOST NO LINE RIGHT NOW...!
Uh...

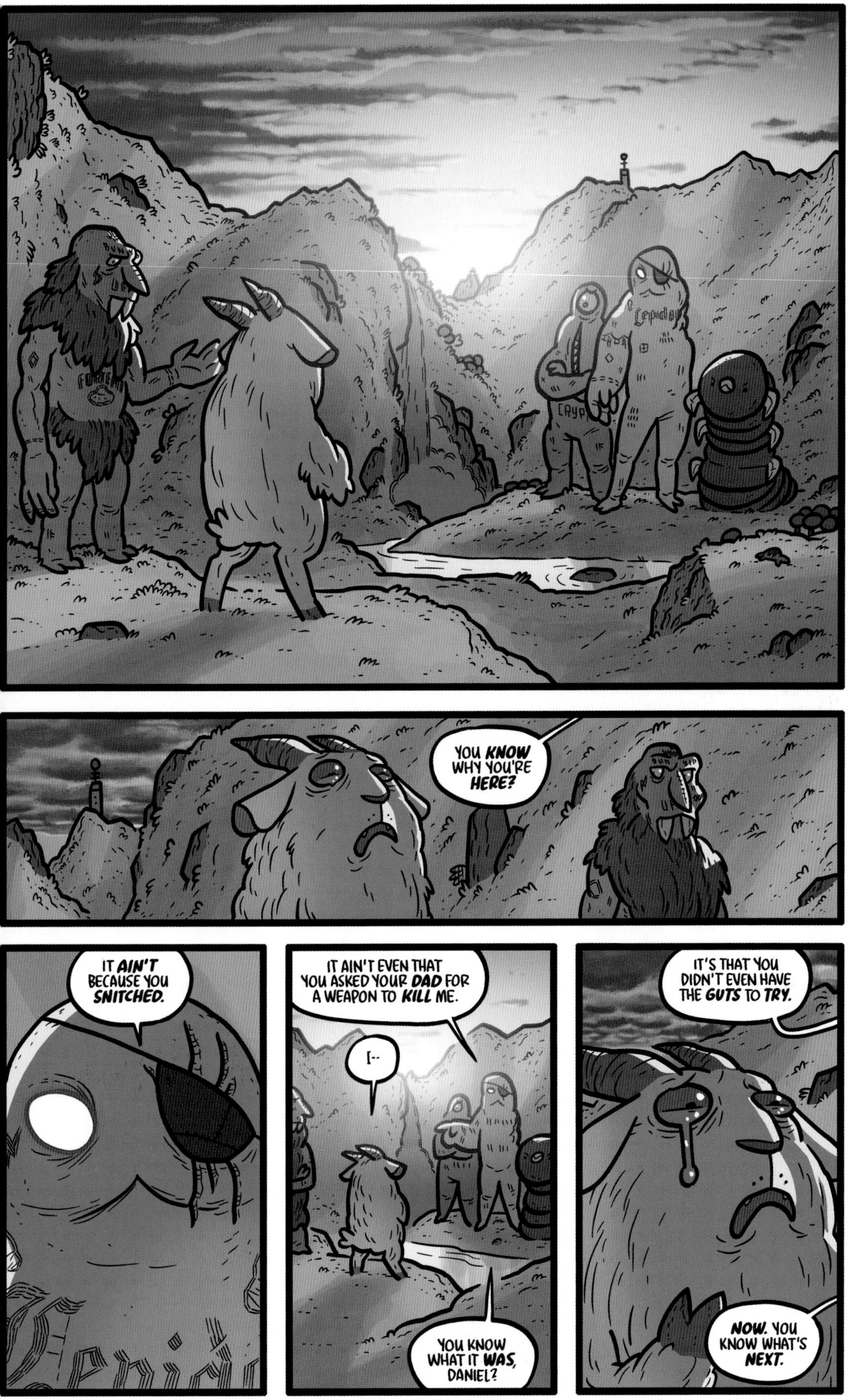
YOU **KNOW** WHY YOU'RE **HERE?**
IT **AIN'T** BECAUSE YOU **SNITCHED.**
IT AIN'T EVEN THAT YOU ASKED YOUR **DAD** FOR A WEAPON TO **KILL** ME.
I--
YOU KNOW WHAT IT **WAS**, DANIEL?
IT'S THAT YOU DIDN'T EVEN HAVE THE **GUTS** TO **TRY.**
NOW. YOU KNOW WHAT'S **NEXT.**

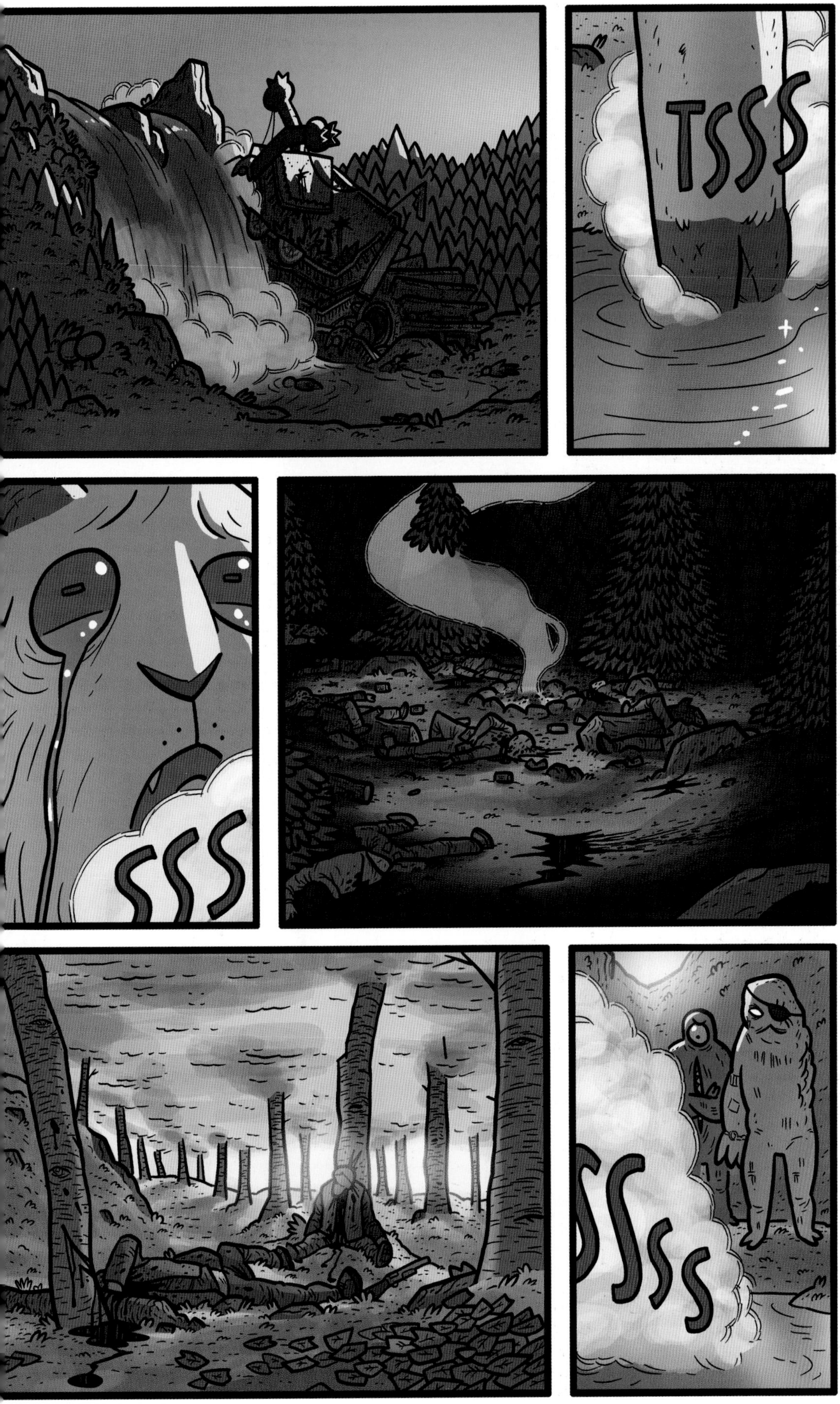
TSSS
SSS
SSSS

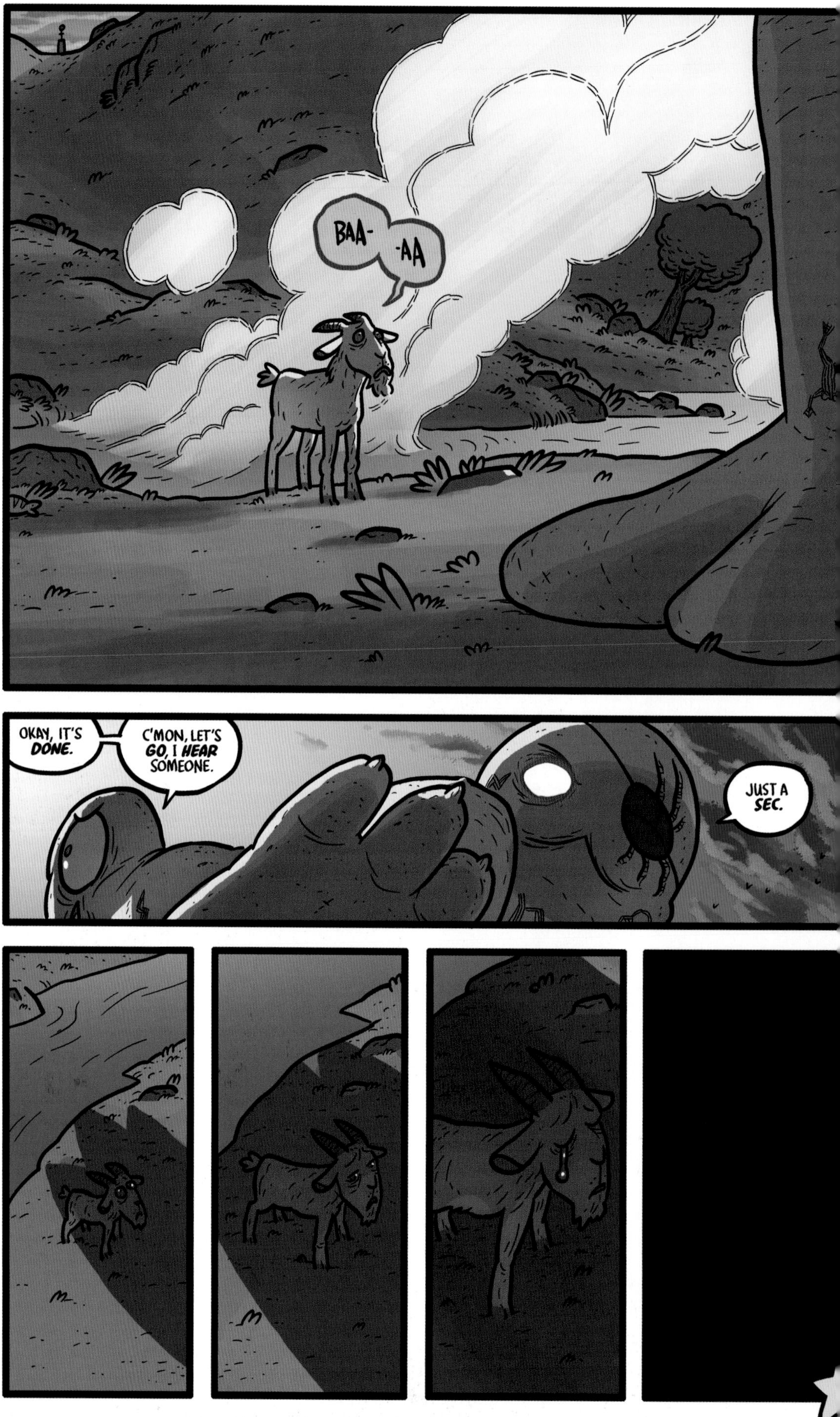
BAA-
-AA
OKAY, IT'S DONE.
C'MON, LET'S GO, I HEAR SOMEONE.
JUST A SEC.

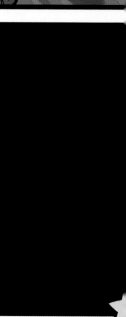

EPISODE 6

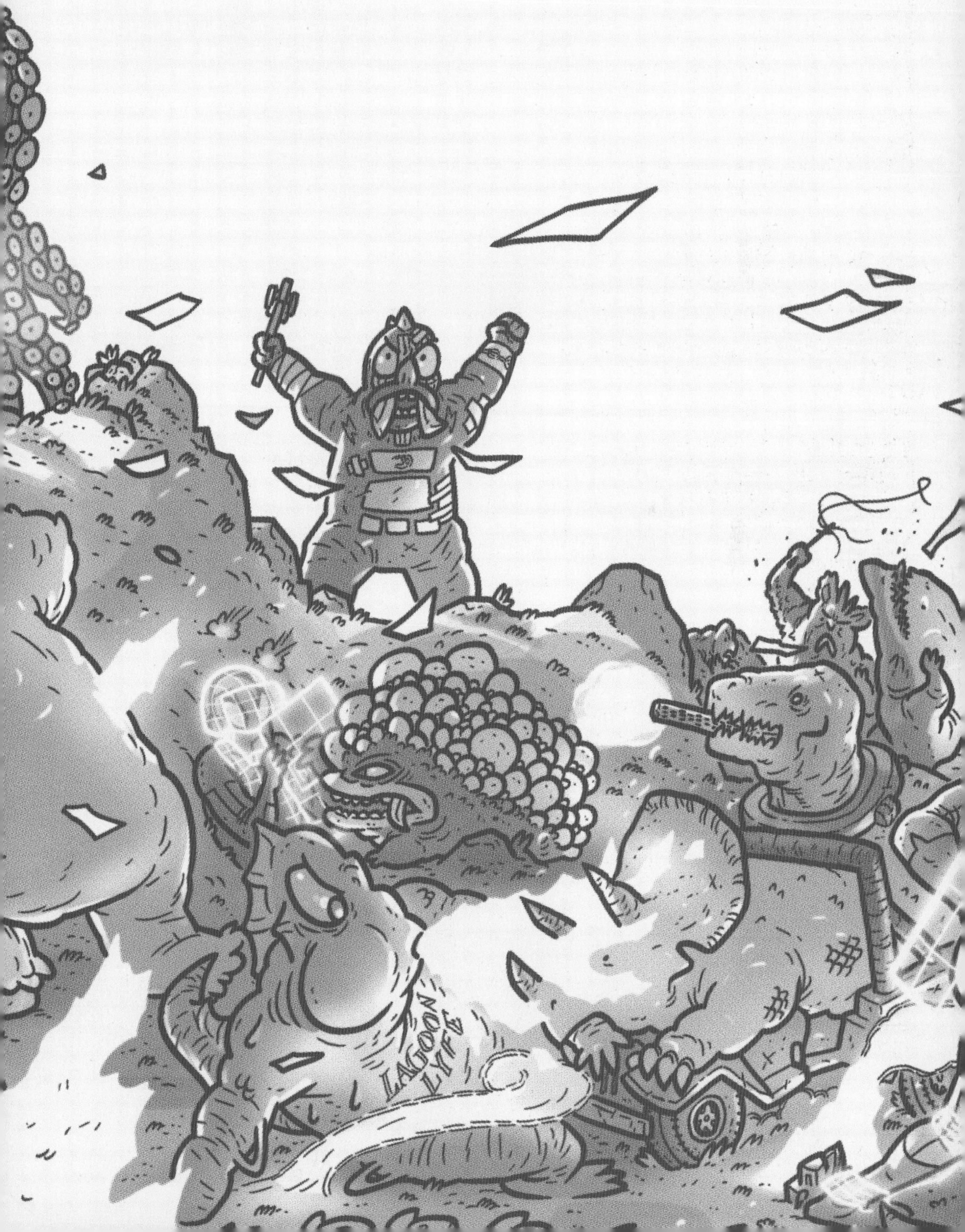

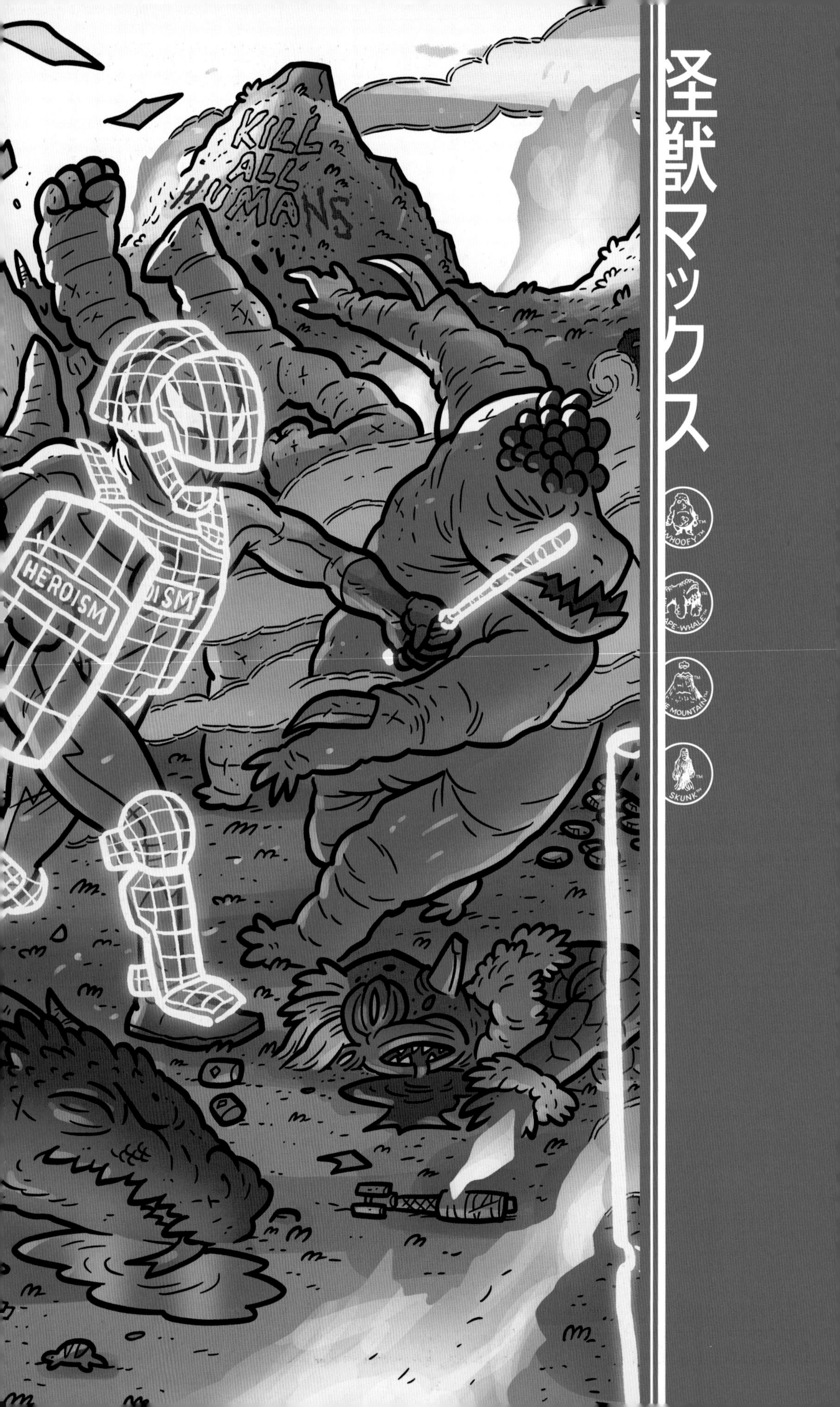

KILL ALL HUMANS
HEROISM
怪獣マックス
WHOOFY™
SKUNK™

THIS IS IT. V.O.T.O.M., FOGRUEDA, GET ELECTROGOR'S *BOY* TO *SAFETY*.

BUT--

GO!

ELECTROGOR, NOW IS THE *TIME*. THIS RIOT IS THE *COVER*. THERE WILL *NEVER* BE A BETTER *CHANCE*. GET A *WEAPON*.

DAD--

VOGO. STAY *CLOSE* TO THEM. I-I GOT TO *DO* SOMETHING. I'M GONNA *FIX* THINGS.

READY?

HE'S FOUR KILOMETERS *THAT* WAY.

NOW...

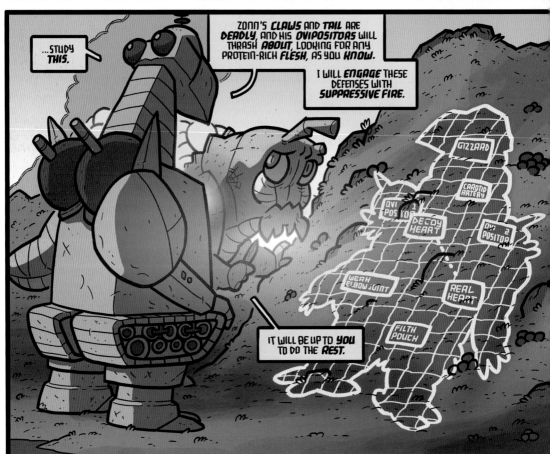

...STUDY *THIS*.

ZONN'S *CLAWS* AND *TAIL* ARE *DEADLY*, AND HIS *OVIPOSITORS* WILL THRASH *ABOUT*, LOOKING FOR ANY PROTEIN-RICH *FLESH*, AS YOU *KNOW*.

I WILL *ENGAGE* THESE DEFENSES WITH *SUPPRESSIVE FIRE*.

IT WILL BE UP TO *YOU* TO DO THE *REST*.

GIZZARD

CAROTID ARTERY

OVI POSITOR

DECOY HEART

OVI 2 POSITOR

WEAK ELBOW JOINT

REAL HEART

FILTH POUCH

HE HAS *TWO HEARTS*. ONE IS *HIDDEN*.

DESTROY IT.

REAL HEART

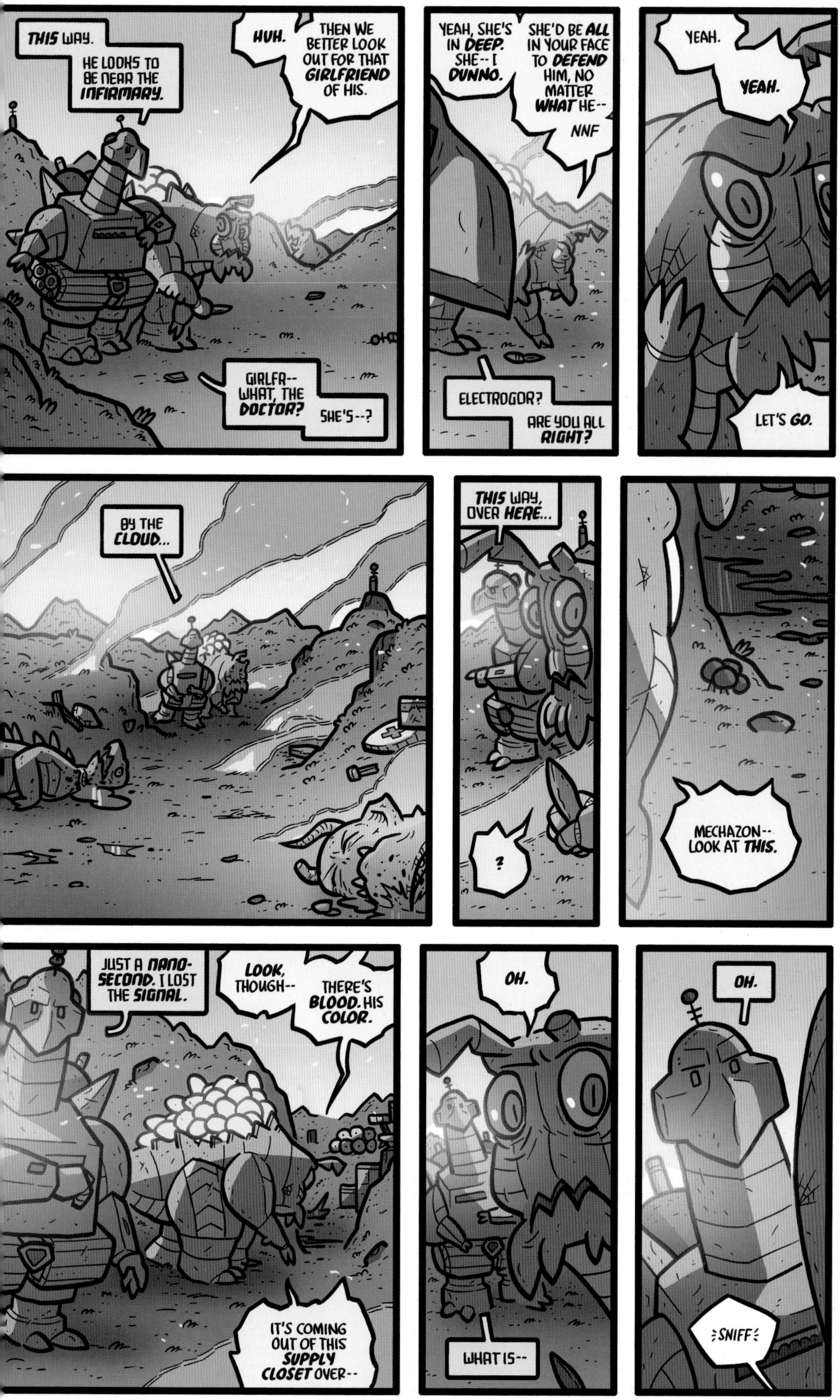
THIS WAY.
HE LOOKS TO BE NEAR THE INFIRMARY.
HUH.
THEN WE BETTER LOOK OUT FOR THAT GIRLFRIEND OF HIS.
GIRLFR-- WHAT, THE DOCTOR?
SHE'S--?
YEAH, SHE'S IN DEEP. SHE-- I DUNNO.
SHE'D BE ALL IN YOUR FACE TO DEFEND HIM, NO MATTER WHAT HE--
NNF
ELECTROGOR?
ARE YOU ALL RIGHT?
YEAH.
YEAH.
LET'S GO.
BY THE CLOUD...
THIS WAY, OVER HERE...
?
MECHAZON-- LOOK AT THIS.
JUST A NANO-SECOND. I LOST THE SIGNAL.
LOOK, THOUGH--
THERE'S BLOOD. HIS COLOR.
IT'S COMING OUT OF THIS SUPPLY CLOSET OVER--
OH.
WHAT IS--
OH.
SNIFF

CONSEQUENCES

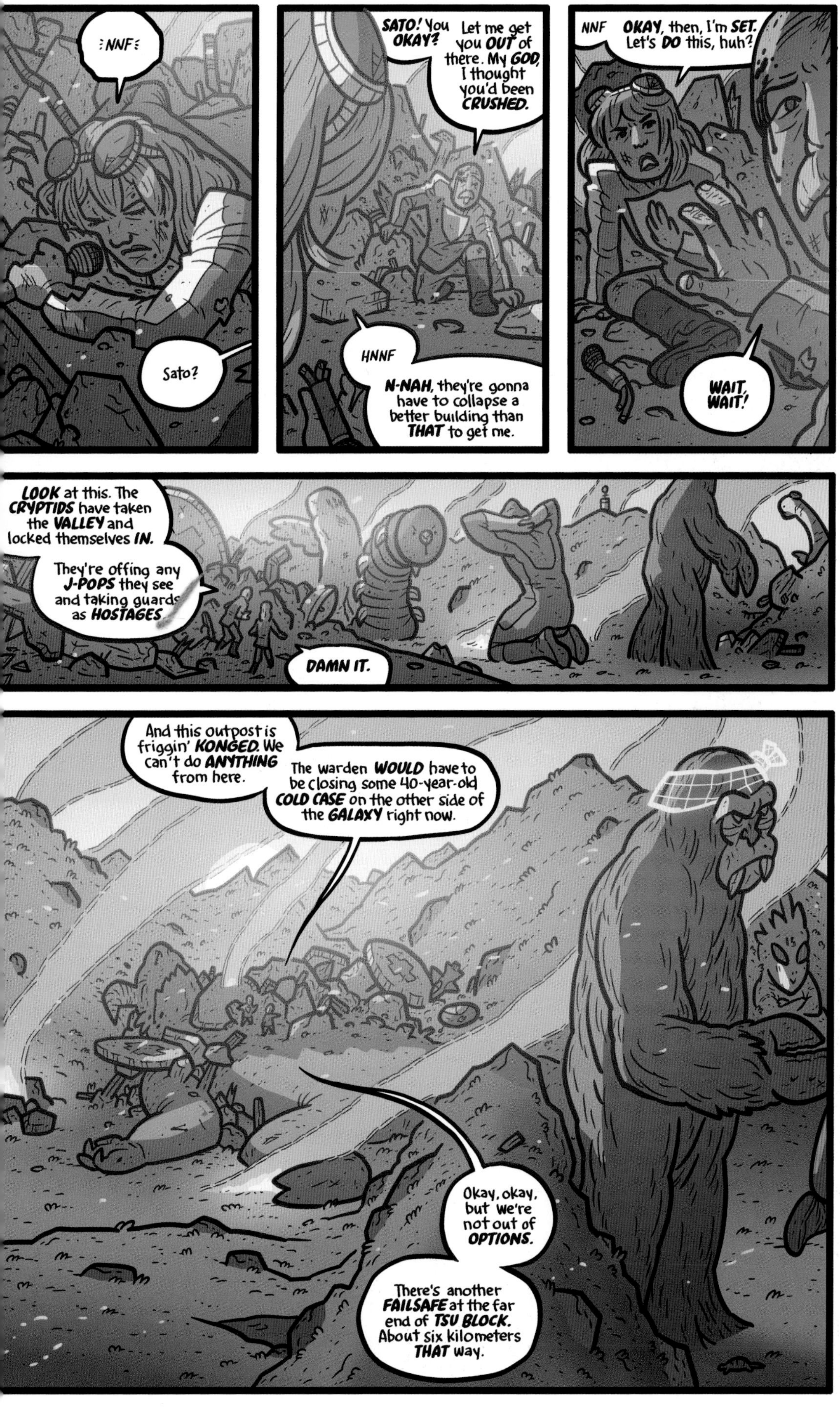
NNF
Sato?
SATO! You OKAY?
Let me get you OUT of there. My GOD, I thought you'd been CRUSHED.
HNNF
N-NAH, they're gonna have to collapse a better building than THAT to get me.
NNF
OKAY, then, I'm SET. Let's DO this, huh?
WAIT, WAIT!
LOOK at this. The CRYPTIDS have taken the VALLEY and locked themselves IN.
They're offing any J-POPS they see and taking guards as HOSTAGES.
DAMN IT.
And this outpost is friggin' KONGED. We can't do ANYTHING from here.
The warden WOULD have to be closing some 40-year-old COLD CASE on the other side of the GALAXY right now.
Okay, okay, but we're not out of OPTIONS.
There's another FAILSAFE at the far end of TSU BLOCK. About six kilometers THAT way.

Yeah. **YEAH. COOL**, we **GOT** this. Time to crack some **CARAPACES.**

LISTEN. I want to settle some scores **TOO**, but this isn't the **TIME** or the **PLACE** to play **ULTRACOP.**

PAP!

They outnumber us **TWENTY** to **ONE**. We make a peep, we'll be **DEVIL'S TRIANGLED**, know what I mean?

Now--

They seem to be **PREOCCUPIED** with getting to **WHOOFY**, that **J-POPS** boss. So they're **DISTRACTED**. We just have to sneak out of this **CRATER** and over to that **PEAK.**

PFF. They can **HAVE** him as far as **I'M** concerned.

Let's **GO.**

SNF SNF

DAMN it-- They **SAW** us!

Sato, **GO!** Get to the **FAILSAFE!** I **GOT** this!

SHING

But--

HURRY!

"**BE RIGHT THERE!**"

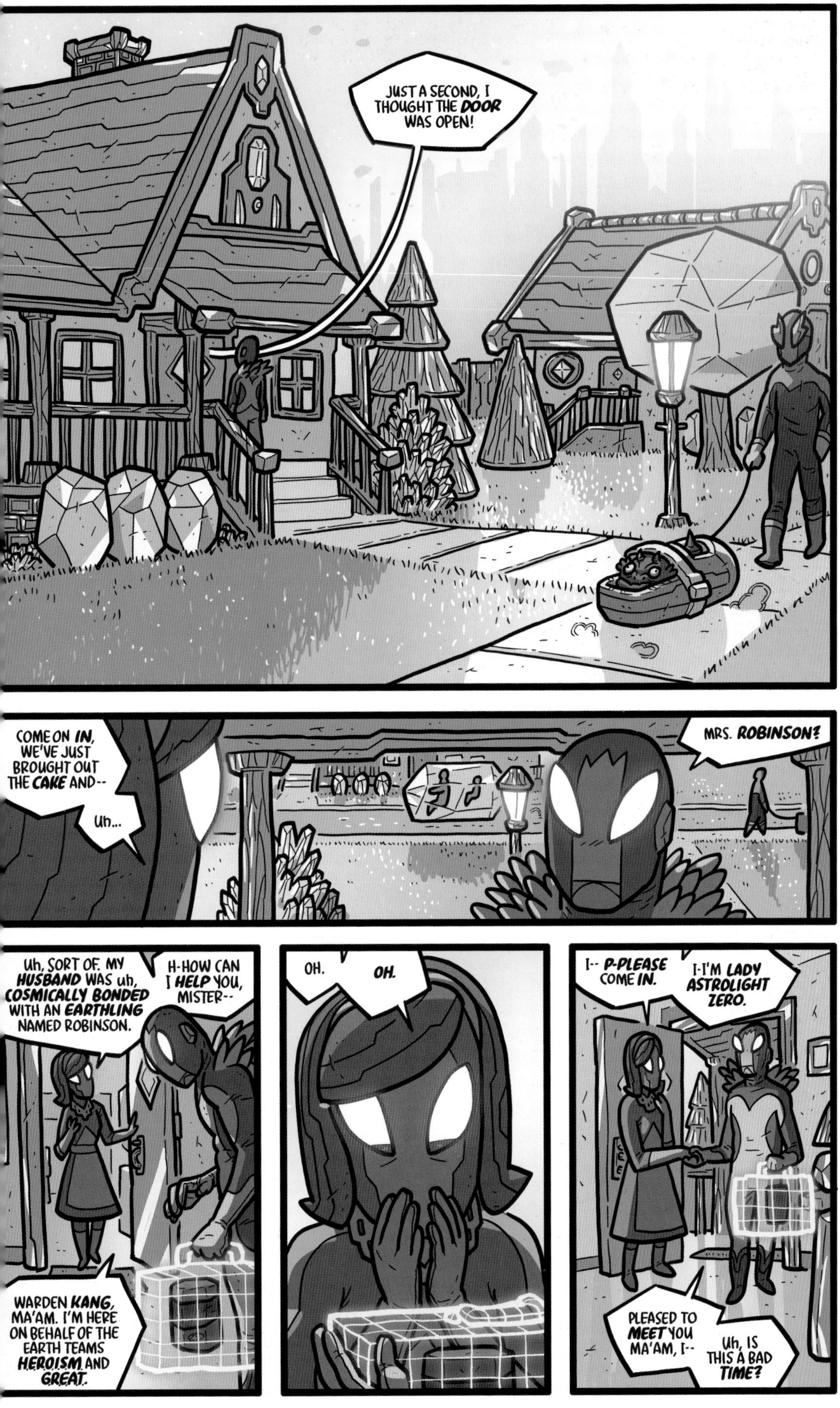

JUST A SECOND, I THOUGHT THE DOOR WAS OPEN!
COME ON IN, WE'VE JUST BROUGHT OUT THE CAKE AND--
Uh...
MRS. ROBINSON?
Uh, SORT OF. MY HUSBAND WAS uh, COSMICALLY BONDED WITH AN EARTHLING NAMED ROBINSON.
H-HOW CAN I HELP YOU, MISTER--
WARDEN KANG, MA'AM. I'M HERE ON BEHALF OF THE EARTH TEAMS HEROISM AND GREAT.
OH.
OH.
I-- P-PLEASE COME IN.
I-I'M LADY ASTROLIGHT ZERO.
PLEASED TO MEET YOU MA'AM, I--
Uh, IS THIS A BAD TIME?

I-IS THERE EVER A *GOOD* TIME?

ASTRO PHONEBOOTH

ASTROLIGHT ZERO JUNIOR, WHAT ARE YOU GOING TO *WISH* FOR?

I WISH FOR A *SPACE PUPPY* OR A *BABY BROTHER!*

C-CAN I GET YOU A CUP OF *COFFEE?*

THIS DAY WAS ALWAYS GOING TO *COME*, I SUPPOSE.

I-I MEAN, YOUR *EARTH OFFICIALS* HAD SAID THEY COULDN'T RULE OUT THE *POSSIBILITY* HE'D BEEN *TRANSFERRED* TO ANOTHER *BODY*, OR SUCKED INTO A *TIME-HOLE*, OR EVEN JUST *REBOOTED*.

AND I GUESS I HELD *ON* TO THAT.

I-I DIDN'T EVEN KNOW *HOW MUCH* I HELD ON.

I-I NEVER *REALLY* BELIEVED WHAT I'VE TOLD JUNIOR, THAT HE'S OUT THERE ON SOME *GLOWING GRID* IN *SPACE*, TRYING TO FIND HIS WAY *BACK* TO US.

THAT WOULD BE *SILLY*, A STORY FOR *CHILDREN*, BUT...

...STRANGER THINGS HAVE *HAPPENED*, RIGHT?

136

HKK

KNCH

NO, NO!

THAT'S RIGHT, YOU LITTLE 'NILLA.

WE'RE COMIN' IN THERE.

COMIN' FOR YOU.

Y'THOUGHT YOU COULD BE THE BOSS FOREVER?

YOU? BUMBLING AROUND WHILE OUR MASTER SPECIES KEEPS GATHERING STRENGTH?

YOU NEVER HAD A SNOWFLAKE'S CHANCE IN CENTRALIA.

NO--

NO, NO, NO, NO NO, NO

THEY'RE RIGHT, YOU KNOW.

!!

L-LI'L BOY! YOU--YOU GOT TO HELP ME! TH-THEY GONNA KILL ME--

HUH.

YEAH THEY ARE.

I MEAN, YOU THOUGHT YOU COULD GO UP AGAINST THE CRYPTIDS?

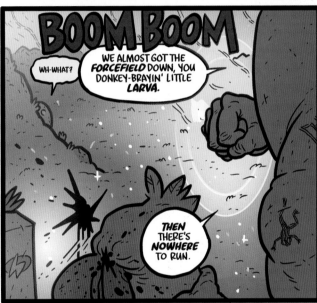

BOOM BOOM

WH-WHAT?

WE ALMOST GOT THE FORCEFIELD DOWN, YOU DONKEY-BRAYIN' LITTLE LARVA.

THEN THERE'S NOWHERE TO RUN.

B-BUT LI'L BOY, YOU TOLD ME T-TO-- PLEASE! Y-YOU ARE SMART, YOU GOT TO HELP ME GET AWAY!

WELL, I DON'T SEE HOW. YOU'VE PRETTY MUCH TRAPPED YOURSELF.

SEEMS LIKE YOU GOT IT COMING IF YOU'RE GONNA BE THIS STUPID.

GOT IT--?

B-BUT I NEVER HURTED NOBODY! I NEVER DID NOTHING.

YEAH. THAT'S RIGHT. YOU DID NOTHING. YOU JUST WATCHED AS LIFE HAPPENED AROUND YOU.

RIGHT?

JUST FLOATED THROUGH LIFE LIKE A LEAF ON A RIVER.

OTHERS MADE A PATH, AND YOU FOLLOWED.

HELL, I BET YOU DON'T EVEN REMEMBER SEEING ME.

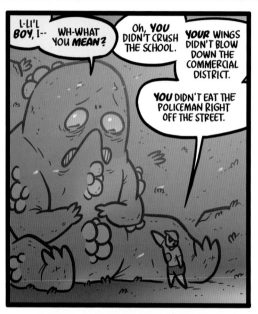

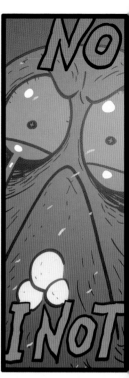

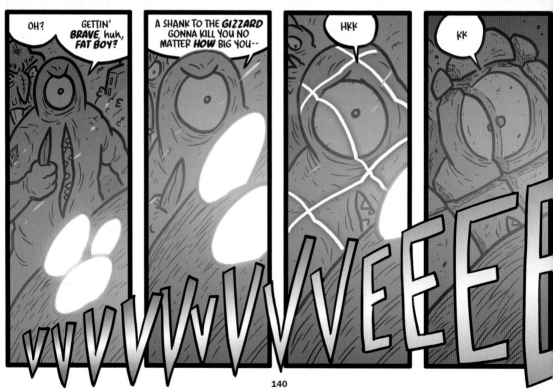

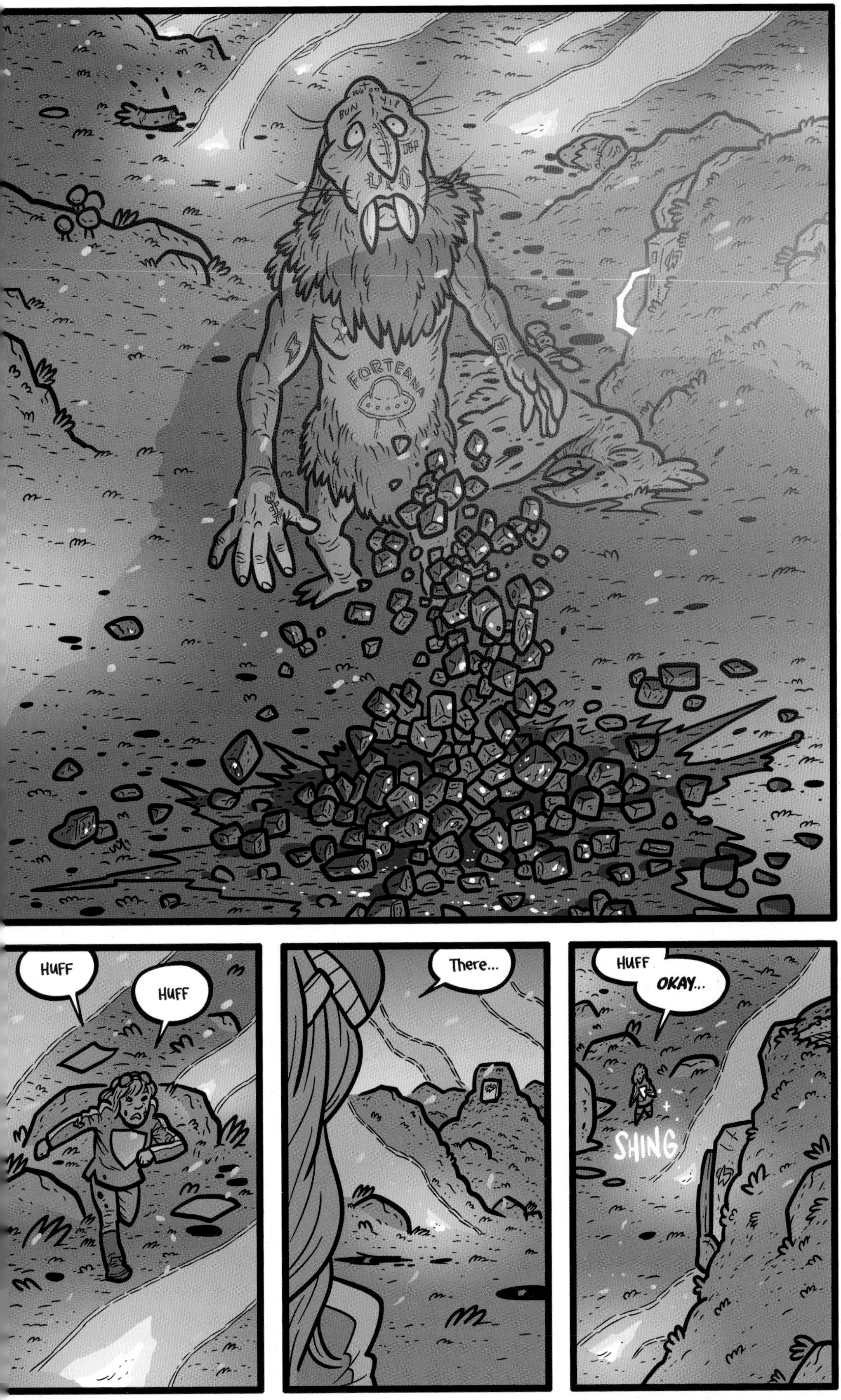
FORTEANA
HUFF
HUFF
There...
HUFF
OKAY...
SHING

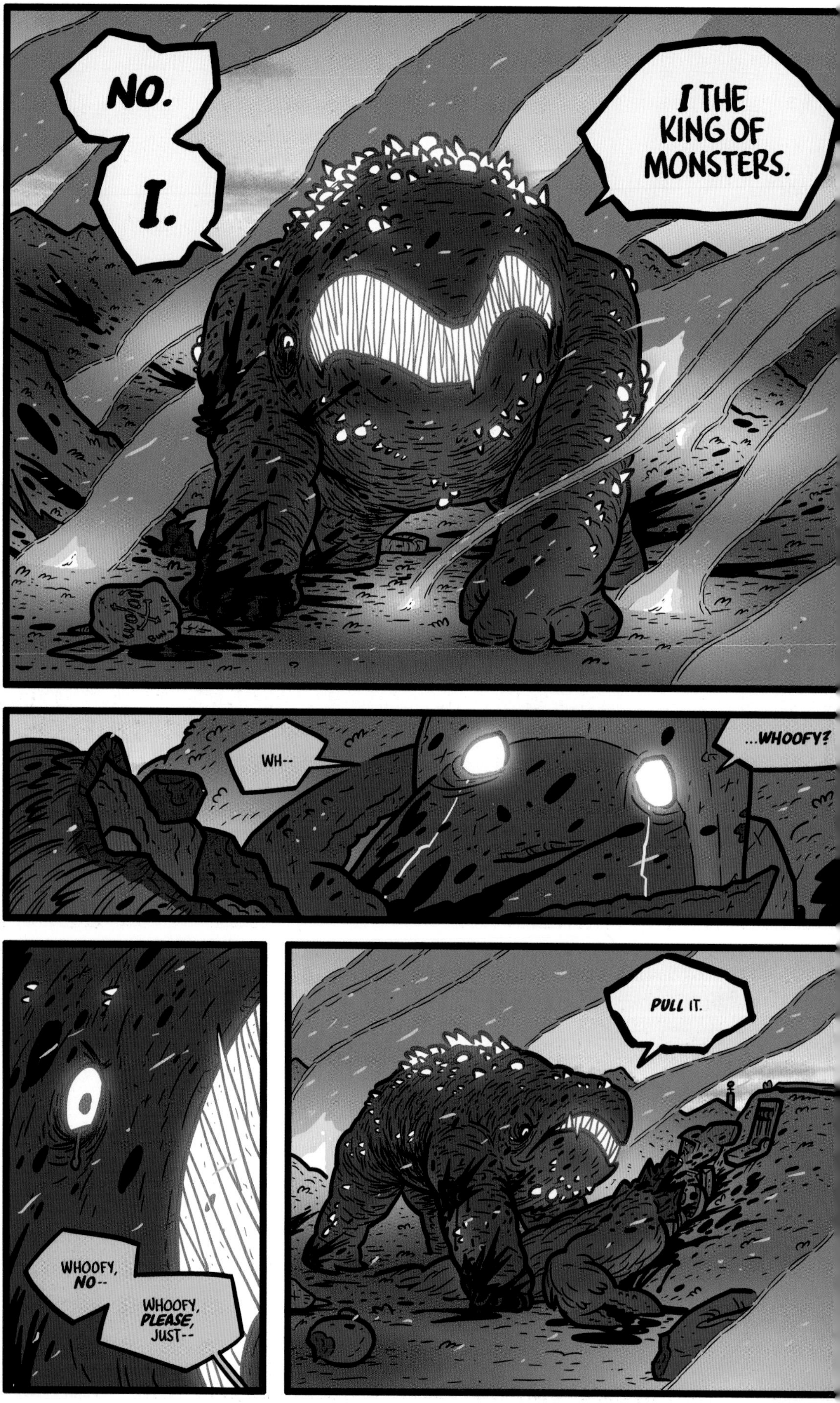
NO.
I.
I THE KING OF MONSTERS.
WH--
...WHOOFY?
PULL IT.
WHOOFY, NO--
WHOOFY, PLEASE, JUST--

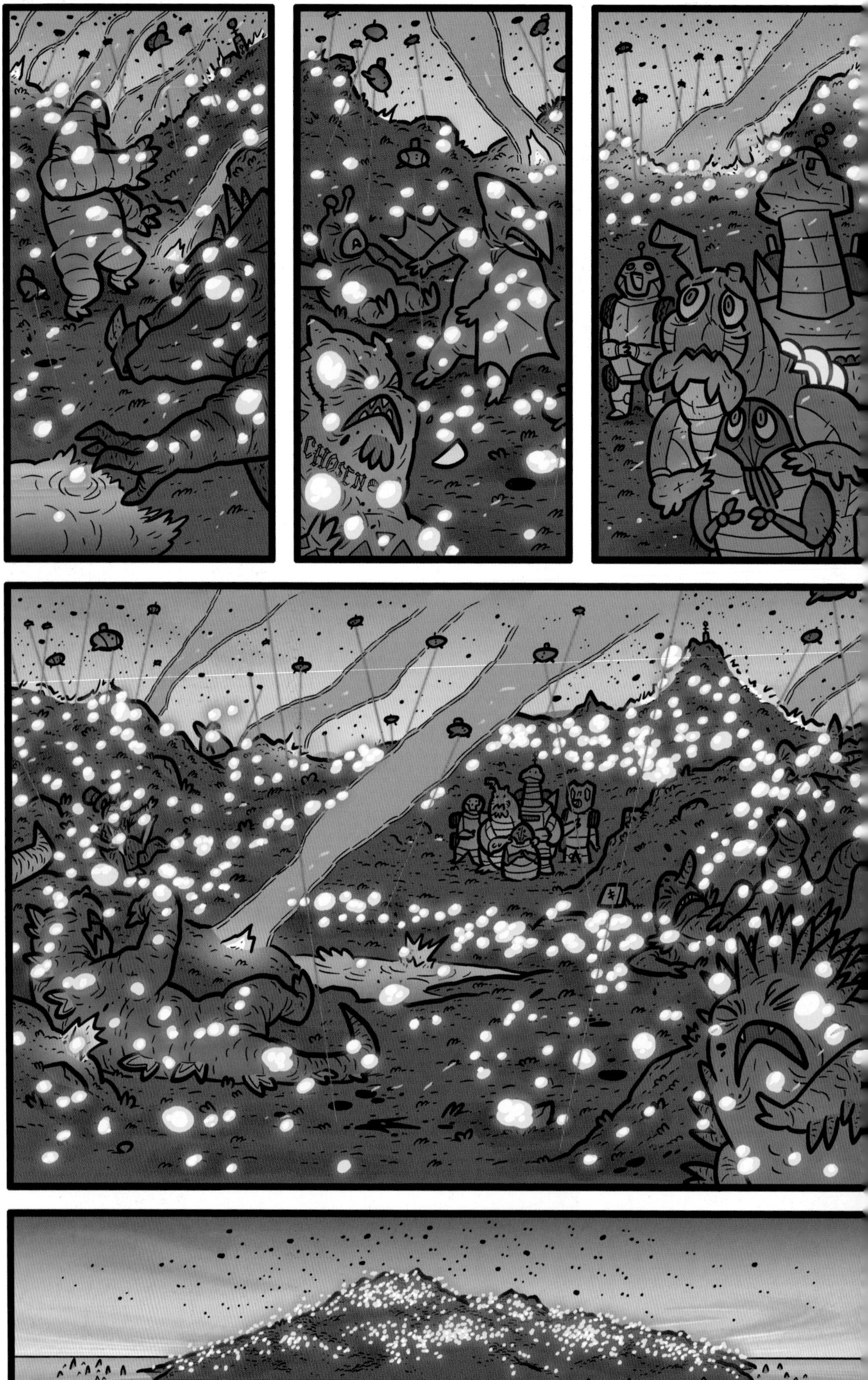
CHOSEN

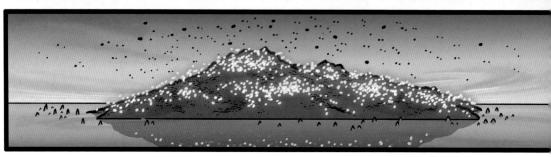

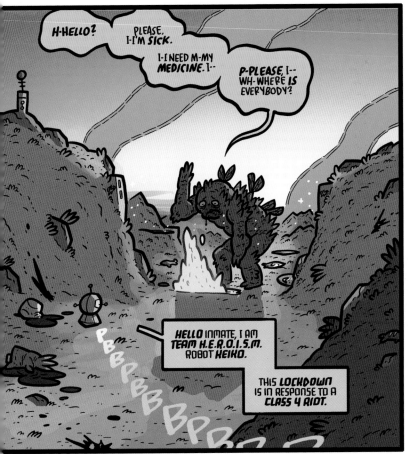

H-HELLO? PLEASE. I-I'M *SICK.*

I-I NEED M-MY *MEDICINE.* I--

P-PLEASE. I-- WH-WHERE *IS* EVERYBODY?

HELLO INMATE, I AM *TEAM H.E.R.O.I.S.M.* ROBOT *KEIKO.*

THIS *LOCKDOWN* IS IN RESPONSE TO A *CLASS 4 RIOT.*

KAIJUMAX IS BACK UNDER TEAM HEROISM *CONTROL,* AND WE WILL BE ADDRESSING *INMATE ISSUES* ACCORDING TO THEIR *SEVERITY* AND ORDER *LOGGED.* HERE IS A RECORDED *MESSAGE* FROM INTERIM CHIEF *SATO:*

You pieces of crap get NOTHING. I hope you like being in LOCKDOWN, because it's all you're gonna KNOW for a LONG-ASS TIME.

THANK YOU AND PLEASE BE *PATIENT.*

WAIT! PLEASE!

WH-WHERE ARE YOU *GOING*??

PLEASE, S-SOMEBODY-- I'M SO SICK. I JUST N-NEED A *HIT.*

P-PLEASE. I'VE GOT *NOTHING!*

E-EVEN ALL MY *SHARKS* ARE GONE.

J-JUST NEED A...

..OVER HERE..

?

..OVER HERE!

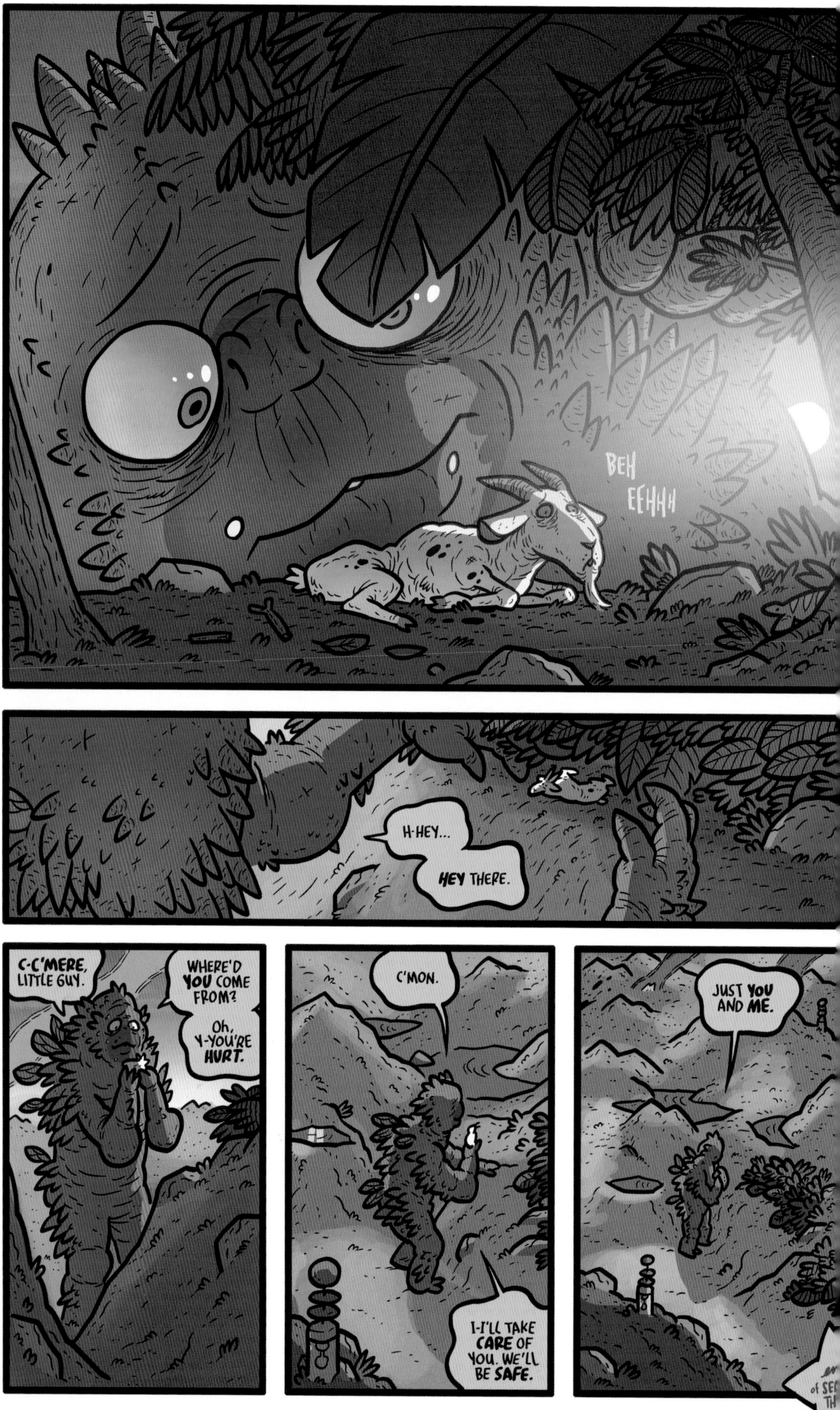

BEH EEHHH
H-HEY...
HEY THERE.
C-C'MERE, LITTLE GUY.
WHERE'D YOU COME FROM?
Oh, Y-YOU'RE HURT.
C'MON.
I-I'LL TAKE CARE OF YOU. WE'LL BE SAFE.
JUST YOU AND ME.

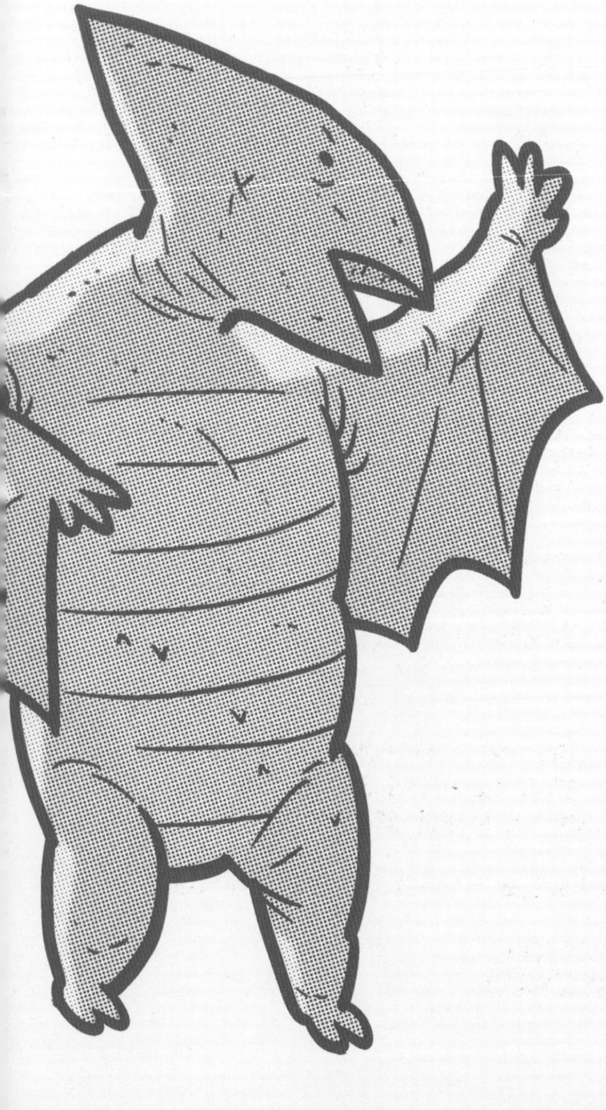

Published by Oni Press, Inc.
Joe Nozemack, founder & chief financial officer
James Lucas Jones, publisher
Charlie Chu, v.p. of creative & business development
Brad Rooks, director of operations
Rachel Reed, marketing manager
Melissa Meszaros, publicity manager
Troy Look, director of design & production
Hilary Thompson, senior graphic designer
Kate Z. Stone, junior graphic designer
Angie Knowles, digital prepress lead
Ari Yarwood, executive editor
Robin Herrera, senior editor
Desiree Wilson, associate editor
Alissa Sallah, administrative assistant
Jung Lee, logistics associate

onipress.com
facebook.com/onipress
twitter.com/onipress
onipress.tumblr.com
instagram.com/onipress

zandercannon.com / @zander_cannon

KAIJUMAX.COM

studiojfish.com / @studiojfish

This volume collects issues #1-6 of the Oni Press series *Kaijumax: Season Three.*

First edition: May 2018

ISBN 978-1-62010-494-1
eISBN 978-1-62010-495-8

KAIJUMAX SEASON THREE: KING OF THE MONSTAS, May 2018. Published by Oni Press, Inc. 1319 SE Martin Luther King Jr. Blvd., Suite 240, Portland, OR 97214.

PRINTED IN CHINA.

Library of Congress Control Number: 2017956255

1 3 5 7 9 10 8 6 4 2

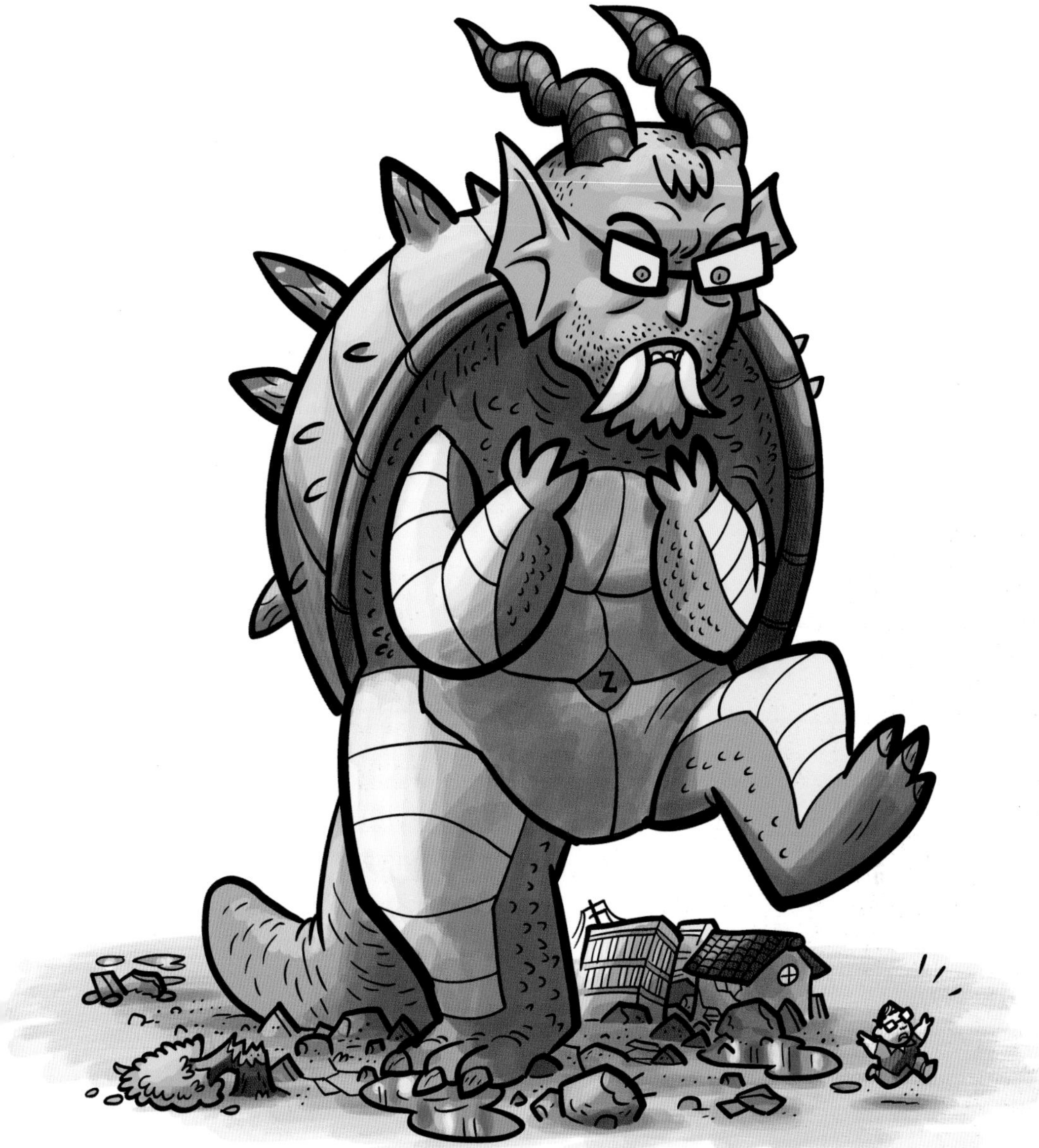

SINCE 1993, ***ZANDER CANNON*** HAS WRITTEN AND DRAWN COMICS ABOUT GODS, ROBOTS, ASTRONAUTS, POLICE OFFICERS, PALEONTOLOGISTS, ALIENS, FENG SHUI MASTERS, SUPERHEROES, AND MONSTERS.

HE LIVES IN MINNESOTA WITH HIS STRONG WIFE JULIE AND ABOVE-AVERAGE SON JIN.

KAIJUMAX.COM
@ZANDER_CANNON